SS HITLER'S FOREIGN DIVISIONS

FOREIGN VOLUNTEERS IN THE WAFFEN-SS 1940–1945

SS HITLER'S FOREIGN DIVISIONS

FOREIGN VOLUNTEERS IN THE WAFFEN-SS 1940–1945

CHRIS BISHOP

SPELLMOUNT

Staplehurst

British Library Cataloguing in Publication Data:
A catalogue record for this book is available
from the British Library

ISBN 1-86227-289-1

First published in the UK in 2005 by
SPELLMOUNT LTD
The Village Centre
Staplehurst
Kent TN12 0BJ

Tel: 01580 893730
Fax: 01580 893731
e-mail: enquiries@spellmount.com
Website: www.spellmount.com

Editorial and design by
Amber Books Ltd
Bradley's Close
74-77 White Lion Street
London N1 9PF
www.amberbooks.co.uk

Project Editor: Michael Spilling
Design: EQ Media
Picture Research: Natasha Jones

Printed in Italy

PICTURE CREDITS
Aerospace/Art-Tech: 13, 28, 37, 49, 61, 69, 77, 82, 86, 91, 100, 102, 105, 111, 117,
118, 119, 139, 144, 145, 153, 157, 160, 166;
AKG Images: 8, 18;
Amber Books: 14, 15, 116, 167;
Cody Images: 9, 10, 11, 16, 20, 23, 24, 25, 27, 30, 32, 34, 35, 38, 39, 41, 43, 44, 46, 47, 50, 52, 54, 55,
56, 60, 71, 78, 87, 93, 94, 96, 99, 107, 112, 114, 123, 124, 125,126, 129, 130, 132, 137,
147, 148, 150, 154, 163, 164, 165, 170, 172, 173, 175, 176, 178, 179, 185;
Ian Baxter: 6, 53, 65, 83, 98, 121, 122, 128;
Popperfoto: 59;
Private collection:155;
Süddeutscher Verlag: 17, 22, 29, 66, 67, 72, 73, 75, 79, 80, 84, 85, 88, 109, 115, 134, 135,
141, 142, 151, 158, 168, 180, 182;
Ukrainian State Archive: 7, 62, 76.

CONTENTS

INTRODUCTION

Even today, more than six decades after the outbreak of World War II, it still seems incredible that thousands of men whose countries had been conquered by the Nazis should have volunteered for service with the SS. Hundreds of thousands more volunteered or were conscripted into the *Wehrmacht*, the *Kriegsmarine* and the *Luftwaffe*. Many had no choice in the matter, but a significant number were willing members of the German armed forces, and those who served with the SS were mostly volunteers. But why did the SS recruit them and, having done so, trust them in battle?

Above: Cossacks in German service ride across the steppe. The German invasion of the USSR in 1941 was seen as a liberation by many minorities which had been suppressed under Stalin, and huge numbers flocked to the Nazi colours.
Left: A ski trooper attached to the 6th *SS-Gebirgs Division Nord* is seen on patrol, armed with a Soviet Tokarev self-loading rifle. The more accomplished skiers in the division came from the *Skijäger Bataillon Norge*.

Above: Although Adolf Hitler was the founder of the SS, it was Heinrich Himmler who gave it a structure. Himmler's desire to expand the fighting SS led to recruitment beyond the borders of the Reich, after Army opposition restricted available manpower in Germany.

During the course of World War II, the *Waffen*-SS grew from an elite force of four regiments composed solely of Germans meeting Heinrich Himmler's exacting physical and racial standards, into a polyglot force of 900,000 men in 39 divisions, with over half of its troops foreign volunteers or conscripts. Even so, at its peak the *Waffen*-SS represented only one-tenth of the strength of the *Wehrmacht* – although it provided a quarter of German panzer strength.

Few people realize just how international were the German forces in World War II. It is estimated that nearly two million foreign nationals served under the Swastika. Although towards the end of the war many were transferred to the SS, large numbers served with the Army, particularly on the Eastern Front. The most committed of the foreign volunteers found a home in the SS, until parts of it were more like a German equivalent of the French Foreign Legion than the elite of the German race. *Waffen*-SS equipment and organization were the same as those of the Army. Units were interchangeable with Army units, and senior *Waffen*-SS officers adopted Army ranks.

The *Waffen*-SS

Although the SS did not welcome non-German volunteers until midway through the conflict in Russia, the idea of recruiting such men dated back to before the war. In his quest for a pan-Germanic Europe, *Reichsführer*-SS Heinrich Himmler had decreed in 1938 that non-Germans of suitable 'Nordic' origin could enlist in the *Allgemeine*-SS. At that point in time the distinction between the civilian 'general' SS, or *Allgemeine*-SS, and the 'armed' SS, or *Waffen*-SS, did not exist. By the outbreak of war in 1939, however, the armed SS had emerged in its own right, as a separate entity from the *Allgemeine*-SS and from the *Totenkopf* units which guarded the concentration camps. The *Waffen*-SS played a small but important part in Germany's early campaigns. Its fighting reputation pleased Himmler greatly, and he wanted to increase the organization's importance. Established primarily as a security force, it would have to become much bigger if it was to play its part in the

Below: Himmler's recruitment drive was made easier by the growth of right-wing nationalist parties in Europe in the 1930s, members of which could easily be persuaded to join a 'crusade' against communism. Here, Staf De Clercq of the *Vlaamsch Nationaal Verbond* addresses members of the Flemish Volunteer Legion before their departure for the Eastern Front.

pan-Germanic future which would come after the war was won. But expansion did not come easily.

The explosive wartime growth of the *Waffen*-SS reflected Himmler's desire to create an instrument of political power that would safeguard the National Socialist revolution inside Germany. In the process, it would provide a counterweight to the influence of the Army. Although a number of former SS officers claimed after the war that the *Waffen*-SS was a purely fighting force, in truth the organization was never completely free of its political origins. As late as 1943, the preface to an SS panzer training manual contained a paragraph which read: '... The SS fulfils a requirement to provide an unflinching force at the disposal of the leadership of the Reich in any situation. This includes the maintenance of order at home by the use of any and all methods.'

The main stumbling-block to this expansion was the Army. With good reason, the generals had feared

the establishment of a powerful party organization answerable only to Hitler. Before the war, the General Staff had blocked SS acquisition of artillery, and had forbidden the formation of an SS field division. Above all, the Army controlled the number of men the SS could recruit. Each year, the *Oberkommando der Wehrmacht* (OKW), or Military High Command, laid down the proportion of men to be conscripted to each arm or service. All men of recruitable age were registered with the local *Wehrbezirkskommando* (WBK), or Military District Headquarters. No volunteer could join a military unit until he had been released by his local WBK, and the Army made sure that as few men as possible were released to join the SS.

Conditions for the SS improved slightly with the outbreak of war. In spite of the rigorous selection process, German volunteers were plentiful. Many were attracted to Himmler's romantic dream of a race of blue-eyed, blond heroes, an elite formed according to 'laws of selection' based on criteria of physiognomy, mental and physical tests, character and spirit. His 'aristocratic' concept would combine charismatic authority with bureaucratic discipline. The SS man would represent a new human type – warrior, administrator, scholar and leader, all in one – whose messianic mission was to repopulate Europe. The SS played on its status as an elite force by using its Nazi connections to recruit the cream of the Hitler Youth movement and the *Reichsarbeitsdienst* (RAD), or Reich Labour Service, before they could be snatched up by the *Wehrmacht*.

Himmler's plans received a major boost when an energetic Swabian SS-*Brigadeführer* named Gottlob Berger was given responsibility for SS recruitment. With recruitment blocked by the Army, it was Berger who suggested to Himmler that he should make use of his control of the concentration camp guards and the police to form two new formations, the *Totenkopf* and the *Polizei* Divisions. As the SS expanded, these were eventually to become the 3rd *SS-Panzer Division Totenkopf* and the 4th *SS-Panzergrenadier Division SS-Polizei*.

Volunteers were still coming in, but early public approval of the *Waffen*-SS was beginning to diminish, and the armed SS began to acquire some of the sinister reputation of other branches of the organization. Heinz Höhne, in his seminal work *The Order of the Death's Head*, quoted a *Sicherheitsdienst* (SD – the SS Security Service) report written in March 1942:

'... it may be stated that by its achievements the *Waffen*-SS has won its place in the popular esteem. Particular reference is made to the good comradeship and excellent relations between officers, NCOs and men ... Unfortunately voices are also to be heard saying that the *Waffen*-SS possesses no trained officers and that therefore SS men are "recklessly sacrificed" ... Critical voices are to be heard saying that the *Waffen*-SS is a sort of military watchdog. SS men are trained to be brutal and ruthless, apparently so that they can be used against other German formations if necessary ... The *Waffen*-SS is a most ruthless force.'

Left: Members of the *SS-Freiwilligen Verband Danemark*, also known as the *Freikorps Danmark*, are sworn in as members of the SS after completing their training at Hamburg in the autumn of 1941. Unlike German SS recruits, the Danish volunteers swore an oath to Adolf Hitler as the commander of the *Wehrmacht*, not the personal oath of absolute loyalty to the *Führer*.

Nordic volunteers

Continually looking for fresh sources of manpower that the Army could not block, Berger now began looking outside Germany's borders for troops. In part, this followed Himmler's romantic vision of a pan-Germanic Europe, in which Germany would annex the 'Nordic' states with the aid of right-wing collaborationist governments.

Himmler believed that once exposed to German propaganda, volunteers from northern and northwestern Europe would flock to the Swastika to take part in a crusade in the East against the 'Judaeo-Bolshevik' enemy. In his dreams, Himmler saw his multi-national SS supplanting the German Army in a new German empire stretching from the Atlantic to the Urals. Curiously his master, Adolf Hitler, was much less excited about such ideas, wanting to win the war before going full speed ahead with reconstructing

Above: Members of an *SS-Polizei Schützen* regiment on the march early in the war. Partially absorbed into the SS in 1940, police regiments were not as highly regarded as *Waffen*-SS units, and many of the early eastern volunteers were assigned to them rather than regular SS units.

Europe in the Nazi image. After the May 1940 *Sieg im Westen*, or 'Victory in the West', the SS began an active programme to recruit suitably 'Nordic' or 'Germanic' volunteers from northern and western Europe to join a number of *Waffen*-SS *Freiwillige* (volunteer) legions. This effort intensified after June 1941, as the SS exhorted volunteers to join the campaign in the Soviet Union.

Norway, Denmark, Holland and Belgium all had their own fascist parties, which in some cases modelled themselves on Germany, while others took their inspiration from Rome. Initially it was Nazi racial doctrine which determined the level of acceptance of volunteers. Danes, Norwegians and Flemish (Dutch-speaking) Belgians were considered 'Aryan', and could volunteer for the *Waffen*-SS, while Frenchmen, Spaniards and Walloons (French-speaking Belgians) were not considered racially pure. Walloon volunteers for the great anti-Bolshevik crusade preached by the Nazis had to join a volunteer legion in the German Army, and the *Légion des Volontaires Français* (LVF) also came under Army control.

However, the LVF was just a small portion of the French contribution to the war effort. Tens of thousands of French speakers became German citizens when the Nazis annexed Alsace and Lorraine. As a result, they became eligible for conscription into the *Wehrmacht*, the *Kriegsmarine* and the *Luftwaffe*. Later in the war some were conscripted directly into the *Waffen*-SS, as Himmler's private army increasingly became a fully fledged member of the *Wehrmacht*.

Racial standards

As the war progressed and manpower grew scarcer to find, the SS lowered its racial standards. Nazi propaganda also changed as more and more 'non-Aryans' joined the *Wehrmacht* and the *Waffen*-SS. Instead of talking about a Germanic empire, the posters, books, magazines, films and radio broadcasts generated the myth of the 'New European Order', which extolled the unification of a continent divided for millennia, and which made much of the battle to overthrow Bolshevik Russia.

However, all this was still in the future, and standards were still high when in September 1940 Hitler consented to the raising of a new *Waffen*-SS division. The formation was originally to be named *SS-Division Germania*, and the backbone of the unit was to be provided by the experienced and combat-tested *Germania* Regiment of the SS-*Verfügungstruppe* (VT) Division (the pre-war forerunner of the *Waffen*-SS). However, the bulk of its strength would be provided by Dutch and Flemish volunteers from the *SS-Regiment Westland* and Norwegians and Danes from *SS-Standarte Nordland*.

Early 1941 saw the addition of a volunteer unit of Finns, the *Finnisches Freiwilligen-Bataillon der Waffen-SS Nordost*, which had been raised in February 1941.

On 20 December Hitler ordered that the division should be known as the *SS-Division Wiking*.

The invasion of the Soviet Union

By the time *Wiking* was formed, the most important boost to the recruitment of foreign volunteers was well under way – the German attack on the Soviet Union. Launched on 22 June 1941, Operation *Barbarossa* was the largest military operation in history. Three huge army groups smashed across the border, punching through the weak Soviet defences with ease. The German plan called for a lightning advance by the *Wehrmacht* to destroy the forward-deployed Red Army, followed by a general pursuit along three main axes: towards Leningrad, towards Moscow, and south to seize the productive wheatfields of the Ukraine and from there on to the oilfields of the Caucasus. It was expected that the onset of winter should see the Red Army completely defeated and Germany in control of much of European Russia. A rump Soviet state might still exist beyond the Urals, but German possession of Russia's major cities and industrial and agricultural regions would secure the resources necessary for the Third Reich to prosper. In the long run, it was to be Hitler's most fatal miscalculation, but the initial stages of the great gamble brought the *Wehrmacht* perilously close to success.

The campaign in Russia was the main driving force in the recruitment of foreign volunteers. Depicted as a crusade against communism, the war in the East attracted many right-wing idealists. Between the wars, politics in Europe had strongly polarized political viewpoints all over the continent, and Soviet support for local communist movements had made the USSR something of a pariah in Europe. It was that attitude which was exploited by German propagandists, who depicted the ongoing struggle as a battle to rid Europe of the 'Red Menace' for ever.

Apart from the volunteers serving with the multi-national *Wiking* Division, early European recruits were incorporated into national volunteer units. These 'legions' could be sponsored and recruited by local collaborationist parties and governments. Nobody knows just who was responsible for the idea: it was probably a spur-of-the-moment plan with a strong propaganda element, inspired by local organizations

keen to be seen taking part in the fight against communism. The first legions were mooted even before Hitler's approval of the use of foreign troops, which came on 28 June 1941.

However, Hitler's approval came with some caveats. The SS would only accept those with 'Nordic' blood, which in essence meant that the only 'Germanic' legions would be those recruited in Scandinavia, Holland and Flanders. However, that did not mean rejecting anti-communist volunteers flocking in from France, Wallonia, Croatia and Spain: these would be assigned to the *Wehrmacht*, which would oversee their equipment and training. To further the image of a multi-national crusade, Germany also persuaded Axis allies to fight alongside the Germans. Troops from Italy, Romania, Hungary and Slovakia were sent to the Eastern Front. Neutral Spain also sent a large volunteer force, the Blue Division. Nominally manned by members of the *Falange*, the local fascist organization,

Above: Members of an SS *Feldgendarmerie* unit take Soviet men into custody. Known as *Kopf Jäger*, or 'Head Hunters', the SS field police worked closely with the death squads of the *Einsatzgruppen* and with volunteer police units recruited in the Baltic states.

the Blue Division was in fact a mix of regular soldiers, civil war veterans and *Falange* militia. Most of the officers were regulars.

Erratic performers

Although the early volunteer formations in the Army and *Waffen*-SS had strong political motivations for fighting, their performance on the field of battle did not match their initial enthusiasm. The Spanish Blue Division was large enough to have some real military value, and could be considered the equivalent of a second- or third-line German infantry division. However, the much smaller French Legion was not a

Sig-Runen

13th Division
Handschar

15th Division
(Latvian)

23rd Division
Nederland (early)

30th Division
(Russian)

5th Division
Wiking

14th Division
Galicia

18th Hungary
Horst Wessel

23rd Division
Nederland (late)

28th Division
Wallonie

30th Division
(Russian)

France

Ukraine
(issue doubtful)

20th Division
(Estonian)

23rd Division
Kama

29th Division
(Russian)

33rd Division
Charlemagne

7th Division
Prinz Eugen

19th Division
(Latvian)

21st Division
Skanderbeg

25th Division
Hunyadi

29th Division
(Russian)

Indian Legion

11th Division
Nordland

Estonian No. 2

22nd Division
(Hungarian)

27th Division
Langemarck

29th Division
(Italian)

British Legion

Opposite: Germany invested a great deal in the recruitment of suitably 'Nordic' volunteers into the *Waffen*-SS. This Dutch recruiting poster is typical of the striking graphic style used to present the SS in an heroic light.

Above: Foreign volunteer units in the *Waffen*-SS did not wear standard 'Sig-rune' collar tabs. Instead, they wore tabs bearing emblems indicating their origins. Foreigners also wore a sleeve shield with their national colours.

success at the front line, and it took considerable effort to make it efficient enough for rear-area security operations. The even smaller Walloon Legion fought reasonably well, but it was too limited in capability to have much effect. The 6000–7000 SS volunteers who served in the various SS legions were more effective. Most were used to man static defences or to carry out rear-area security duties. They did occasionally see brief but intense fighting in mopping-up operations. However, the Danish *Freikorps* saw intense action when used to reinforce the *Totenkopf* Division in the

vicious fighting in the Demyansk pocket in 1942. The Dutch regiment and the Norwegian and Flemish battalions joined the 2nd SS Infantry Brigade in the siege lines of Leningrad, and were eventually incorporated into the SS proper.

In contrast to the legions, the *Wiking* Division was a true elite formation. Commanded by Felix Steiner, one of the most influential officers in the *Waffen*-SS, *Wiking* was the first 'international' *Waffen*-SS division. It proved to be an excellent fighting unit, and as the 5th *SS-Panzer Division Wiking* it gained a combat

Above: A patrol from the 5th *SS-Division Wiking* moves through the Russian snow. The prototype of the multi-national SS division, *Wiking* gained an excellent reputation as a fighting unit in its four years on the Eastern Front.

Opposite: *Obergruppenführer* Felix Steiner, the original commander of the 5th *SS-Division Wiking*, is seen here awarding the Knight's Cross to an Estonian volunteer, *Obersturmführer* (First Lieutenant) Harald Riipalu.

reputation second to none. In the process, it served as the progenitor of a number of other SS divisions.

However, Germans outnumbered Germanics in its ranks, and a sluggish Germanic replacement system kept the proportion of Germans to Germanics quite high. *Wiking* operated exclusively on the Eastern Front, serving as a spearhead unit for Operation *Barbarossa* in 1941, for the drive on the Caucasus in 1942, and for the *Citadel* offensive at Kursk in 1943. The division served in the Cherkassy pocket and in Hungary as the war turned against Germany. Despite at least one allegation of war crimes, *Wiking* earned a tough but fair reputation – or as fair a reputation as

any unit on the Eastern Front could have. Before the withdrawal of the Legions from the Eastern Front in 1943, Himmler had already compromised the exclusive status of his foreign auxiliaries by combining them with each other and with German units. Thus, in September 1942, Himmler reported to Hitler that he would merge the legions with the formerly all-German SS brigades in Army Group North. The Danish volunteers joined one regiment of the 1st SS Brigade, and the Dutch and Norwegian Legions formed a regiment in the 2nd SS Brigade. The reason for this consolidation was straightforward: as individual, independent units the legions were simply too small

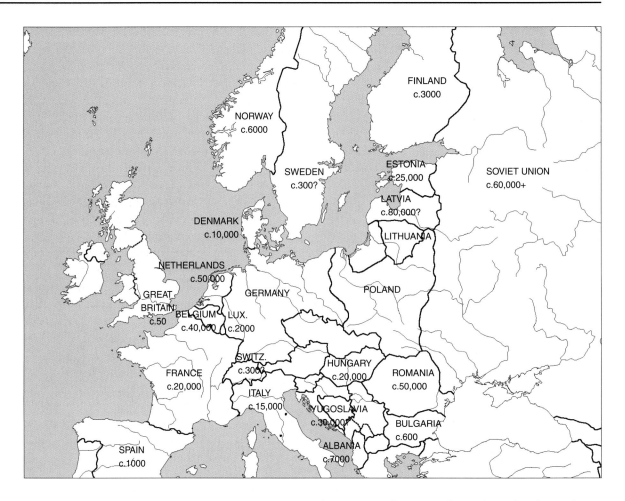

Above: Foreign volunteers serving in the *Wehrmacht*, the *Kriegsmarine* and the *Waffen*-SS came from almost every country in occupied Europe, as well as from Allied nations and from neutrals like Sweden and Switzerland. By the end of the war over half of the *Waffen*-SS was non-German.

to have any effect on operations over the vast distances and in the huge scale of combat on the Russian Front. Additionally, it was proving increasingly hard to recruit volunteers for the legions, since any European enthusiasm for the anti-communist crusade had gradually melted away as the volunteer units began to suffer heavy casualties in the bitter fighting on the Eastern Front.

Himmler now decided to combine the available Germanic volunteers in a new multi-national division modelled on the successful SS *Wiking* Division, as part of the *Waffen*-SS expansion programme which had

begun in 1942. Formed in July 1943, the 11th *SS-Freiwilligen Panzergrenadier Division Nordland* absorbed the SS *Nordland* Regiment from *Wiking*, the remnants of the volunteer legions, and new replacements recruited in Norway, Denmark and Holland under Berger's refurbished recruitment programme.

Western European volunteers who joined the *Waffen*-SS were not treated the same as their German counterparts. They did not take the oath of allegiance to Hitler, most being motivated by their own idealistic beliefs in the fight against communism. They were certainly exposed to less political and racial indoctrination than Germans. However, there were many problems, not least being the fact that in the early days they were treated with some disdain by their German cadres. Communications were also a problem, with units from several different countries speaking different languages often being brigaded together for combat. In the later stages of the war, the Western and Nordic *Freiwillige* divisions were among the most disciplined and fanatical of all SS units. This was possibly because as the war turned against Germany, they realized that their countrymen back home would look on them as traitors, and that their only hope would be to fight as hard as possible for an unlikely Nazi victory.

The *Volksdeutsche*

Although more than 125,000 Western Europeans volunteered for the *Waffen*-SS, it was still not enough to satisfy the organization's ever-growing need for manpower. Once again, it was Gottlob Berger, by now an *Obergruppenführer* in charge of the SS-*Hauptamt* (SS Main Office), who came up with a solution. He proposed expanding SS recruitment to include the *Volksdeutsche* – ethnic Germans scattered in communities all over Central and Eastern Europe.

The origins of many of the German-speaking communities dated back to the Middle Ages. Others were remnants of the former Austro-Hungarian Empire and of the Kaiser's empire. As well as the loss of Germany's colonial empire, the Versailles Treaty of 1919 had seen German border territory ceded to Denmark, Poland and Belgium. Closer to home, Germany lost the important coalfields of Alsace-Lorraine, which went back to France after having been captured by Prussia in 1871. The desire to undo the perceived iniquities of Versailles and to bring the Germanic territories of Europe from their current foreign control into a greater German state was an article of faith for Hitler and the Nazis.

In Europe there were several countries and regions with large populations for whom German was their first language. Poland, Hungary, Transylvanian Romania and the Sudeten area of Czechoslovakia had German-speaking communities of between one and five million, while in Yugoslavia there were up to a million German speakers. Within Europe the Nazis were actively engaged in political and propaganda activities in Hungary and Yugoslavia, while pro-Nazi political movements of varying sizes existed in almost every other country. For Hitler and his pan-German mentors, a long-term goal was the creation of Greater Germany, a country that united those people who were ethnically German, or *Volksdeutsche*, into one nation. As far back as November 1937 Hitler explained his plans: 'The aim of German policy is to secure and preserve the racial community – and to enlarge it.'

For many Germans or German communities living abroad, Hitler's Third Reich seemed a dynamic and vigorous nation that had grown out of defeat and the decadence of the Weimar Republic. It was exciting to be involved as *Auslandsdeutsche*, whether at a distance or as close neighbours. When the SS began recruiting *Volksdeutsche*, that attitude led to a flood of new recruits. However, there were problems. Despite their ethnic background, many of the *Volksdeutsche* recruits had only a rudimentary command of German, and the hard discipline typical of SS training meant that their motivation and commitment to the cause often failed to match that of members of the western legions. Some *Volksdeutsche* units fought well, but as a whole the ethnic Germans had a mixed reputation. Many of the *Reichsdeutsche* members of the SS felt that the *Volksdeutsche* were cowardly and untrustworthy. The flood of volunteers also began to dry up fairly quickly, and Germany leaned heavily on the governments of various puppet states to allow the conscription of men of the right age straight into the SS.

New divisions

The next two SS divisions to be formed made extensive use of *Volksdeutsche* volunteers to fill out their respective orders of battle. The *Waffen*-SS had started the war as the most poorly equipped troops in the German armed forces. Most SS formations had gone into battle on foot, with horse-drawn transport. SS equipment was procured through the Army, and as long as the Army saw the SS as a potential rival, it refused to supply the latest weapons. Even though the big-name units like the *Leibstandarte* and *Das Reich* were grudgingly supplied with the latest weaponry, less favoured SS units were much less well equipped.

The 7th *SS-Freiwilligen Gebirgs Division Prinz Eugen* was one such unit. Created for anti-partisan operations in the Balkans, the bulk of its strength consisted of *Volksdeutsche* volunteers and conscripts from Romania, Hungary and Yugoslavia. Formed as a mountain division, *Prinz Eugen* was equipped with

Above: A propaganda picture of Cossacks in German service. In the original French magazine article it was captioned, 'Fighters for a New Europe: Gathered in their hundreds and commanded by German officers, Cossacks hunt down partisan bandits behind the lines.'

obsolete and captured equipment such as Czech machine guns and French light tanks.

Despite this poor equipment, it was one of the most effective counter-insurgency units the Germans fielded in Yugoslavia, and was greatly feared by the partisans. However, that reputation was gained primarily by brutality and utter ruthlessness. The conflict in Yugoslavia combined guerrilla war with civil and tribal warfare, and neither side was prone to giving quarter. The 8th *SS-Kavallerie Division Florian Geyer* was also used on anti-partisan operations, and quickly gained an equally unsavoury reputation. The origins of the unit dated back to the formation of cavalry units

within the *Allgemeine-SS Totenkopf Standarten* late in 1939. These cavalry units were then consolidated under the command of the *Kommandostab-RFSS* (Command Staff *Reichsführer*-SS) for Operation *Barbarossa*. Their primary function was security, being used behind the front lines to mop up bypassed Soviet Army units.

Gradually, their main function became the waging of an extremely ruthless anti-partisan campaign. Formed in 1942, the *Florian Geyer* Division continued with these security duties but did see some front-line service. The Soviet Army destroyed the division during the siege of Budapest in February 1945.

The success of his troops in Russia prompted Himmler to expand the *Waffen*-SS still further. Four new divisions were authorized, three of them armoured. These were the 9th *SS-Panzer Division Hohenstaufen*, the 10th *SS-Panzer Division Frundsberg*, the 11th *SS-Freiwilligen Panzergrenadier Division*

Nordland and the 12th *SS-Panzer Division Hitlerjugend*. All began forming in 1943, but none were ready to take part in the summer offensive that year. Only the *Nordland* Division made extensive use of foreign volunteers.

In the spring of 1944 the SS Panzer Corps was a shadow of the powerful force that had spearheaded Operation *Citadel* at Kursk the previous year. Most units had been withdrawn to Western Europe to rest and refit, becoming fully fledged panzer divisions in the process. However, the 9th and 10th Divisions had now completed their training, and went into action at Tarnopol in April 1944. By now, the SS could no longer sustain itself on volunteers alone, and conscripts manned the two divisions. Nevertheless, they had been given full SS-style training, and they fought at least as well as the original divisions. By accepting conscripts, the SS solved at least part of its manpower problem. Even *Volksdeutsche* volunteers could not fill out the rest of the manpower needs of the SS, so Himmler began looking for volunteers from beyond the German 'race'.

The bulk of the early non-Germanic volunteers fighting for Hitler served with the *Wehrmacht*. Those from Eastern Europe were initially used in secondary roles, serving in police battalions or as prison camp guards, working as labourers or moving supplies on the long lines of communication. But gradually, as the pressure on German manpower increased, they were used more and more often as combat troops. Some fought extremely well, while others were worthless in battle. Some of the auxiliary units, particularly those employed by the *Einsatzgruppen* and as camp and ghetto guards, were among the worst perpetrators of war crimes.

Later, as manpower demands grew apace with Himmler's ambitions, SS racial standards were relaxed still further and units were formed from Muslims, Slavs, Indians and other 'Asiatics'. The first such division was raised in 1943. The 13th *Waffen-Gebirgs Division der SS Handschar* was a *Waffen*-SS division of Bosnian Muslim volunteers. Most had joined the division in order to protect their homes and families from *Ustase/Chetnik* and partisan attacks. The fascist Croat puppet government disapproved of the formation, since they felt that the SS recruitment in Bosnia violated their sovereignty. A small-scale mutiny during training in France was instigated by partisans who had infiltrated the ranks.

Enter the Slavs

Following the defeats at Stalingrad and Kursk, Himmler began to reappraise the SS attitude towards the 'subhuman' Slavs of Eastern Europe. The 14th *Waffen-Grenadier Division der SS* was formed in Galicia in mid-1943. The region of Galicia, covering southeastern Poland and western Ukraine, was colonized by German settlers in the fourteenth century. It had became a province of Maria-Theresa's Austro-Hungarian Empire by the 1770s, with the provincial capital at Lemberg (L'vov). Although the region was considered Germanic by the Nazis, the main cultural influence there was in fact Ukrainian, as were most of the troops in the division.

The next major units came from the Baltic. In June 1940, the Soviet Union annexed the republics of Estonia, Latvia and Lithuania. Stalin claimed the take-over had been at the instigation of the three countries themselves, but it was in effect a military conquest. The communists moved large forces into the area, and immediately enacted repressive measures against opposition and liberation groups. As a result, the Balts welcomed the 1941 German invaders as liberators, and when the SS formed a Latvian unit there was no problem with recruitment. Early in 1943, the *Lettische SS-Freiwilligen Legion* was formed from several SS-linked Latvian internal security units, known as *Schutzmannschaft* battalions

The largest number of foreign volunteers in German service came from the Soviet Union, although it was not until late in the war that SS racial standards were relaxed to permit Russian SS units to be formed. Almost from the beginning of the campaign in Russia, huge numbers of individual Soviet Army prisoners and deserters offered their services to the Germans. Known as *Hilfswillige* – literally 'willing helpers' but more often known as 'auxiliary volunteers' and generally nicknamed '*Hiwis*' – these men served in non-combat and support units in such roles as drivers, cooks, labourers and medical orderlies. Initially serving in their Soviet uniforms, many were later issued with basic German uniforms.

Left: An instructor holds a Soviet DT light machine gun. The first volunteers to rally to the Germans after the *Barbarossa* invasion were local defence units that had risen against the Soviets. Armed with Soviet weapons at first, many of these *Selbstschutz* formations were incorporated into police and later into SS formations.

centuries, and gained a reputation as skilled horsemen. However, like other Russian minorities, they had been persecuted under the communist regime, and initially welcomed the Germans as liberators. They were recruited in small squadrons and served as local auxiliaries, but their numbers grew as the war progressed until an entire division was formed in 1943.

Allied recruits

Not all of the foreign volunteers in the SS served in the SS divisions. One of the most interesting units, given Himmler's racial obsessions, was the *Indische Freiwilligen Legion der Waffen-SS*. It was founded by the Indian nationalist leader Subhas Chandra Bose, whose dream it was to raise a German-sponsored Indian Legion that would be in the vanguard of the German advance in the Caucasus. The Indian Legion would then push on through Persia, Afghanistan and onward to liberate their homeland. The *Indische Freiwilligen Legion* (transferred to the *Waffen*-SS in 1944) never did fulfil the martial dreams of its founder, the polyglot force of Sikhs, Muslims and Hindus being relegated to garrison duty.

Less successful was Himmler's attempt to recruit SS members from British prisoners of war. John Amery, son of Conservative minister Leo Amery and a pre-war fascist, suggested the idea of a volunteer legion of British POWs soon after being captured in 1940. It was not until 1943 that the *Waffen*-SS expressed interest in the project, creating the 'Legion of St George'. Despite promises of cash bonuses, limited freedom and access to prostitutes, the SS recruitment efforts were essentially a failure, with less than 50 men

More significant to the conduct of the war were the *Osttruppen*. These were former Soviet units incorporated into the German forces, the bulk of which were non-Russians from the Baltic, the Ukraine and other Soviet republics. These were armed units, but were mainly used for security behind the lines. However, they were never entirely trusted, and as a result thousands were sent to the West. As early as 1942 there were more than 72 *Ost-Bataillonen* doing occupation duty in Western Europe, which freed up large numbers of German troops for service in the East. The Cossack communities, or 'hosts', had provided light cavalry for the armies of the Tsars for volunteering. This was too few to have any military value, and the men were too unreliable to have any propaganda impact. The British Freecorps (BFC) spent most of its existence in training, but apart from half a dozen individuals who volunteered for the front in 1945, it never saw action. After the war, Amery was hanged for treason.

The foreign volunteer programme remained central to the development of the *Waffen*-SS, but the value of the non-German contribution to the war in the West and in Russia ranged from excellent to very poor. In the case of the Western European volunteers, the SS was able to tap a useful source of high-grade manpower, which the German armed forces would otherwise have found unavailable. After a generally poor start, the western volunteers fought well. The SS had one major criticism levelled against it, as far as the western volunteers were concerned, however, which was the inability of its training grounds and officer and NCO schools to readily accommodate non-German recruits, a systemic weakness that was corrected far too slowly.

With regard to the Eastern European volunteers, SS policy can only be seen as an almost unmitigated disaster. Given the wide range of nationalities involved, the German suggestion that the invasion of the Soviet Union was a 'European' undertaking to rid the world of communism was valuable propaganda. But the military evaluation is more critical. The small Finnish SS detachments were obviously good soldiers, but would have fought just as well in their own national uniforms. Some of the Baltic divisions also fought well, especially in the defence of their homelands, but the remaining units ranged from poor to appalling.

The programme might have made sense even as late as 1942, if only for its propaganda potential. However, the fortunes of war changed considerably from 1943 onwards, after Soviet successes at Stalingrad and Kursk forced the Germans onto the defensive. In such difficult circumstances it made no sense to keep expanding the SS with units of questionable value – units which generally needed an experienced German cadre for training. Deploying combat-tested German officers and NCOs desperately needed elsewhere was not a good idea at a time when manpower and material shortages began to bite.

Right: Himmler's search for manpower took some exotic turns as the war progressed. He hoped – erroneously – that an Indian Legion would be the nucleus of a force that could be used to overthrow British rule in India.

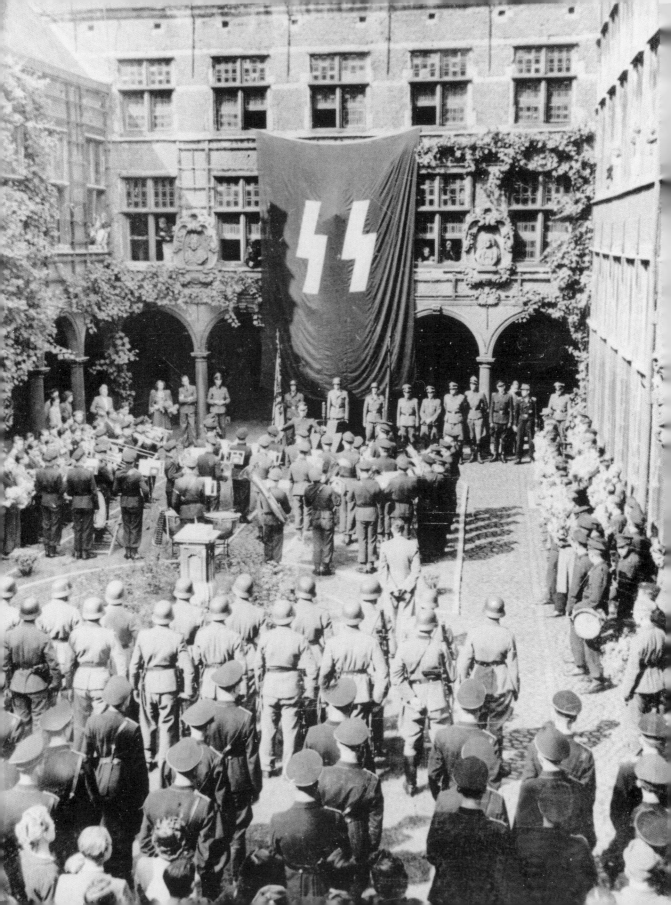

WESTERN EUROPE

The SS had high expectations that European volunteers would provide a real boost to German fighting power. In particular it was hoped that troops of northern European origin, considered racially Germanic, would be able to fit into the *Wehrmacht's* fighting plans with little trouble. In the event, the early volunteers performed badly. Too few came forward to join, and those that did were unhappy with German discipline. However, as the war progressed, several Western European formations became effective combat units. Some of the toughest of the defenders of Berlin in 1945 were members of these divisions.

Above: An SdKfz 232 heavy armoured car of the 11th *SS-Panzergrenadier Division Nordland,* bearing the division's *Sonnenrad,* or 'Sunwheel', variant of the Swastika on the front (next to the headlamp).
Left: SS men on parade in Brussels at the end of July 1944. Even at this late stage in the war, with the Nazis on the defensive everywhere, fresh volunteers were sought to fill the ranks of Himmler's ever-expanding SS.

NETHERLANDS

DATE OF OCCUPATION: MAY 1940
NUMBER OF VOLUNTEERS: 50,000
MAIN SS UNITS INCLUDING VOLUNTEERS: 23rd SS-Freiwilligen Panzergrenadier Division *Nederland* (niederlandische Nr. 1); 34th SS-Freiwilligen Grenadier Division *Landstorm Nederland*

Although the Netherlands is related linguistically and culturally to its much larger neighbour, Germany, a strong sense of independence has meant that Holland has never been overwhelmed by Germanic power. During the 1930s the *Nationaal Socialistische Beweging* (NSB, or National Socialist Movement), led by Anton Mussert, tried to emulate the success of the Nazi Party in Germany, but the people of the Netherlands never rallied to its support in any great numbers.

On 10 May 1940, Germany invaded, and Holland was swiftly overrun and occupied. Mussert and the NSB saw this as their chance to seize control of the nation, but their lack of popular or political support meant that they had little value to, and hence little influence with, their masters. One way of trying to increase what little influence they had was by fighting for the Germans. After the fall of the Low Countries in June, the SS began to recruit new members from Holland and Flanders, the Dutch-speaking part of Belgium. Seen as suitably 'Aryan' by the Nazis, the Dutch volunteers were funnelled into the SS *Westland* Regiment, a counterpart to the *Nordland* Regiment which was recruiting in Norway and Denmark. Mussert initially dreamed that the Dutch volunteers would fight in their own uniforms under their own colours, but the Germans would have none of it. The Dutch volunteers were inducted into the *Waffen*-SS. The Nazis made it clear that the Netherlands would eventually be integrated into Greater Germany, and to

The Netherlands provided more recruits for the Waffen-SS than any other European country. Most had been influenced by Anton Mussert's home-grown national socialist party, the NSB.

that end Himmler insisted on the formation of a Dutch *Allgemeine*-SS. This organization was intended to help to Nazify the Dutch people and make them ready for the final integration.

Although Mussert had urged closer ties with the Nazis, he was primarily a Dutch nationalist, and did not want to see his country absorbed into the Reich. However, opposition to German plans would have meant the marginalization of the NSB. Mussert chose to collaborate, and on 11 September 1940, shortly after a meeting with Hitler, he established the *Nederlandsche*-SS. Although almost identical with the German *Allgemeine*-SS, the Dutch version was officially a part of the NSB. In September 1940, Hitler approved Himmler's request to form a fifth SS division. Centered on the *Germania* Regiment, which had been withdrawn from the SS-VT Division (which later became *Das Reich*), it was intended that the bulk of its strength would come from the Nordic volunteers of the *Westland* and *Nordland* Regiments. The division, then named *SS-Germania*, would be equipped as an Army motorized division. Late in 1940, the division was renamed *SS-Division Wiking*, to avoid confusion with the *Germania* Regiment.

The German occupation forces established recruiting centres in all the major cities of Holland. Many Dutchmen volunteered to join, and in May 1941, a contingent of 631 Dutch recruits with a cadre of German personnel were incorporated into the *Wiking* Division. Many of the volunteers knew exactly what they were doing when they signed up.

However, quite a few were tricked: hundreds thought that they were signing on for political, police or sports education in Germany. They only found out the truth when they arrived at the SS barracks. However, *Wiking* was multi-national more in theory

Above: *SS-Standarte Westland*, made up from suitably 'Germanic' volunteers from the Low Countries, was formed in July 1940 even before the war in the West had ended. These Dutch members wear the 'Wolfshook' insignia above their 'Deathshead' cap badge.

than in practice. In June 1941, as the division formed up to cross the Soviet border, it numbered only 1564 foreign volunteers in a total strength of 19,377 men. The remainder consisted of German SS men, with a scattering of *Volksdeutsche*. However, those 1500 volunteers provided grist to the German propaganda mill as the *Wiking* Division amassed a combat record

second to none. The coming war with Russia saw the SS needing more volunteers to enable it to expand further, and in April 1941 Hitler gave Himmler permission to recruit up to 2500 Flemings and Dutch nationals for a new volunteer regiment, *SS-Nordwest*. By 25 May, some 920 Dutchmen had arrived in Hamburg-Langenhorn, and they were joined by a further 560 Dutch, Flemish and Danish volunteers over the next three months.

SS planners foresaw separate battalions of Flemish and Dutch volunteers, but too few volunteers meant that the SS had to scrap the scheme. It was decided to form a purely Dutch formation on the lines of the *Nordwest* Regiment, but without the 'Greater Dutch' ethos which permeated that Flemish/Dutch formation.

A contingent of 2000 volunteers entrained for the SS basic training camp at Debica in Poland, and by the end of August 1941, two battalions of volunteers were formed into the Dutch Legion. The volunteers wore SS uniforms with a sleeve shield in the Dutch national colours of red, white and blue. Command was given to the former chief of staff of the Dutch Army, 69-year-old Lieutenant-General H.A. Seyffardt. Although the Dutch provided one of the

Below: Dutch SS volunteers arrived in the East in the winter of 1941. They made their combat debut on the Volkhov front around Lake Ilmen, being thrown into battle against the Soviet winter offensive.

largest of all the volunteer legions, most of the officers and NCO cadre were German. In September, the legion was moved to East Prussia for further training. Later that month, it absorbed the Dutch contingent of the *Nordwest* Regiment, and was declared operational as the *Freiwilligen Legion Niederlande*.

The Dutch Legion blooded

Like many of the foreign legions, the Dutch Legion had very little of the order and discipline inculcated into the German units of the *Waffen*-SS. Partly this was due to the curiously mixed nature of the Dutch recruits, who included in their number volunteers ranging from political idealists and true believers to thrill-seekers and criminals. *Waffen*-SS training personnel had little regard for their Dutch charges, and relations were bad from the beginning.

Sent to the Volkhov front early in 1942, the legion arrived at Lake Ilmen at the height of the Soviet winter offensive, and suffered 80 per cent casualties in its first major combat in March of that year. After refitting, in June 1942 it was attached to the German 2nd SS (Motorized) Infantry Brigade. In spring of 1943, the legion was withdrawn to Grafenwohr, Germany, and disbanded.

By 1943, the experiment with the European 'Germanic' legions had pretty much failed, since such small units were simply not effective in the titanic conflict which had evolved in Russia. Mussert then suggested that a Dutch SS division be formed, but finding 20,000 men in the time scale envisaged proved to be impossible. However, a brigade-sized formation was possible, and the *SS-Freiwilligen Panzergrenadier Brigade Nederland* was formed in

Above: New recruits for the *Waffen*-SS take the oath of loyalty to Adolf Hitler. After the loss of so many men on the Eastern Front, the organization was forced to scour Europe for suitable replacements.

October 1943 as part of the further expansion of the *Waffen*-SS. Some 2500 veteran legionnaires joined with an additional 3000 volunteers from the *Nordland* Regiment. This brigade was composed of two regiments: the *General Seyffardt* (named after the first legion commander, who had been assassinated by the Dutch resistance earlier that year) and the *De Ruyter* Regiment (named after the seventeenth-century Dutch admiral Michael de Ruyter). Renamed 4th *SS-Freiwilligen Panzergrenadier Brigade Nederland*, it saw action in Yugoslavia. In December 1944 the brigade was expanded to become the 23rd

SS-Freiwilligen Panzergrenadier Division Nederland (niederlandische Nr. 1), though it was never brought up to full divisional strength.

One further Dutch unit should be mentioned. On 1 January 1942 the SS raised the *SS-Wachbataillon Nordwest*. Although nominally part of the *Waffen-SS*, the *Wachbataillon* had much lower physical entry standards and accepted recruits up to the age of 40. It also included a company of Ukrainian volunteers transferred from the Eastern Front.

The reason for the lower standards was simple: *Wachbataillon Nordwest* was responsible for guarding German concentration camps in the Netherlands. The new *Wachbataillon* consisted of six companies:

Below: Flemish volunteers in the SS prepare to fire an MG34 machine gun during training. Belgian members of the *Waffen*-SS reflected the divided nature of the country, coming as they did from both Dutch-speaking Flanders and French-speaking Wallonia.

two companies served at the police detention camp at Amersfoort; one was based at St Michielsgestel, which was a camp for intellectuals and hostages from prominent families; two more were responsible for the concentration camp at Vught; the sixth company was based at Haaren. One further company was intended to take up guard duty at Westerbork concentration camp, but this unit was transferred to the garrison at Scheveningen, where it became an anti-tank company.

Criminals and conmen

The irregular nature of its duties and the poor quality of its recruits meant that *Wachbataillon Nordwest* was 'an irregular lawless mess' in the words of Dutch World War II historian Lou de Jong. The *Wachbataillon* was also an attractive option for those who wished to avoid German forced labour, which was starting to make increasing demands of the male population of the Netherlands. Poor-quality recruits

who were less than honest meant that it was not long before the military police began to receive regular complaints about the unit. *Nordwest* men were accused of large numbers of thefts, burglaries and episodes of looting. The unit commander was held responsible for the incidents, but he claimed that it was not his fault. He claimed that since his men had not been provided with enough alcohol or with decent food, they had simply gone crazy.

A senior SS investigating judge was to recall after the war that 'the battalion had a very high crime rate, without even considering purely military crimes such as desertion, absence without leave, abandoning sentry duties, and disobedience. The men of the Wachbataillon committed every single crime that is known in common criminal law: crimes like theft, looting, fraud, and blackmail.'

Landstorm Nederland

In November 1944 the *SS-Wachbataillon Nordwest* was transferred to the Ardennes front, where it was combined with two *Landstorm* battalions to form the *SS-Freiwilligen Grenadier Brigade Landstorm Nederland*. The *Landstorm* had been formed (originally as the *Landwacht Nederland*) on 12 March 1943 as a territorial defensive unit. The name was changed to *Landstorm Nederland* in October 1943. The unit consisted of Dutch volunteers and was stationed in Den Bosch, Vught, Roermond and Hoogeveen.

Some took part in the Arnhem campaign. Many of the volunteers joined simply because the *Landstorm* was a source of employment, shelter and food (the latter in short supply in Holland in 1944). Also, by joining the force workers escaped the *Arbeitseinsatz* – the all-embracing German forced labour programme. In February 1945, the *Brigade Landstorm Nederland* was expanded, in name only, to become a division. The 34th *SS-Freiwilligen Grenadier Division Landstorm Nederland*, like most of the late-war *Waffen*-SS divisions, was smaller than brigades had been less than a year before.

BELGIUM

DATE OF OCCUPATION: JUNE 1940
NUMBER OF VOLUNTEERS: 40,000
MAIN SS UNITS INCLUDING VOLUNTEERS: 27th SS-Freiwilligen Grenadier Division *Langemarck* (flämische Nr. 1); 28th SS-Freiwilligen Grenadier Division *Wallonien*

Adjectives like 'plucky' and 'courageous' are often used to describe Belgium in World War II, but there was a darker side to the nation's experience between 1940 and 1944. Although the government had set itself up in exile in London, most of the civil service remained, along with the king, and continued to run the country under the Germans. However, pre-war rivalries between the Dutch-speaking Flemings and French-speaking Walloons added a great deal to the tension.

How much the government and local police helped the Germans identify Jews for deportation is difficult to say, but certainly some right-wing organizations collaborated actively with the Nazis. It is known that in Antwerp, the German Army and SS battalions staffed with Flemish volunteers relied on local police units to help catch Jews earmarked for deportation. Those same organizations provided much of the volunteer manpower who fought alongside the German Army on the Eastern Front.

On 27 June 1941 the *Führer* approved the establishment of national legions from the occupied nations which would take part in the struggle against communism. Belgium would provide two legions. One was to be a Flemish unit, which being considered Aryan would be attached to the *Waffen*-SS. The other, to be manned by Walloons, was not considered to be suitably Nordic, and as such would come under the aegis of the German Army. The right-wing parties in the Flemish region of Belgium,

Above: Belgian SS men on parade. Belgian volunteers fought hard for Germany, most notably in the struggle to hold back the Red Army in the fierce battles on the Narva River, where both Flemish and Walloon elements were under the command of III *Germanisches Korps*.

from which the Germans expected to recruit racially acceptable volunteers, were far from united. Some wanted an independent state, some a union with Holland, while the more extreme parties were believers in the pan-Germanic ideal of a Nordic super-state. Differences between these parties meant that Flemish volunteers were not forthcoming in any great numbers when in 1940 the SS sought to form the *Westland* Regiment of the *Wiking* Division.

Nordwest Volunteers

In an attempt to tap into Flemish manpower, the *Nordwest* volunteer unit was created. Manned by both

Dutchmen and Flemings, the regiment used the *Vlaamsch Nationaal Verbond* led by Staf De Clercq as the nucleus of Flemish participation. De Clercq encouraged party members to volunteer, and three companies were formed in April 1941. However, not all German commanders were keen on the 'Greater Dutch' sentiments which were common in *SS-Nordwest*, and a more broadly based Flemish volunteer unit was established in September 1941. The *Legion Flandern* benefited from anti-communist feeling engendered by the invasion of Russia, and over 1000 men (including a cadre of 150 German professionals) reported for training at Radom in Poland. The legion was the foundation of the Flemish SS units which were to fight on the Eastern Front and which will be covered in more detail later in this volume.

The formation of Flemish volunteer units caused considerable concern in the French-speaking part of Belgium. To counter any influence the separatist

Flemings might have gained with their German masters, Belgian unionist forces announced that a *Corps Franc Wallonie* would be recruited for service in the great crusade against the Russians. This would draw its strength from the fascist Rexist Party, led by the charismatic Léon Degrelle. Although they had made some political gains in the 1930s, the largely Catholic Rexists had fallen into disarray mainly due to internal rivalries. The German campaign in Russia allowed Degrelle to use anti-communist sentiments to force the party in a new direction. Up to that point, the occupying authorities had seen little value in the Rexists, who in spite of their pro-German stance had minimal support among the Belgian people.

However, control of the new volunteer units was seized by Fernand Rouleau, Léon Degrelle's deputy and head of the Rexist militia, the *Formations de Combat*. Because the Walloons were considered to be non-Aryan, the volunteers were taken into the German Army rather than the SS, where they were designated the *(Wallonische) Infanterie Bataillon 373*. On 8 August 1941, 869 Walloon volunteers embarked at Brussels for the long rail trip to a training camp at Meseritz, near the Polish border. Volunteer number 237 was Léon Degrelle, serving as a private soldier but acting as political leader. He had been forced to volunteer to prevent Rouleau from seizing control of the legion, and had announced his intention at a Rexist meeting in Liège on 20 July.

The name *Corps Franc Wallonie* was intended to echo the name of a volunteer *Freikorps* which had operated in the Baltic after the end of World War I, but it was quickly changed to the *Légion Belge Wallonie*. It was hoped that this title would foster a unionist spirit in the Belgian troops operating in the East, but the Flemish separatists would have no part of it. Eventually the name was changed to the more accurate *Légion Wallonie*. The legion included three members of the Belgian nobility and a handful of White Russians who had fought the Bolsheviks in the Russian Civil War. A small cadre of professional officers was joined by a number of reserve officers,

Initially considered to be non-Germanic, French-speaking volunteers from France and Wallonia were recruited by the German Army in 1941. They were incorporated into the **Waffen-SS** *late in 1943.*

most of whom were veterans of World War I. It was agreed that the legion was to be employed as a light infantry unit, with no front-line duties. In fact, the only combat it was intended to see would be mopping-up operations well back behind the lines. Degrelle was more ambitious, however, and sought a more active role for his Walloons, secretly fearing that the fighting would all be over before he and his men could take part. However, he found matters difficult to arrange from his position as a private soldier. Repeated requests to be made an officer were refused on the grounds that he lacked military experience.

Training was completed on 15 October, and the next day the 373rd Infantry Battalion of the German Army set off by train for the Ukraine, where it would join Army Group South. The battalion commander was Captain Georges Jacobs, a former officer of Belgian colonial troops. The legion was really too small to have any independent existence, and the Germans deployed it on security duties on lines of communication around Dnepropetrovsk. For the next six months, the *Légion Wallonie* was attached to various units in the First Panzer Army and the Seventeenth Army. The Germans did not regard it with any respect and morale plummeted. Relations went from bad to worse in December, when the Germans took most of the Walloons' heavy weapons for redistribution to 'real combat units'.

A report by the operations section of the Seventeenth Army noted that: 'We are having some difficulties with the Walloon Battalion. Members of the battalion complain about unfair treatment by our command to OKW, while IV Corps reports that the behaviour and non-cooperation of the Belgian troops borders on treason. The only use we can see is to transfer them to the rear areas of LII Corps.' At the beginning of 1942 the Germans tried to correct matters by appointing a new commander and a new German liaison officer. But before any reorganization could take effect the Walloons found themselves directly in the path of a Soviet counter-attack through the Donetz basin.

Opposite: Léon Degrelle, leader of Belgium's fascist Rexist Party, joined the Walloon Legion as a common soldier. In three years of combat in the East he rose to command the 28th *SS-Freiwilligen Grenadier Division Wallonien*.

Above: The Walloons fought alongside the *Wiking* Division in the Cherkassy pocket. Surrounded by overwhelming Red Army forces, the beleaguered SS men led a breakout in February 1944, losing half their number in the process.

Combat experience

The legion was ordered to eject Soviet troops from the village of Gromovayabalka. Having done so, on 28 February the Walloons, stiffened by an SS company attached from the *Germania* Regiment of the *Wiking* Division, fought off a counter-attack by two Soviet infantry regiments supported by tanks. After fierce house-to-house fighting, the legion was relieved by German forces on 2 March, by which time only two officers and some 250 men were still in action. Léon Degrelle, slightly wounded, won promotion to sergeant for bravery on the field of battle. In spite of their losses, proof that they could fight meant that morale in the legion improved. Sent to the rear to recuperate, the Walloons awaited reinforcements from Belgium. However, these were

hard to find. The legion had little popular appeal in Belgium, and replacements had to come from Rexist Party members alone. Men were drafted from the political leadership of the party and from its youth corps. These recruits reported to Meseritz for training in April 1942, and by May the legion was nominally up to strength.

On 21 May 1942, the Walloon Legion was assigned to the 97th Light Infantry Division. Lucien Lippert, a professional artilleryman, assumed command, and combat-tested NCOs, including Léon Degrelle, became junior officers. On arrival at the front, the Walloons were initially restricted to the reserve, where they carried out security duties until true unit cohesion could develop. The battalion was moved to the front lines in June, holding a supporting position on the Donetz River during the German summer offensive. The Walloons stayed at the rear, securing lines of communication as German panzer units smashed through the Don Basin and into the Caucasus.

Their first major action, a mopping-up operation in the village of Cheryakov, took place on 21–22 August. It was something of a milk run, assigned to the Walloons for propaganda purposes. The legion cleared Cheryakov by the end of the 22nd, capturing 35 Russians and an anti-tank gun. Walloon casualties were light, with only one man killed and 10 or so wounded. Minor though the fighting was, the action report was passed up through division, corps and onwards up to OKW.

The Walloon Legion was commended, and much was made of Lieutenant Léon Degrelle's leadership and bravery. Eventually it emerged as a press release which was widely distributed by the German propaganda organs.

However, the true combat value of the Walloons is a matter for conjecture. Within a week of the battle at Cheryakov the legion was withdrawn from the front after mounting casualties. Restricted to flank security duties, the Walloon Legion was briefly attached to the elite *SS-Division Wiking*. Degrelle was deeply affected by the leadership qualities of *Gruppenführer* Felix Steiner, and the Rexist leader started trying to build SS-style ideological zeal into his men after orders came for their withdrawal for rest and refitting. In September Degrelle was sent to Berlin to help organize the formation of a second battalion, made up from Rexist volunteers among the Belgian POWs held by the Germans since 1940. Most of the rest of the legion returned to Belgium, apart from one company which remained with *Wiking* through the withdrawal from the Caucasus after the disaster at Stalingrad.

The legion began to reassemble at Meseritz in March 1943. Its strength had grown rapidly, with surviving veterans being joined by released POWs and men recruited from Belgian civilians working in Germany. As many as 2000 men were now serving under German colours, but their future was no longer with the Army. Degrelle, using his new-found celebrity, was negotiating with Himmler and SS personnel chief Berger to transfer the legion to the *Waffen-SS*, where it would form the nucleus of an SS *Sturmbrigade*, eventually growing to become the 28th *SS-Freiwilligen Grenadier Division Wallonien*.

FRANCE

DATE OF OCCUPATION: JUNE 1940
NUMBER OF VOLUNTEERS: 20,000
MAIN SS UNITS INCLUDING VOLUNTEERS: 8th Französische SS-Freiwilligen Sturmbrigade; 33rd Waffen-Grenadier Division der SS *Charlemagne*

The defeat of France in 1940 and the one-sided armistice which followed fostered a pessimistic and cynical spirit in the French people. The octogenarian Philippe Pétain, Marshal of France and lionized as the 'Victor of Verdun', was called upon by President Lebrun to form a government on 17 June 1940. The 84-year-old marshal consented, signing an armistice with Germany on 22 June. Under the terms of this agreement, the only one Hitler ever signed with a defeated enemy, only part of France was to be occupied. The rest would be free of the enemy's presence – but in both occupied and unoccupied zones the authority of the French Government would apply … theoretically. Vichy, in the unoccupied zone, became the seat of the new government after it had established itself in the city.

Right-wing parties in both zones of France would become fertile recruiting grounds for the Nazis. The outbreak of war with Russia had a similar effect on anti-communists in France as it had elsewhere in Europe. The war in the East brought the prospect of the destruction of communism; at the same time

active combat over a huge area might reduce German pressure upon France. The war strengthened the positions of the collaborationist parties, since it fostered the idea that a German victory was far more acceptable than the 'Bolshevization' of Europe. However, Vichy France was never allowed an official role in the war in the East, unlike Germany's allies and satellites such as Italy, Finland, Hungary, Slovakia, Romania and Bulgaria. That is not to say that the French did not play a part in the German war effort. In fact, more Frenchmen worked directly for the Germans than did any other Western European nationality.

Not all were volunteers, however. Over 140,000 men from Alsace and Lorraine were conscripted into the German armed forces after their territories were annexed by Hitler. The Nazis believed that Alsace and Lorraine were rightly part of Germany, so their citizens were considered to be Aryan, unlike the rest of

Above: Right-wing recruits for the *Légion des Volontaires Français* depart to become part of the German Army. In common with other legion units, French volunteers who continued to fight were transferred to the SS in 1943.

the French population. At least another 150,000 men were conscripted into the *Organisation Todt* to help build the massive defences of the Atlantic Wall, and a further 25,000 worked for the *Kriegsmarine* in the Breton and Biscay ports. Many thousands of former POWs were forced to work in factories in Germany, where they were joined by members of the *Service du Travail Obligatoire* (STO), who were labourers conscripted on the Germans' behalf by the Vichy government.

But not all of those who served in German uniform were unwilling conscripts: about 45,000 Frenchmen volunteered to serve in the branches of Germany's armed forces and in various paramilitary arms. As in other countries, the early volunteers chose to fight for political or idealistic reasons, primarily to fight against communism. More than 6000 served with the *Légion des Volontaires Français* (LVF), while a company of some 212 men, *La Phalange Africaine*, fought with the 754th Panzergrenadier Regiment against the British in North Africa.

The Paris *Fronde*

The idea of a French legion to fight at the side of the Germans came neither from Vichy nor the Germans. Rather, it was the creation of the group of Paris collaborationist parties known collectively as the Paris *Fronde*. The main collaborationist political parties included *le Rassemblement National Populaire* (RNP),

Below: Not part of the German forces, but extremely active alongside the *Gestapo* in Metropolitan France, the collaborationist *Milice*, or 'Militia', hunted down Jews and resistance fighters for the Nazis in Vichy France.

founded in February 1941 by Marcel Déat, a former socialist who admired the order and discipline of European fascists; *le Francisme*, an overtly fascist pre-war movement led by Marcel Bucard that received financial support from Mussolini in the 1930s and which enjoyed a new lease of life in occupied France; the *Mouvement Social Revolutionnaire* (MSR), led by Eugene Deloncle; and the *Parti Populaire Français* (PPF), established by Jacques Doriot with the backing of numerous financiers and industrialists. Doriot was formerly a leading member of the French Communist Party, who had been expelled in 1934 after disagreeing with the party leadership.

An admirer of the achievements of Mussolini's Fascists, he formed the PPF soon afterwards, and through the remainder of the pre-war years used *Le Cri du Peuple*, the party newspaper, to advocate collaboration with Germany. Support for these Parisian collaborationist parties in France was limited. Historian Yves Durand estimates that less than one

Right: French volunteers in the German Army featured strongly in German propaganda photos, but they were not highly regarded by the *Wehrmacht*. However, those that stayed in German service after 1943 were much more highly motivated, and French SS units fought to the death in the defence of Berlin in 1945.

per cent of the French population ever became members. Even so, they were the driving force behind the formation of the French volunteer legion to fight against the Soviets on the Eastern Front.

Hitler (who despised the French) reluctantly approved the recruitment of a volunteer anti-communist legion in July 1941, though he denied the collaborationist request to form a full division. Public meetings, propaganda campaigns, and the formation of symbolic committees of party leaders and intellectual notables all took place through July and August, amid a feverish anti-Bolshevik atmosphere. The usual *Wehrmacht* health and racial regulations were applied to the recruits raised by this campaign, but the more stringent racial and physical strictures of the SS did not apply. Even so, there is some evidence that the Germans rejected many otherwise passable recruits to ensure that the French volunteer unit remained small.

Volunteers

Records indicate that some 3600 legionnaires enlisted and were accepted by the German Army through February 1942, and a further 3000 through May 1943. Those accepted were mainly members of the right-wing parties which had supported the formation of the LVF; others were veterans of the *Légion Etrangère* (Foreign Legion), including some of White Russian, Georgian and Armenian origin, as well as Arab and black colonials and veterans of the Spanish Civil War – both those who had fought under the 'Jeanne d'Arc' banner for the Nationalists and disenchanted ex-Republican International Brigade members.

The *Légion des Volontaires Français contre le Bolchevisme* mounted their first parade on 27 August 1941 at the Borguis-Desbordes Barracks at Versailles. Unfortunately, an assassination attempt carried out by an infiltrator, from within the ranks of the legion, wounded ministers Pierre Laval and Marcel Déat.

Nationalsocialistische Kraftfahrkorps

Less well known than the LVF, but offering far more to the German war effort, was the 4th NSKK Regiment, part of the NSKK *Motorgruppe Luftwaffe*. The NSKK, or *Nationalsocialistische Kraftfahrkorps*, was the original Nazi motorized organization, and during the war it provided logistic support to the *Wehrmacht*. The 4th NSKK Regiment was a logistics unit of some 2500 French drivers and engineers attached to the *Luftwaffe*. Formed in July 1942, it saw service on the Eastern Front and in the Balkans before returning to France in 1944 to provide motor support to the V-1 missile sites being built in the Pas de Calais. Later the unit was to see service in Italy, Denmark and Hungary before finally surrendering in Austria.

This unlucky beginning proved to be an omen for the legion's experiences in Russia. Sent by train from Paris, the LVF began training at Deba, Poland, through September and October. The unit swore fidelity to Adolf Hitler, but only as overall commander of the forces fighting against communism. By the end of October the legion was ready to be shipped to Smolensk as the *Französisches Vestartktes Infanterie Regiment 638* (French Reinforced Infantry Regiment 638) of the German Army. The regiment was reinforced only in name: the LVF would never be deployed as more than a light regiment with only two battalions.

The members of the LVF were a strange mixture of idealists, adventurers, political opportunists and professional soldiers. Doriot himself had joined as an NCO. Command had been given to Colonel Roger Henri Labonne, formerly military attaché to Turkey. Labonne, a veteran of World War I and a former commander of a French colonial regiment, was, at 65, far too old for the rigours of a winter campaign in Russia. Without adequate leadership and with incomplete training, the Germans held out little hope that the LVF would be of any use in combat. That judgement appeared to be vindicated when they were attached to the German 7th Infantry Division near Smolensk.

First blood

The LVF's baptism of fire came at the end of November during the advance towards Kubinka. The unit performed poorly, but did much better a few days

later in a series of small engagements during which they inflicted casualties on the Russians but suffered heavy losses themselves. The weakened unit had no answer to the heavy Soviet counter-offensive which began on the night of 5 December. The battalion was so heavily mauled that it had to be withdrawn after only a few hours of combat. In just two weeks the LVF had lost 150 men in battle – with another 300 killed or severely frost-bitten by the icy Russian weather.

In January 1942 the LVF was withdrawn to Smolensk for reorganization. Incompetent officers were removed and Russian *Hilfswilliger* (volunteer auxiliaries) were attached. Even though it was assigned to relatively easy security duties, the LVF's performance remained poor, and after the Germans decided that the regiment had zero combat capability, it was pulled back to Poland. The two existing battalions were merged, while a new battalion was raised after reinforcements arrived from France. However, the French were considered the worst of all the foreign volunteer units serving with the *Wehrmacht*, and the LVF was destined to remain on anti-partisan duties for the remainder of its existence. Surviving members of the legion were transferred to the SS in 1943. Under SS tutelage the French proved vastly more capable, and by the time they returned to front-line duty in 1944 they were able to earn the respect which had never been offered to the LVF.

Smaller units worked for organizations as diverse as the 21st Panzer Division, which had a French logistics company, and the *Kriegsmarine*, which employed some 4000 sailors, shore workers and policemen.

There were also 180 Frenchmen in the 8th Company of the 3rd Regiment of the Brandenburg Division. They were used in anti-partisan actions, but their primary mission was to infiltrate resistance groups in the South of France.

Police units

There were approximately 10,000 French members of German police units, who controlled as many as 30,000 civilian auxiliaries and informers. Many of the more active collaborators worked directly for the German intelligence services, including the *Abwehr*, the *Sicherheitspolizei* (Security Police), the *Gestapo* and the SD. The Germans also operated alongside the right-wing Vichy militia, the *Milice*.

Up to 20,000 Frenchmen served in the *Waffen*-SS, the majority after Himmler's men had taken control of most foreign volunteer units in the last two years of the war. However, individuals served in a number of

SS units before that, including at least two members of the *Leibstandarte*, Hitler's SS bodyguard. By late 1943, the remaining French volunteers were inducted into the Waffen-SS *Französische SS-Freiwilligen Grenadier Regiment*, which was later upgraded to the 8th *Französische SS-Freiwilligen Sturmbrigade*. At the end of the war the *Sturmbrigade* saw considerable action, suffering 90 per cent losses in Galicia and in the Carpathians.

The survivors were absorbed into the 33rd *Waffen-Grenadier Division der SS Charlemagne*. This too suffered heavy losses, initially in Pomerania and then in the final battle for Berlin.

Below: In spite of the impression of comradeship between *Luftwaffe*, SS, *Wehrmacht* and the LVF suggested by this photo, the early French volunteers in Russia did not perform well, and the German high command withdrew them from combat.

ITALY

DATE OF OCCUPATION: 1943
NUMBER OF VOLUNTEERS: 15,000
MAIN SS UNITS INCLUDING VOLUNTEERS: Waffen-Grenadier Brigade der SS (italienische Nr. 1); 29th Waffen-Grenadier Division der SS (italienische Nr. 1)

Italian troops had fought alongside the *Wehrmacht* in North Africa, the Balkans and on the Eastern Front since 1940. After the disaster at Stalingrad, where the Italian Eighth Army was among German satellite forces, Mussolini formed a new government in February 1943, *Il Duce* personally taking over from Ciano as foreign minister. Two months later, after Axis troops capitulated in North Africa and the Germans were being driven back through the Ukraine, Mussolini visited Hitler at Salzburg and urged him to make a settlement with the USSR.

By July 1943, Italy had lost all of its colonies in Africa, and most of its army, and was being invaded. Mussolini was deposed by a revolt within his own Fascist Grand Council, and Victor Emmanuel III, the king of Italy, who had been reduced to a figurehead by Mussolini, appointed Marshal Badoglio to be the new prime minister. Arrested as he was leaving the palace, *Il Duce* was bustled off in an ambulance to a succession of heavily guarded hiding places, ending at an isolated hotel located in the highest mountains of the Apennines, the Gran Sasso d'Italia. Badoglio told the Germans that he was going to continue to fight, while at the same time beginning to negotiate in secret with the Allies. Even though Hitler knew nothing of the Italian plans, he suspected that they might be about to surrender, and so pushed forward his own plans to occupy the country.

On 3 September, as the British Eighth Army crossed the Straits of Messina and landed in Calabria, the Italians signed an armistice to become effective on 8 September. Some Italian troops were able to surrender to the Allies, but although their leaders slipped away to comfortable exile, the surrender was

a disaster for most ordinary soldiers. Across Italy, the Balkans and Greece, German garrisons turned on their erstwhile allies. Italian units were disarmed and hauled off to Germany for use as slave labour. In some cases, as depicted in Louis de Bernières' novel *Captain Corelli's Mandolin*, they were massacred.

Meanwhile, Adolf Hitler had plans for *Il Duce*. The *Führer* maintained his high regard for Mussolini long after it became clear that Italy could offer little to the Axis cause, and ordered his friend's rescue. A specially picked team of SS and *Luftwaffe* parachutists commanded by Otto Skorzeny made a daring descent on the Gran Sasso on 12 September. After his dramatic rescue, Mussolini was bundled into a tiny Fieseler Storch reconnaissance plane and flown off the mountain. Once in German-occupied territory he was flown immediately to see Hitler.

To occupy his friend, the *Führer* set up a fascist puppet state in northern Italy, which would continue to fight alongside the Germans. He installed the 'cardboard Caesar' under heavy SS protection as head of the 'Salo Republic'. Its seat was the village of Gargnano on the western shore of Lake Garda. As an early item of business Mussolini established a tribunal to avenge the *coup d'état* of 1943. His son-in-law Count Ciano was among those ordered executed on 11 January 1944. Although a titular head of state, Mussolini remained a somewhat pathetic figure for the remainder of his life. He continued to inspect military formations, and went about the business of running his republic with the aid of Marshal Graziani. But he was a broken man.

New formations

However, Italian troops still had a considerable part to play in the Axis war effort. Nominally

Opposite: Long after Mussolini had been overthrown, Hitler continued to treat him as a head of state. However, surviving Italian Fascist troops were incorporated into the *Wehrmacht* structure under German control.

Prima Brigata d'Assalto della Legione SS Italiana – the Italian SS

Some Italian Fascists came under direct German control. After the 1943 armistice, the SS began recruiting for an Italian Volunteer Legion among the 800,000 disarmed and 250,000 interned members of the former Italian Army. In November 1943 the *Italienische Freiwilligen Legion* was established after more than 15,000 Italians volunteered to join the *Waffen*-SS. Many of the would-be recruits had been members of the 'Fortunato' *Bersaglieri* unit which had fought hard as part of the Italian Army on the Eastern Front. In January 1944 the unit was renamed 1st *Sturmbrigade Italienische Freiwilligen Legion*. It was also known as the 1st *Italienische Freiwilligen Sturmbrigade Milizia Armata*, while to the Italians themselves it was the *Prima Brigata d'Assalto della Legione SS Italiana*.

Of the SS but not actually part of it, the Italian Legion wore a similar uniform but with green rather than black trimmings. However, following a hard-fighting contribution to the struggle around Anzio in the spring of 1944, the Italian SS men received a sign of approval from Heinrich Himmler, who in June wrote: 'For valour and devotion to Duty, the Sturmbrigade Italienische Freiwilligen Legion shall hereafter adopt the black collar and rank insignia of the German SS, and shall be eligible for all duties and rights thereto.'

In September 1944 the unit was renamed the *Waffen-Grenadier Brigade der SS (italienische Nr. 1)*. Early in March 1945 the unit was nominally expanded to divisional size, becoming the 29th *Waffen-Grenadier Division der SS (italienische Nr. 1)*. It was a 'second-hand' divisional number, which was applied to the Italians after the 29th *Waffen-Grenadier Division der SS (russische Nr. 1)* was disbanded. It was intended to be brought up to strength by fresh drafts of German and Italian troops but the war ended before the formation could approach its planned strength.

Those divisional members – in fact, almost any Italian in SS uniform – who surrendered to the partisans at the end of the war were almost invariably executed.

independent, the former Fascists were actually under *Wehrmacht* control, and were treated as part of the German armed forces. In July 1943, the German high command ordered the formation of a new Italian Army.

By March 1944 four new divisions had been formed, the 1st Infantry Division *Bersaglieri*, the 2nd Infantry Division *Camice Nere*, the 3rd Infantry Division *Granatieri* and the 4th Infantry Division *Alpini*. These were joined by Fascist militiamen from the *Milizia Voluntaria Sicurezza Nationale* (MVSN), which by the end of 1944 had put seven Blackshirt battalions into the field.

Opposite: A poster that circulated through northern Italy at the end of 1943 calls for volunteers to join the Italian SS, claiming that the only way for Italy to escape defeat is through a real fighting force – the *Waffen*-SS.

Nominally under the command of Marshal Graziani, the four infantry divisions were actually under the control of *Oberbefehlshaber* Southwest. The 1st Division was attached to the German Fourteenth Army, and went into action around Parma at the end of 1944. Early in 1945 it was in action in the Parma/Fidenza/Salsomaggiore area alongside the 162nd (Turkistani) Infantry Division. The 2nd Division, by now renamed the *Littorio* Division, went into action near Parma in November before being transferred to the Alps in December 1944. The 3rd Division was renamed the *San Marco* Division. Most of its personnel had been transferred from the Italian Navy. In July 1944 it was sent to the Ligurian coast, where it was used for coastal security and anti-partisan duties. One infantry regiment was later detached and sent to the Alps where it became part of a *Kampfgruppe* of the German Army's 4th

Left: The German Army and the SS oversee the disarmament of Italian forces in German occupied Italy after Badoglio's government switches to the Allies in the autumn of 1943. Many Fascist units remained loyal to Mussolini, however, and were soon rearmed and under German control.

to Garfagnana where it was thrown into battle against the US 92nd Infantry Division. The 8th *Kampfgruppe* stayed in Liguria until March 1945, when it was also sent to join the 5th German *Gebirgsjäger* Division in the Alps.

The four infantry divisions were only the tip of the iceberg, however. Early in 1944, a *Wehrmacht* report recorded 18 Italian coastal fortress battalions under German orders or forming. Most of these had German officers or NCOs. These units were supplemented by six coastal artillery battalions. In addition, six German-led pioneer battalions were in service, and another 38 wholly Italian labour battalions were being formed. These were supported by up to 15 signals, transportation and supply units, and by 42 medical units distributed around northern Italy. More Italian units served in the Balkans under *Oberbefehlshaber* Southeast. Seven Blackshirt battalions were used on anti-partisan and security operations in the Balkans.

The *San Marco* Legion was formed in Croatia in 1943 under the aegis of the V SS Mountain Corps. Other Italian volunteer legions were formed by committed Fascists on the Greek islands of Crete, Samos and Rhodes, after Germany disarmed the Italian garrisons there in 1943.

Gebirgsjäger Division. The 4th Infantry Division was formed at Munsingen between March and May 1944. It too was sent to Liguria, where it suffered heavily in the anti-partisan war.

In September two battalions were disbanded after losing most of their men in the guerrilla campaign, and a mountain regiment and an artillery regiment were transferred to the 5th German *Gebirgsjäger* Division in the Alps. Much of the rest of the division was reorganized by the Germans into two *Kampfgruppen*. The 7th *Kampfgruppe* was transferred

DENMARK

DATE OF OCCUPATION: APRIL 1940
NUMBER OF VOLUNTEERS: 10,000
MAIN SS UNITS INCLUDING VOLUNTEERS: 5th SS-Panzer Division *Wiking*; 11th SS-Panzergrenadier Division *Nordland*

In April 1940, the Germans invaded Denmark and conquered the country after encountering virtually no resistance. Denmark was looked on as a Nordic nation with suitably Aryan bloodlines, so on 23 April 1940 – just two weeks after the invasion – Himmler ordered a recruiting drive to be mounted in both Denmark and Norway (rather presumptuously, as parts of the country at that time had yet to fall to the Germans). As has already been seen, the German Army's stranglehold on recruiting in Germany proper blocked Himmler's ambitions to increase the size of the SS, so northern European volunteers were seen as a way around the problem.

Suitable volunteers from Denmark and Norway between the ages of 17 to 23 were encouraged to sign on for a minimum enlistment of two years. By doing so, they would receive German citizenship, with all the rights and privileges of *Reichsdeutsche*, while also retaining their Danish citizenship.

However, only some 200 Danes initially volunteered, not the flood into German service that Himmler had hoped for, but ethnic Germans from Schleswig, on the German border, provided enough manpower, along with the Norwegians, to establish the *SS-Standarte* (Regiment) *Nordland*, which was to become one of the constituent parts of the *SS-Division Wiking*. Over 1000 German Danes also joined the SS individually, most serving with the *Totenkopf* Division and with the 1st SS Brigade, which gained a sinister reputation on the Eastern Front. As in other European nations, Operation

Above: Three brothers from Copenhagen take a break from physical training as they prepare to join the *Nordland* Regiment. Soon to become part of the SS Division *Wiking*, *Nordland* numbered several hundred Danes and Norwegians in its strength.

Barbarossa in June 1941 provided the impetus for a much more successful recruiting drive. By now, both the SS and the German Army were recruiting foreign volunteers into a new kind of formation: the legion. These units tried to avoid association with out-and-out Nazis, an anti-communist theme being used to attract members of right-wing political groups who were not necessarily national socialists.

Most of the SS legions – those from Norway, the Netherlands and Flanders – were the result of a combined effort between the SS *Hauptamt* in Berlin and local national socialist or Nazi-inspired parties. The local parties expected to gain political capital with the Germans, which could be used in the post-war 'New Order' which at that time, in 1941, they expected to be in place within a year. In Denmark, the DNSAP (Danish National Socialist Workers Party) were willing helpers of the SS. Party leader Frits Clausen used the *Barbarossa* offensive to call upon Danes to fight for Europe against the *Weltfeind* or 'World Enemy'. In a speech on 23 June 1941, he urged Danes to join *SS-Standarte Nordland*. Other party officials, however, recommended that a new, all-Danish unit be established. It was to be a national legion, similar to one which had fought for the Finns against the Russians during the Winter War.

Clausen and the DNSAP needed a military man to help set up the new unit, so they called on Artillery Lieutenant-Colonel Christian Peder Kryssing for assistance. Kryssing, a well-known Danish nationalist, did more than the Nazis expected. He sought and obtained the acceptance of the Danish Government for the legion's formation, and got permission for Danish citizens, including regular military officers, to take service under a foreign power. The War Ministry passed a regulation to that effect on 8 July, some weeks after the initial recruiting drive started. The new formation would differ from other volunteer legions in two main ways. Firstly, since it was officially sanctioned by the Danish Government, serving members of the Danish armed forces were free to volunteer. Indeed, regular soldiers were to retain their Danish ranks, and service with the *Waffen*-SS would count equally with their Danish military service when it came to pension rights. Secondly, the new unit was to be officially sponsored by the Danish Government, unlike other legions whose primary support was from local fascist parties like Vidkun Quisling's *Nasjional Samling* in Norway, or Léon Degrelle's Rexist Party in Belgium.

Danish Legion formed

The formation of the legion was officially announced by the Danish Government on 28 June 1941. Press releases and public notices giving details of the new legion were posted on 8 July 1941, and recruiting offices were opened all over Denmark. The legion was to be open to men between 17 and 35, preferably serving soldiers or reservists who had completed their national service in the previous 10 years. The new legion received the official German designation of *SS-Freiwilligen Verband Danemark*, or SS Volunteer Group *Denmark*. However, it was more generally known as the *Freikorps Danmark*.

An initial draft of 430 volunteers was placed under the command of Colonel Kryssing, and the new battalion was sent to Hamburg for training in July. Most volunteers still wore Danish uniforms, but once in Germany they were issued with *Waffen*-SS equipment. The members of the *Freikorps* wore standard *Waffen*-SS uniforms, with a 'FREIKORPS DANMARK' cuff-band worn on their lower left tunic sleeve and a shield above this title bearing a white cross on a red background, the Danish national flag. SS flashes were worn on all ranks' collar tabs. More volunteers, together with a cadre of 200 Danes who had been transferred from *SS-Standarte Nordwest*, arrived in August to form a second battalion. By the end of 1941, the legion had grown to more than 1200 men.

Some 40 per cent of the *Freikorps* members had some previous military experience, but only 30 or so had recent combat experience, having served as

> **The Danes raised the only volunteer legion that had the full backing of the government of their country; legions elsewhere in Europe were usually inspired by local right-wing nationalist political parties.**

Above: SS troops escorted by a Panzer 38(t) move across the Russian steppe in the winter of 1941–42. While many of the volunteer legions served in the north, the Danes of the *Wiking* Division were in action in the Ukraine.

volunteers with the Finns during the Winter War. Like German SS members, they had to prove their 'Aryan' racial heritage before being accepted. A criminal record meant automatic rejection, as did being in debt. The motives of Danes for volunteering were varied. A few joined because they were professional soldiers and the Germans had the only war going at that time. Others were simply adventurers, who were looking for excitement in the thrill of combat. However, over three-quarters of the 6000 Danes who were to serve in the SS over the next four years did so because they were anti-communist, pro-German, or were connected with the Danish Nazi Party. As with the pre-war SS in Germany, the

bulk of the other ranks were working class, many being unskilled labourers or farmhands.

As the Danish volunteers gathered in Hamburg to begin their training, SS headquarters issued orders to organize them as an independent motorized battalion of three infantry companies and one weapons company. Sent to Russia in the spring of 1942, *Freikorps Danmark* was thrown into the battle of the Demyansk pocket, suffering heavy casualties.

NORWAY

DATE OF OCCUPATION: MAY 1940
NUMBER OF VOLUNTEERS: 6000
MAIN SS UNITS INCLUDING VOLUNTEERS: 5th SS-Panzer Division
Wiking, Den Norske Legion

The driving force behind Norwegian collaboration with the Germans during World War II was Vidkun Quisling, whose name has since become synonymous with treasonous collaboration with an enemy. Born in Fyresdal, Telemarken, Quisling joined the Norwegian Army in 1905 and was commissioned as an artillery officer. He spent long periods abroad as a military attaché and diplomat, before becoming war minister in 1931. Quisling resigned in 1933 to form the Nazi-style *Nasjional Samling* (NS, or National Unity Party). On 9 April 1940 Quisling gave orders that no NS member should participate in armed resistance against the German invasion, but most ignored this order, among them his own 'minister of defence', Major Ragnvald Hvoslef. Following the German conquest Quisling declared himself prime minister, but his regime had no popular support, which made him useless to the Nazis, and he was replaced by a German administration.

Below: Vidkun Quisling (centre right) accompanies *Reichsführer*-**SS Heinrich Himmler (left) during a visit to Germany. Quisling had formed a pro-German government in Norway, but the Nazis did not trust him and later replaced Quisling with a German administration.**

Even before the conquest of Norway had been completed, the SS began seeking recruits for the *SS-Standarte Nordland*. Initial numbers volunteering were not great, most of the few hundred signing on being members of the NS. Late in 1940, *Nordland* combined with the Dutch/Flemish *SS-Standarte Westland* and the German *SS-Standarte Germania* as the nucleus of what was to become the *SS-Division Wiking*. Quisling was rather disappointed, since he had had visions of a 50,000-strong Norwegian Army serving alongside the Germans.

Formation of the DNL

As in other occupied countries, the invasion of Russia brought an increase in the numbers volunteering. On 29 June 1941 *Reichskommissar* Josef Terboven announced the creation of a Norwegian legion to fight against the USSR. Known as *Den Norske Legion* (DNL), or *Legion Norwegen* in German, the first battalion carried the name *Viken*, after a historical Norwegian Army unit from Oslo. The Germans carefully orchestrated a call for volunteers based upon the 'flood of requests ... to take part in the opposition against Bolshevism'. The *Legion Norwegen* formed at

the end of July under the command of Major Joergen Bakke. Several thousand men volunteered, many being members of the *Hird*, the NS militia. About 1000 of these volunteers were accepted.

Quisling supported the effort, and assumed that the unit would fight in Finland. He also believed it would form the core of a new Norwegian Army after the expected German victory. Many Germans favoured this idea, since it would inspire the spirit of Scandinavian solidarity which had arisen during Finland's Winter War with the Russians. However, OKW squashed the notion, saying that there was not enough transport available. The DNL would have to go wherever they said it would go. Training began near Kiel. The men wore standard SS uniforms, but with the Norwegian lion replacing the 'Sig-runes' on collar patches, and the uniform carried an arm patch of the Norwegian flag. *Hird* members also wore a silver-on-black version of the St Olaf's Cross on their left sleeve.

Early in 1942, the legion was moved up to the front, but not to Finland. It was sent to take part in the siege of Leningrad. By this time, Adolf Hitler had declared war on the USA, which did not sit well with many of the Norwegian volunteers, many of whom

SS-Skijäger Kompanie Norge

Another unit was the *SS-Skijäger Kompanie Norge*, formed in 1943 by the Danish-born Gust Jonassen, who was the leader of the sports section of the NSUF, the NS equivalent of the Hitler Youth. A keen skier, he had fostered the sport within his organization. The 6th *SS-Gebirgsdivision Nord*, fighting in central Finland, had a requirement for a specialised ski company, and Jonassen proposed the formation of a Norwegian ski unit which would be used for reconnaissance and long-range patrolling. Jonassen was sent on an officer training course at the SS officer school at Bad Tolz, and began to recruit 120 skiers from the NSUF. Late in the spring of 1943, the unit joined *Nord*. Jonassen was killed soon afterwards when he stepped on a mine, but the ski company had proved its worth, and it was decided to

expand it to battalion size. Unlike other volunteer units, the ski battalion had no difficulty in finding volunteers. Most of the Norwegians in the *Waffen*-SS had originally expected to serve in Finland, and a number transferred from the *Norge* Battalion and from the *Luftwaffe*. In October 1943 it was joined by a company raised from the Norwegian police. The ski battalion distinguished itself in the fighting against the Soviets over the next two years. On 4 September 1944 Finland signed an armistice with the Russians, and the Norwegians retreated through Finnish Lappland towards Norway, often providing the rearguard for the 20th *Gebirgsarmee*. They reached Narvik by mid-December, where the battalion was reformed into a security police unit, in which form it fought until the end of the war.

had relatives in America. On 10 March 1942, the Norwegians entered the German siege lines around Leningrad, part of a mixed Army/SS battle group. It was intended to free up first-line divisions for a counter-attack on the Volkhov pocket. The legion at this time numbered about 1150 officers and men. Even though static operations called for less military skill than other forms of combat, SS headquarters was not satisfied with the Norwegian Legion.

Towards the end of 1942 the SS removed Major Bakke and his second-in-command, Major Andersen, from the legion. The Germans described Bakke as obstinate, and his fiercely nationalist attitude also made co-operation difficult. SS Personnel Chief Berger instructed his staff not to employ him in any other role, saying that 'his unpleasant personality and

independent character combined with his age make him of little value in a political or training role'. Bakke was replaced by Major Arthur Quist, a much more diplomatic former Norwegian Army officer.

The Norwegian Legion remained at Leningrad until the spring of 1943. Whether it was because of the appalling conditions under which they served, or the poor quality of their leaders, most Norwegian legionnaires declined to extend their enlistments. The *Reichsführer*-SS ordered the replacement of the Norwegian Legion with the Latvian Legion at the front in February 1943. Because of the legion's bad experiences, the Germans encountered problems in the recruitment of Norwegian volunteers for the rest of the war. In 1943, the *Nordland* Regiment was removed from the *Wiking* Division to form the nucleus of a new multi-national SS division. The 11th *SS-Freiwilligen Panzergrenadier Division Nordland* incorporated its Norwegian troops into a new unit, the *SS-Panzergrenadier Regiment 23 Norge*. Organized in September 1943, the regiment included those

Below: Norwegian volunteers are sworn in as members of the SS. *Waffen-SS* recruitment in Norway lagged significantly after an initial outburst of enthusiasm, and only with the war against the USSR did it pick up again.

Above: The *Den Norske Legion* was thrown into action on the Leningrad front. Poor leadership and heavy casualties meant that only one in five surviving volunteers re-enlisted after their two-year terms expired at the beginning of 1943.

members of the DNL who had been persuaded to re-enlist, together with surviving Norwegian members of the *Nordland* Regiment – about 700 men in all.

The regiment was brought up to strength with Hungarian *Volksdeutsche*. *Norge* was to be the second infantry regiment of the *Nordland* Division, but the Danish Government was slow to approve the formation of *SS-Panzergrenadier Regiment Danmark*, so *Norge* took its place. Again the number of Norwegian volunteers was to disappoint Quisling, who had expected more than 3000 recruits. However, those that served gained a much better reputation than their predecessors. Training was far more intense, and its core of combat veterans made *Norge* a far tougher unit than the Norwegian Legion.

Serving the cause

Not all of the Norwegian volunteers fighting for the Nazis were members of the *Waffen*-SS. The German administrators of occupied Norway did not trust the ambitious Quisling, and so they formed a branch of the *Allgemeine*-SS as a counter to Quisling's NS. Established in May 1941, it was renamed the *Germanske SS Norge* (GSSN) in 1942. The GSSN attracted those more fanatical and often younger members of the NS who saw Norway as a part of a Greater Germanic Europe. Most of them considered the NS to be an old-fashioned organization that placed the good of Norway ahead of the good of Europe as a whole. Officially Quisling approved of the GSSN, though in private he must have been less than delighted.

The only purely Norwegian unit in the SS, and one of the most controversial, was the *SS Vaktbataljon Norge*, also known as the *SS-Wachbataillon Norwegen*. Like the Dutch *Wachbataillon*, it was set up to provide

Left: By the second winter of the war in the Soviet Union, German troops had been issued with more effective winter uniforms. This Norwegian NCO of the *Wiking* Division is seen at Cherkassy, wearing *Waffen*-SS winter camouflage parka.

force, manned exclusively by older men beyond the normal age of military service. Also, after the occupation of Norway in 1940, a number of members of the Norwegian Air Force volunteered to join the *Luftwaffe*, but most were diverted into the *Waffen*-SS. About 100 men joined the *Luftwaffe* individually, with two serving as pilots (including Alf Lie, who had previously served in the *Wiking* Division), and about 500 Norwegians served as individuals or small groups in the German *Kriegsmarine*. Some are known to have served on the old pre-dreadnought battleship *Schlesien* in the Baltic. Some of the younger recruits were provided by the *Unghirdmarinen*, the naval youth movement of the NS. Many thousands more Norwegians served in the *Germansk Landtjeneste*, a labour organization, and in the *Organisation Todt*. They were employed all over Europe on the building of roads, forts and other military structures: large

guards for concentration camps. Manned by older NS members, its training grounds were at Holmestrand. Some 360 men served as *Konzentrationslager* guards, mostly in northern Norway.

Norwegians also served in the other German armed forces. As many as 1500 Norwegians served in the German Army, most having joined independently as individuals. Some had been students in Germany at the outbreak of war in 1939. The German Army actually established an all-Norwegian unit in 1942, though it was far from being a true combat unit. The *Wachdienst Norwegen* was a kind of home defence

numbers of Norwegians worked on the building of the *Westwall* fortifications in Germany and the Atlantic Wall in France, the Low Countries and Norway. Some also served with the *Reichsarbeitsdienst*, or Reich Labour Service.

Over 350 Norwegian women served as front-line nurses. *Frontsisters* over the age of 21 saw duty in Finland, the Baltic States, the USSR, Poland, Croatia, Italy and France. Those under 21 generally served in Norway and Germany. At least 13 *Frontsisters* were killed in action, and one, Anne Moxness, was the only non-German woman to be awarded the Iron Cross.

FINLAND

DATE OF OCCUPATION: ALLY – NOT OCCUPIED
NUMBER OF VOLUNTEERS: **3000**
MAIN SS UNITS INCLUDING VOLUNTEERS: **SS-Regiment** *Nordland*; **Finnisches Freiwilligen-Bataillon der Waffen-SS**

The Winter War of 1939–40 began when Finland, formerly a Russian province, refused Soviet demands for border adjustments. Germany gave moral support to the Finns in their disagreement with Stalin, but would not give material support, Adolf Hitler being as yet unready to take on the USSR.

The Soviets attacked Finland on 30 November 1939, launching half a million men with massive armoured and air support against a Finnish Army less than half as strong. But the Finns proved to be ferocious fighters, and the Soviets made no headway until they committed a further 500,000 men under Marshal Timoshenko. Battered by sheer numbers in a war of attrition they could not win, the Finns signed an armistice in March 1940, after losing some 25,000 men. Soviet losses were at least 10 times higher, many soldiers freezing to death in the Arctic cold which on occasion fell to –50°C (–58°F). Finnish stubbornness and the sheer fighting qualities of Finnish soldiers meant that Moscow did not treat the Finns as they

Below: Although vastly outnumbered, the Finns had fought overwhelming Soviet strength almost to a standstill in the Winter War, 1939–40. Most Finns served in their own units, but a few joined the *Waffen*-SS.

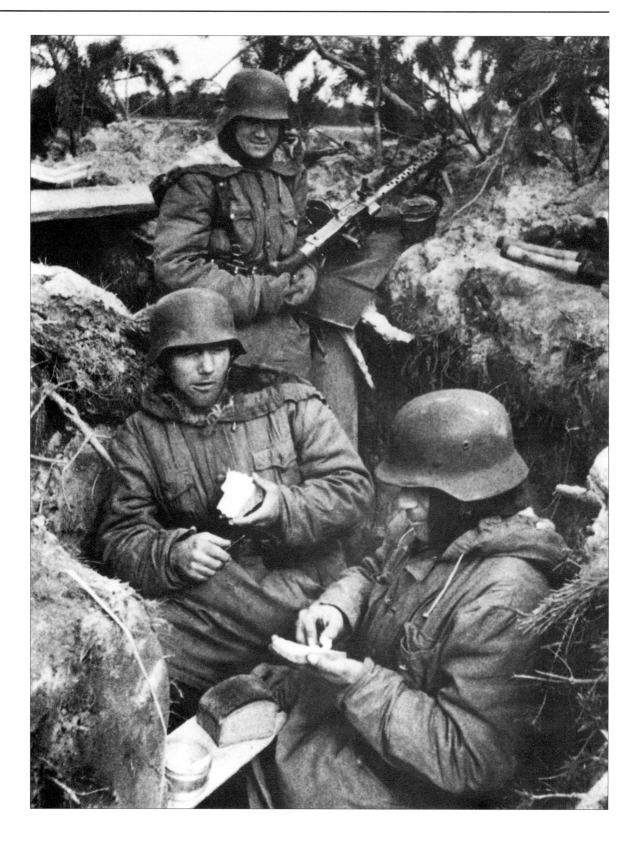

had the other Baltic States, leaving Finland a measure of independence that was denied to Latvia, Lithuania and Estonia. The Soviet failure to dominate Finland convinced many Germans – Adolf Hitler and the high command included – that the Soviet Union was a paper giant, and would be easy to conquer.

The Finns had impressed the Germans with their fighting qualities, and Himmler sought to include Finnish volunteers when he accelerated the expansion of the *Waffen*-SS in 1941. Moreover, the Finnish government was in secret negotiations with the Germans to join in the forthcoming invasion of Russia, Operation *Barbarossa*. But there was a clause in the agreement that while Finnish troops would take part in the Axis campaign, no Finns would be used against Britain or Greece, who were the only nations actively fighting against Germany at that time.

Wiking volunteers

Several months before this, however, the first 1000 Finnish volunteers for the *Waffen*-SS had been assembled. In an effort to avoid complications with the Russians, the volunteers were described as industrial workers taking up employment in Germany, but it would be several months before the Finns actually arrived in Germany: they were delayed by details, including the refusal of many individual soldiers to take the SS oath of unquestioning obedience to Adolf Hitler.

Eventually these problems were settled, and between May and June 1941, somewhere in the region of 125 officers, 110 NCOs and 850 other ranks joined the SS on the Eastern Front, ready for Operation *Barbarossa*. Because most of the volunteers had recent military training and combat experience, they were assigned directly to the *Wiking* Division, which by now was a fully motorized formation.

Two more groups of volunteers, this time made up from those who lacked a military background, were sent to Vienna for full *Waffen*-SS training. These would form the nucleus of a new battalion, the *SS-*

Opposite: The Finns were respected by the Germans, since they were masters of Arctic warfare. However, the Finnish Government insisted that Finns enlisting in German units must only be used to fight against the Soviets.

Freiwilligen Bataillon Nordost. As more recruits arrived for training, the unit was renamed the *Finnisches Freiwilligen-Bataillon der Waffen-SS*. The Finns considered themselves an elite light infantry unit, and described themselves as *Jäger* (literally 'Hunters', the north European term for light infantry). In August 1941, the battalion transferred for advanced training to the *Truppenlager* Gross Born. Training was completed by the middle of October, and the unit was declared combat ready. It was eventually sent by rail to the Eastern Front early in December 1941.

Although the Finns were good soldiers, they had some problems integrating with their German counterparts. Admittedly, they looked like any other *Waffen*-SS unit, but they were very much their own men. Unlike other volunteer legions, the Finns would only accept their own officers and NCOs. They made that point clear by refusing to accept any orders given in German. The legendary Finnish stubbornness eventually prevailed over German parade-ground discipline, and the Finns got their way.

Disbandment

The Finnish volunteers came to the end of their two-year enlistments in March 1943, and the Finnish Government made it clear that it expected its men to be returned home. In May 1943 they were pulled from the front lines, and after rest and recuperation at Grafenwohr, were sent by rail to Tallinn, from where they were shipped back to Finland. There, on 2 June 1943 the men of the *Finnisches Freiwilligen Bataillon der Waffen-SS* were sent on a month's leave. The unit was officially disbanded on 11 July 1943, and its members were transferred back into the Finnish Army. The last official ceremony, commemorating those members of the battalion who had fallen in action, was held in Helsinki on 19 September 1943.

There was now no Finnish unit in the official *Waffen*-SS order of battle. However, a number of Finnish troops were still serving in the *SS-Standarte Nordland*, which in July 1943 was detached from the *Wiking* Division to become part of the 11th *SS-Freiwilligen Panzergrenadier Division Nordland*. These men were allowed to remain in German service, and the Finns were still in action with the division when hostilities ceased in May 1945.

LUXEMBOURG

DATE OF OCCUPATION: MAY 1940

NUMBER OF VOLUNTEERS: 2000

MAIN SS UNITS INCLUDING VOLUNTEERS: Not known – Luxembourgers were classed as German and served in all branches of the _Wehrmacht_

The Grand Duchy of Luxembourg, the tiny country southwest of Belgium, had retained its independence for centuries. However, its strategic position on the Belgian and German borders meant that it stood astride the _Wehrmacht_'s invasion route in the West, and it was overrun on 10 May 1940, the first day of the Western campaign.

Like Alsace and Lorraine, Luxembourg was looked on by the Nazis as an integral part of Greater Germany. There had been some attempts to establish a German-style national socialist party after Hitler's accession to power in 1933, but without success. It was not until July 1940, after the German occupation, that the _Volksdeutsche Bewegung_ (VDB) was formed under the leadership of 62-year-old Professor Damian Kratzenberg. The VDB's motto was _Heim ins Reich_, or 'Home to the Reich'. This was not strictly accurate: Luxembourg had been an independent member of the German Confederation between 1815 and 1867, but it had never officially been part of the German Reich.

After the campaign in the West ended, on 28 June 1940, Luxembourg was formally linked to _Gau_ Koblenz-Trier. _Gaue_ were the main Nazi territorial units, corresponding to the old _Reichstag_ electoral districts and civil defence regions. _Gaue_ were also set up after 1938 in Austria and Czechoslovakia, and by the outbreak of war there were 43 – the 43rd being the _Auslands_ organization for overseas Germans which was administered from Berlin by _Gauleiter_ Ernst Wilhelm Bohle. Territories like Luxembourg, which were annexed into the Reich proper rather than simply being occupied were attached to existing _Gaue_. In February of 1941 _Gau_ Koblenz-Trier was renamed _Gau_ Moselland.

A rigid policy of Germanization was forced on Luxembourg. German organizations were set up and rapidly made compulsory. From January 1941, manual and industrial workers had to join the _Deutsches Arbeits Front_ (DAF) or face dismissal. Compulsory service in the _Reichsarbeitsdienst_ (RAD) was introduced for school-leavers of both sexes. By 1942 a German report showed that 110 Luxembourgers were in the _Allegemeine_-SS, 1100 had joined the _Sturmabteilung_ (SA, or 'Brownshirts'), nearly 1500 were members of the NSKK and as many as 60,000 had joined the DAF.

More than 14,000 Luxembourgers fought for the Germans as part of the _Wehrmacht_ between 1940 and 1945, but since Luxembourg was regarded by the Germans as an integral part of the Reich, there was no 'Luxembourger Legion'. However, the _Wehrmacht_ mounted an intensive recruitment campaign in the tiny Duchy soon after the victory in the West was completed at the end of June 1940.

Volunteers and conscription

The spectacular German triumph over France made finding volunteers for the unit relatively easy, and the first German recruitment drive brought in as many as 2000 volunteers from a total population of only 290,000. In August 1942 Luxembourg was officially made a part of the German Reich, and all of its citizens were subject to conscription into the armed forces of the Reich. Soon afterwards, all of the classes of (that is to say, men born in the years) 1920 to 1926 were drafted. In the two years before liberation at the end of 1944, the Germans called up 12,035 men from Luxembourg.

Over 2750 Luxembourgers were killed or missing in action, 1500 were severely wounded or disabled, and 3516 deserted. Luxembourg volunteers and conscripts served in various units of the Army, _Luftwaffe_, _Kriegsmarine_ and _Waffen_-SS, but since they were classed by the _Wehrmacht_ as Germans they were not identified by their origin.

SPAIN

DATE OF OCCUPATION: NEUTRAL

NUMBER OF VOLUNTEERS: 1000

MAIN SS UNITS INCLUDING VOLUNTEERS: Spanische Freiwilligen Kompanie der SS 101; 3rd (Spanish) Company of the 1st Battalion, 28th SS-Freiwilligen Panzergrenadier Division *Wallonien*

Despite Adolf Hitler's best efforts, the wily Spanish dictator Francisco Franco refused to bring his nation into the war on Germany's side. 'Dealing with Franco is like pulling teeth,' the *Führer* is reported to have said, after one particularly difficult meeting. Hitler wanted Franco's help in eliminating the key British naval base at Gibraltar, but the Spaniard could not be persuaded.

That is not to say that Spain did not contribute to the Axis war effort. Franco knew that he owed Germany and Italy a debt for the aid which they had provided during the Spanish Civil War – and he had a score to settle with Stalin, who had supported the Republicans in the same conflict. It was after the German invasion of the USSR that he saw the chance to repay some of that debt, without actually becoming a belligerent. Within a day of the launch of Operation *Barbarossa*, the Spanish Government

Below: Many of the Spanish volunteers who served with the *Wehrmacht* on the Eastern Front were veterans of the Spanish Civil War. However, their free-and-easy ways infuriated the German instructors who had to train them.

Aged 45, he had been a successful corps commander in the Civil War, and was a former secretary general of the *Falange*. He oversaw the raising of four infantry regiments at Madrid, Seville, Valladolid, Valencia, Barcelona, Zaragoza, Corunna, Burgos and at Ceuta in Spanish Morocco. Divisional artillery and support services were formed from veteran Spanish Army units.

It took less than four weeks to assemble the new division, and it was sent to Grafenwohr training ground in Bavaria in the middle of July 1941. The division arrived at Grafenwohr on 17 July. There, the four regiments were reduced to three to match German Army practice. Soon afterwards, the Spanish volunteer contingent was included into the German Army order of battle as the 250th Infantry Division. Total strength in August 1941 was 641 officers, 2272 NCOs and 15,780 other ranks.

As with most of the foreign volunteer formations, the ferocious discipline of the instructors at Grafenwohr caused problems. The German NCOs in particular felt that the Spanish soldiers were slovenly and lacked respect for parade-ground routines. To the Spaniards, most of whom were veterans of one of the most bitterly fought civil wars of the century, what mattered was what was done on the battlefield, not the parade ground. Nevertheless, training proceeded quickly, and by the end of August the division was classified as combat-ready.

From the beginning, the German high command regarded the Spanish Volunteer Division more as a political and propaganda symbol than as a real contribution to the *Wehrmacht*. In the war diary of the Ninth Army for September 1941, it was said that '... the deployment of the division from Spain is less a military advantage than a political and propaganda

offered to raise a unit of volunteers to fight alongside the Germans in the East. The plan was to call for volunteers from the regular army and from members of the ruling fascist party in Spain, the *Falange*. Response was enthusiastic: only three years before, the Spanish fascists had been fighting a bitter civil war against an enemy backed by the international communist movement, and the thought of playing a part in bringing down the home of communism was exciting. The idea was to form a full infantry division of volunteers, some 18,000 men, which would become known as the *Azul*, or 'Blue', Division – a reference to the blue shirts worn by *Falange* members.

The Blue Division formed

So many potential fighters appeared at the recruiting stations set up in army barracks and at *Falange* offices that they could have manned several divisions, not just one. Many of the recruits were ex-Civil War combatants, and a number of flyers also volunteered which enabled an *Esquadra Azul* to be formed to serve with the *Luftwaffe*. Franco appointed General Agustin Munoz Grandes to command the volunteers.

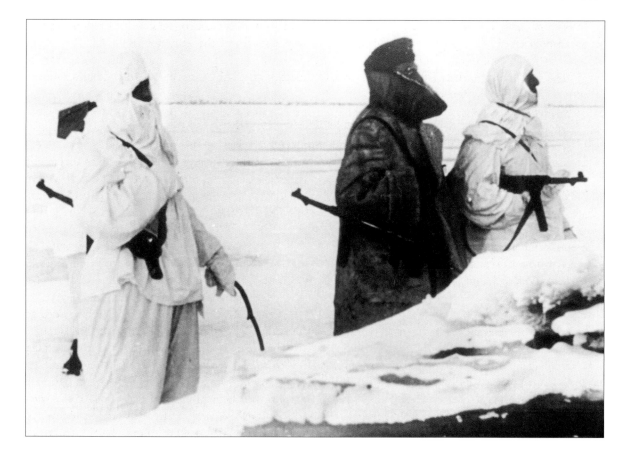

Above: Although Spanish troops were fighting in unfamiliar terrain, and under extremely unfamiliar weather conditions, the Blue Division performed about as well as a second-line German division on the Eastern Front.

effect. Therefore, despite any lack of ability, they should be welcome as comrades in the struggle.'

Delivered by train to Sulwalki in Poland, the *Division Azul* now began a gruelling 1000km (621 mile), 40-day march to Vitebsk in northern Russia. Setting out on 29 August, they had no mechanized transport, and their problems were compounded by having been issued with the worst of the *Wehrmacht's* horses. Nevertheless, the exhausted division reached Vitebsk in October. There they were assigned to the XVIII Army Corps of Army Group North. The Spanish/German difficulties which had emerged during training continued during the long march. German liaison officers with the division reported that the Spaniards were 'stealing chickens on the

march; associating with persons of Jewish race; threatening civilians; they lack march discipline; they do not care for their horses, nor their weapons, nor their equipment. Above all, junior officers and non-commissioned officers seem to be unable to enforce their orders to the troops.'

Over the next month the Spaniards saw considerable action along the Volkhov front, and were the recipients of several 'human wave' attacks by the Red Army. Far from the sun of Spain, the division also had to face the horrors of a Russian winter, made even worse by continual Soviet attacks. On Christmas Eve 1941, a company of Spanish grenadiers at Lubkovo was overrun. The position was retaken, but the Spaniards found the stripped and mutilated bodies of one platoon which had been cut off. Their comrades had been nailed to the frozen ground with their own bayonets. A revenge attack by two companies of the *Azul* ripped through a Soviet battalion, who were slaughtered to a man.

In spite of the Spaniards' capacity to fight with a ferocity which should have gone down well with their allies, German documents concerning the Spanish are filled with criticism of their attitudes and skills. While their sacrifices on the Volkhov front were recognized, the Germans did not like what they saw as excessive Spanish pride and a reluctance to accept German orders. In a note to Field Marshal von Leeb in November 1941, Chief of the General Staff Franz Halder commented that 'Spanish troops do not measure up to German norms of general discipline and care of horses, weapons, and equipment'.

'Russia is guilty of causing our civil war and our pain, and the destruction of Russia can only be for the well-being of Europe.'

Spanish Foreign Minister Serrano, 1941

Heavy losses

In June 1942, after several months of rebuilding, the Blue Division again suffered heavy losses during the final mopping-up of the Volkhov pocket. According to the *Kampfgruppe* commander, the Spaniards should not have suffered such losses in a simple mopping-up operation, and the reason that they had was down to Spanish ineptitude and inexperience.

The two German battalions taking part in the operation suffered around one-fifth of the losses sustained by the two Spanish battalions involved. The Spanish, by contrast, claimed that their losses were because they had failed to receive promised support from the Germans. Ultimately, the military value of the early volunteer formations of the Army

and *Waffen*-SS must be measured at the time of their withdrawal in the summer of 1943. The large Spanish division had shown itself capable of performing as a second-line German infantry unit in limited offensive and static defensive missions. Thanks to its size, its employment of regular army officers and its replacement system, it performed reasonably well under a harsh climate and in a demanding military situation. The changing face of the war in 1943 saw Franco seeking to distance himself from the Axis cause, which was clearly on a downwards slide. In October, he changed Spain's status from non-belligerence to strict neutrality.

As a neutral, the Spanish could not be seen to provide any support to one of the warring factions, so Franco ordered the withdrawal and disbandment of the Blue Division. Several thousand hard-line anti-communists refused to leave, and they formed the last of Germany's foreign legions, the *Legion Espanola de Voluntarios*, more commonly known as the *Legion Azul*, or Blue Legion. This did not last long, since it was disbanded six months later on 15 March 1944.

New recruits

Even as the Blue Legion was returning home, however, hundreds of young Spaniards were crossing the Pyrenees clandestinely to join the *Waffen*-SS.

Einheit Ezquerra – the last Spanish survivors

Miguel Ezquerra, a veteran of the Blue Division and then a captain in the *Waffen*-SS, led another small Spanish unit, later to be called the *Einheit Ezquerra*, or 'Unit Ezquerra'. This had originally been formed as part of the Brandenburger, or special forces, organization, and had worked for the *Gestapo* in France, fighting the French resistance (which included many Spanish exiles in its numbers).

After taking part in the Battle of the Bulge, Ezquerra was instructed to gather up all the Spanish survivors he could to form a single unit. By mid-April, he had about 100 men left out of three companies which had been cobbled together in January. After being attached to 11th *SS-Freiwilligen Panzergrenadier Division Nordland*, the men of Unit Ezquerra were amongst the last troops fighting the Russians in the rubble of Berlin.

Some were adventurers, but many were young Falangists, idealists who wanted to play their part even now in the anti-communist crusade.

More volunteers were found among the tens of thousands of industrial workers and labourers Franco had sent to Germany. By 6 June 1944, the day the Allies launched Operation Overlord, over 400 Spaniards were in training at Stablack-Sud camp in East Prussia.

By the middle of July numbers of this 'ghost battalion' had risen to 550. After rapid training, they were formed into two companies, the *Spanische Freiwilligen Kompanie der SS* 101 and 102. Other small units of Spaniards, left as flotsam after the retreating tide of the war, were attached to German units in northern Italy and Yugoslavia.

Over a hundred Spanish volunteers joined Léon Degrelle's 28th *SS-Freiwilligen Panzergrenadier*

Opposite: A StuG III assault gun and a motorcycle combination of the Wiking *Division move through Hungarian mud in the last months of the war. By this time, about a third of the neutral Swiss and Swedish volunteers who had joined the unit had died for the* Reich.

Division Wallonien where they formed the 3rd (Spanish) Company of the 1st Battalion. Some Spanish platoons were attached to the 3rd Mountain Division and the 357th Infantry Division.

The 101st Company of Spanish Volunteers served against the Red Army in Romania until the Romanians switched sides on 27 August 1944. What was left of the 101st began a slow, painful retreat northwest, eventually joining up with the equally mangled remains of the 102nd Company at Holabrunn, north of Vienna, which had been fighting partisans in northern Italy and Yugoslavia.

SWEDEN

DATE OF OCCUPATION: NEUTRAL
NUMBER OF VOLUNTEERS: 300
MAIN SS UNITS INCLUDING VOLUNTEERS: 5th SS-Panzer Division *Wiking*; **11th SS-Freiwilligen Panzergrenadier Division** *Nordland*

Unlike Spain, Sweden was strictly neutral during World War II, and did not allow the belligerent powers to recruit from amongst its population. However, the government did allow some 10,000 men to fight for Finland against the USSR during the Winter War, and when Germany launched Operation *Barbarossa*, the Swedes allowed Finland to recruit a further 1500 volunteers. A few individuals are known to have joined the *Wehrmacht* between 1939 and 1941. After the invasion of Russia, the *Waffen-SS* began a clandestine recruitment programme, working through the German Embassy in Stockholm and funnelling any such volunteers through Norway.

There are several estimates of the number of Swedes who fought for the Germans, ranging from 150 to 330. Swedes are known to have served with the 5th *SS-Panzer Division Wiking*, the 11th *SS-Freiwilligen Panzergrenadier Division Nordland*, and the 23rd *SS-Freiwilligen Panzergrenadier Division Nederland*. It is known that 11 Swedish SS men went through the SS Officer School at Bad Tolz. Several Swedes worked as SS war correspondents. One unit, the 3rd Company of *Nordland*'s Armoured Reconnaissance Battalion, had a large proportion of Swedes; so many that the 4th *Zug* (platoon) of the company was known unofficially as the *Swedenzug*.

The *Swedenzug*, along with the other Swedes in the *Nordland* Division, were among Hitler's last defenders in the Battle of Berlin. After seeing action in the Baltic and Courland late in 1944, it was withdrawn to the Oder front early in 1945. It was practically wiped out in an attempt to break out of Berlin on 2 May 1945.

SWITZERLAND

DATE OF OCCUPATION: NEUTRAL
NUMBER OF VOLUNTEERS: 300
**MAIN SS UNITS INCLUDING VOLUNTEERS: 5th SS-Panzer
Division *Wiking*, SS-Standarte *Kurt Eggers***

Like Sweden, Switzerland was strictly neutral
during World War II. As a neutral, it could not
allow a belligerent power to recruit among its
citizens. To the Nazis, the German-speaking Swiss
would have made natural recruits for both the
Waffen-SS and for the *Wehrmacht*, but official Swiss
disapproval meant that no real recruiting effort, open
or clandestine, was made. Nevertheless, without
official approval, a small number of Swiss citizens
volunteered for service in the East, primarily in the
ranks of the SS. Between 700 and 800 Swiss
volunteers are thought to have become members of

the *Wehrmacht* during World War II. Of these, at
least 300 are thought to have been killed in action.

No single national unit of Swiss volunteers was
formed during World War II since all Swiss
volunteers had joined the *Wehrmacht* individually.
The vast majority of Swiss volunteers found
themselves in the ranks of the *Waffen*-SS, most of
these being assigned to the 5th *SS-Panzer Division
Wiking*, although a number were assigned to the *SS-
Standarte Kurt Eggers*.

This was the SS *Kriegsberichter*, or war reporters'
unit. It was named after the former editor of the SS
magazine *Das Schwarz Korps*, who had been killed in
action near Kharkov while serving with *Wiking* in
1943. Many non-Germans were attached to the unit,
usually being assigned to report on the activities of
their own national formations.

EASTERN EUROPE

From the very beginning of the German invasion of the Soviet Union in June 1941, the *Wehrmacht* made extensive use of 'native' volunteer and conscript units in the front line and in rear-area security roles. Many were volunteers who had actually approached the Germans first, reflecting the internal opposition to Stalin's regime. Communist oppression had been fiercest in areas with long and proud national histories, and the German invasion gave them hope that they might eventually throw off the Soviet yoke.

Above: On a Silesian plain, a Latvian SS man prepares to fire a *Panzerfaust* 30 or *Faustpatrone* 2 recoiless anti-tank rocket in the last days of the war.
Opposite: Soviet Central Asian *Freiwillige* – 'volunteers' – served the *Wehrmacht* in large numbers. It was not until late in the war that the SS relaxed its racial standards and recruited from such nationalities.

SOVIET UNION

DATE OF OCCUPATION: JUNE 1941
NUMBER OF VOLUNTEERS: 60,000+
MAIN SS UNITS INCLUDING VOLUNTEERS: 29th Waffen-Grenadier Division der SS (russische Nr. 1); 30th Waffen-Grenadier Division der SS (russische Nr. 2); XV SS Kosaken-Kavallerie Korps

Although Adolf Hitler's primary racial hatred was directed at the Jews, he also despised Slavs. Slavs occupied the land into which the Greater German Reich must expand; Slavs had spawned world communism; Slavs were seen as *Untermenschen* ('Subhumans'). Given that such ideas filtered down from the very top of the *Führer* state, eventually they permeated every corner of Nazi society. It is all the more surprising, then, to discover that more Slavs fought on Germany's side than any other racial group, and that Soviet citizens made an essential contribution to the *Wehrmacht* war machine on the Eastern Front. From very early in the German occupation of Russia, which began in June 1941, the *Wehrmacht* made extensive use of local volunteers and conscripts. Originally employed to provide labour, they were also used later in combat roles. Mostly they provided rear-area security, but they were also sent out to hunt down partisans, and occasionally they found themselves fighting on the front line.

First volunteers

The first volunteers were employed by German front-line units on their own initiative. As the *Wehrmacht* pushed ever deeper into Soviet territory, it became clear that the sheer size of Russia meant that lines of logistics would be strained almost to the limit. Although the men of the *Wehrmacht* were greeted as liberators by many of the non-Russian populations of the USSR, any initial good feeling was quickly squandered. Germany intended to have European Russia for itself and its people. German administrators arrived soon after the armies, and proceeded to loot the Nazi Party's victims, and the SD, SS and the *Gestapo*

instituted a reign of terror. Welcome quickly turned to hatred, and partisan activity grew at an increasing rate. However, the manpower resources of the Reich, even at this early stage of the war in the East, were strained almost to breaking point.

Unable to divert enough of their front-line units to combat partisans in the rear, the Germans had to draw manpower from somewhere, and the 'Eastern peoples' seemed to provide the perfect answer. Anything which freed German soldiers from such mundane (but vital) tasks as protecting supply routes gave the Army a reinforcement of reliable, trained troops who could then be used in combat. Then someone remembered the prisoners in POW cages.

The original German estimate of the number of Soviet prisoners that would be taken during Operation *Barbarossa* was far too low. OKW had made plans to deal with prisoners by the tens of thousands. What they got after the great battles of encirclement of the summer of 1941 were prisoners by the hundreds of thousands, often taken in a single day. By the autumn of 1941, the number of Soviet soldiers in POW camps had reached the millions. Official German contempt for Slavs meant that they were kept in overcrowded barbed-wire pens, with little food and even less shelter. The arrival of the Russian winter would see many of these POWs dying of starvation or disease. The POWs represented a huge potential labour force, which could be used for slave labour back in Germany. However, by the time the German authorities realized that fact, millions had died from neglect. Among those who died were many from non-Russian ethnic minorities, who would have been all too willing to fight against Stalin's oppressive and murderous regime. The whole question of POW treatment was an huge waste of a usable resource for the Germans, as well as an immense tragedy and, for the wider world, a criminal act.

Hilfswillige

With the manpower shortage starting to bite, divisions, regiments and even battalions organized

Left: Germany's triumphant advance
through Soviet territory in the summer
of 1941 created a major problem for the
Wehrmacht. Nobody on the General Staff
had anticipated the sheer numbers of
Soviet prisoners that would be taken.

(*Schutzmannschaft*, or self-defence
units) were formed. These were
intended primarily for border and
rear-area security in their own Baltic
states. In the event, they served all over
the Eastern Front, eventually being
converted into regular police
battalions. They had an unsavoury
reputation, since many such units
were used by the SS and SD as 'hands-
on' thugs when committing atrocities.
By the spring of 1942, there were at
least 200,000 Russians serving in the
German rear areas. By the end of that
year, the numbers of Russians in
German uniform or taking German
orders has been estimated variously as
between 800,000 and one million.

The next step taken by the German
commanders in the East – again
behind Hitler's back, since the *Führer*
would never have approved – was the
organization of volunteer armed units, known as
Osttruppen. Wearing German uniforms, they were
recruited or conscripted to guard lines of
communication, to fight partisans in the rear of the
German armies, and sometimes even to reinforce and
hold positions along the front line. Volunteers were
plentiful, since the Germans were able to capitalize on
the real hatreds generated among ethnic minorities by
the brutality and oppression of Stalin's regime. Most
Osttruppen units were of battalion size or smaller. By
the summer of 1942, there were six *Ost-bataillonen* in
Army Group Centre alone.

Osttruppen volunteer units

Cossacks, Turkomans, Kalmyks, Estonians, Latvians
and many other groups which had been absorbed into
the USSR or the preceding Russian Empire had

their own support units. They acquired the necessary
manpower by taking in Soviet deserters, drafting in
prisoners and calling for volunteers from among the
local population. Known as *Hilfswillige* ('volunteer
helpers'), commonly shortened to '*Hiwi*', the Russian
auxiliaries were employed in non-combat posts such as
drivers, porters, orderlies, storesmen and labourers.
Obviously, given Nazi racial policies and the attitude
of senior German authorities towards Slavs and
Asiatics, those units that chose to employ *Hiwis*
initially kept quiet about the fact. But by the autumn
of 1941 the reality of combat on the Eastern Front
forced a grudging change of attitude on the part of the
high command. In October 1941, the first semi-
official groups of Soviet prisoners were allowed to be
used in road construction behind German lines, and
during the winter the first Baltic *Schumas*

distinctive cultures, histories and national identities. Such individualism was not tolerated in the USSR, and most were victimized by communist rule. Serving with the Germans, they believed, offered a chance at getting revenge on the Russians. Also, they hoped that the defeat of the Soviet Union might give them the chance of gaining independence. The *Osttruppen* were organized roughly on the basis of ethnicity, the majority of a battalion's personnel being drawn from a single nationality. Command and cadre positions were usually filled by German officers and NCOs.

There were two main types of unit as defined by the German Army. These were generally known as *Ost-Bataillone* and *Turk-Bataillone*. *Ost-* units were drawn from European Russia, and their personnel were mostly a mix of Russian and Byelorussians, with a few Ukrainians thrown in for good measure. *Turk-* battalions generally referred to units formed from the 'Asiatic' Turkic peoples of the Caucasus and beyond, such as Turkomans and Kalmyks. Eastern battalions attached directly to a corps staff used the number of the corps plus 400 as their designated number, so a battalion belonging to the XXXIV Corps would be known as the 434th *Ost-Bataillone*. Battalions answering to army headquarters and operating in rear areas received a number in the 600 series. Battalions assigned directly to a division used the number of the division, combined with *Ost-Bataillon* (or other appropriate title) as their designation. All of these battalions were referred to as the *Osttruppen*, although by 1943 many had been given designations reflecting their main ethnic component – typically, units with a majority of Cossacks would be known as *Kosaken-Bataillone*.

The organization of the *Osttruppen* was co-ordinated by the *Fremde Heere Ost*, the Foreign Armies East section of the Intelligence Department of the Army General Staff. It was clear to much of the German Army that an anti-Soviet Russian army fighting on the German side could be a serious contribution to victory in the East. Many senior commanders were keen to establish such an army. In

The German invaders were greeted as liberators by many of the subject peoples of the USSR, but any good feelings were quickly negated by the brutal and short-sighted way in which the occupiers went about their business.

the autumn of 1941, Field Marshal Fedor von Bock sent the OKW a proposal to create a liberation army of around 200,000 men. He also suggested giving the area around Smolensk some form of independent local anti-communist government. But nobody told the *Führer*. The proposal was returned in November 1941 with the comment that 'such thoughts cannot be discussed with the *Führer*', and that 'politics are not the prerogatives of Army Group Commanders'. Field Marshal Keitel, who lacked the spine to present anything remotely controversial to the Nazi leadership, knew what Hitler's feelings about the Russians were, and he did not present such a radical idea to his leader.

Russian National Army of Liberation

One of the first Russian volunteer formations was the *Russkaya Osvoboditelnaya Narodnaya Armiya* (RONA, or the Russian National Army of Liberation). In the autumn of 1941, the mayor of Lokot, a town with about 6000 inhabitants just south of Bryansk, raised a small militia unit to defend the town against partisans. The mayor and most of his staff were later killed in a partisan attack, and the unit was taken over by Bronislav Vladislavovich Kaminski. Born to a Polish father and a German mother, Kaminski expanded the militia from its original strength of some 400 men. In June 1942, the unit took part in Operation *Vogelsang*, a major German anti-partisan operation in the Bryansk Forest.

His 'army' – which in fact never exceeded the strength of a division – at first fought against Soviet partisans, and later at the front. In the summer of 1944, after considerable losses, RONA was withdrawn to East Prussia, It was renamed *Volksheer-Brigade Kaminski* shortly before being taken over by the Waffen-SS in July 1944, as *Waffen-Sturm-Brigade RONA*, with Kaminski himself receiving the rank of *Waffen-Brigadeführer der SS*. The SS had plans to expand the brigade to a full division, the 29th *Waffen-Grenadier Division der SS (russische Nr. 1)*. The unit was used during the obliteration of the Warsaw Rising, committing numerous atrocities. Later, Kaminski was

Eastern legion shields

Because of the increasing numbers of foreign volunteers entering the service of the Third Reich from all over Europe, the Germans authorized and issued national insignias to be worn on *Wehrmacht* uniforms. Most foreign volunteers served in the German Army and the *Waffen*-SS, and the majority of such insignias were issued by these organizations.

During the early stages of Operation *Barbarossa*, which commenced in June 1941, many of these foreign contingents wore their own home-made patches to distinguish their nationality. Eventually German regulations prohibited their use, and the intention was to replace them with standardized badges of German manufacture. By 1943, most of the foreign volunteer legions had been disbanded and incorporated into the *Waffen*-SS.

Manufacture

The SS shields were machine embroidered onto black wool base cloth – earlier badges issued to units serving the German Army had been made in the BeVo machine-woven style. BeVo was the abbreviation for *Bandfabrik Ewald Vorsteher*, a principal maker of wartime woven insignia. The later SS shields and SS collar insignia are commonly referred to as 'DACHAU' issues because many were made – and many were found unissued – at the SS clothing depots at Dachau. Another firm that made these shields was Troltsch & Hansemann of Berlin. Shields were at first worn above the cuff title, and later beneath the SS arm eagle.

A variety of armshields were worn by members of the *Ost-Legionen*, which were the administrative

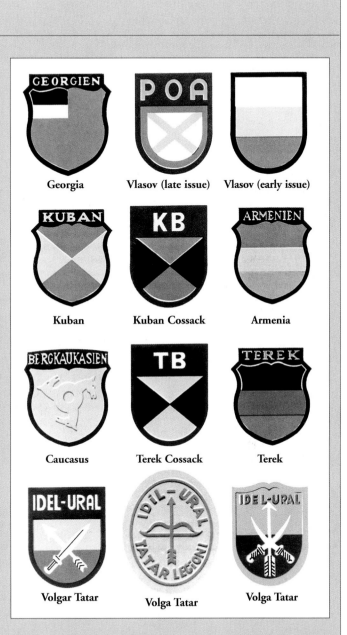

Georgia   Vlasov (late issue)   Vlasov (early issue)

Kuban   Kuban Cossack   Armenia

Caucasus   Terek Cossack   Terek

Volgar Tatar   Volga Tatar   Volga Tatar

centres for the eastern units. These were worn on either the upper left or upper right arm. Initially, they were the same shape as those worn by other foreign legions, and bore the name of the region of the Soviet Union from which the unit was recruited. Many units, especially those formed late in the war, had shields designed and made but never issued.

Above: Russian volunteer cavalrymen on patrol are watched warily by local civilians. Such units were used primarily on anti-partisan duties, though German manpower shortages meant that more and more were sent to the front line.

called to Lodz to attend an SS leader's conference. What happened next is not entirely clear. The official version was that he was killed by Polish partisans in an ambush, but some sources say that the activities of his troops in Warsaw had sickened even the SS; placed in front of a military tribunal, he was then shot by a firing squad. Others claim that he was arrested and shot out of hand by the *Gestapo*.

Rodionov's SS

In April 1942 the Fighting Union of Russian Nationalists, or BSRN (*Boyevogo Soyuza Russkaya*

Naroda) was formed in the town of Suvalki. It was headed by the former chief of staff of the Soviet 229th Rifle Division, V.V. Gil, who took the pseudonym 'Rodionov'. This was the first Russian national unit to be taken into the SS, and was known as the *Druzhina* (which is the Russian word for militia unit). With a strength of some 500 men, the *Druzhina* was formed to provide rear-area security and to fight partisans. In December 1942 a second Russian SS detachment was formed under the command of former NKVD (Soviet secret police) Major E. Blazhevich. In March both detachments were combined into the 1st Russian SS Regiment with Gil-Rodionov as its commander.

In May the regiment, some 2000 strong, was deployed to the town of Luzhki in Byelorussia, where it was again expanded, becoming 1st Russian SS Brigade. Although the brigade took part in many anti-partisan operations, it was never particularly effective, and the change in the tide of war after the Battle of Kursk in 1943 convinced many of its members that they had chosen the wrong side. On 16 August 1943 the brigade destroyed their German liaison headquarters and deserted *en masse* to the partisans.

Also in the autumn of 1941, a White Russian émigré, S.N. Ivanov, suggested to the *Abwehr* chief Admiral Canaris that he should form a unit made up of Soviet prisoners of war and deserters. Its mission would be to infiltrate deep behind Soviet lines. The unit came into existence in March 1942. It wore Soviet uniforms with the addition of the old Tsarist colours, and it used Soviet equipment.

The unit's Russian members believed that they would be the nucleus of a future great Russian 'liberation' army, and called themselves the *Russkaya Natsionalnaya Narodnaya Armiya* (RNNA, or Russian Nationalist Patriotic Army). By the end of 1942 it had grown to be a brigade-sized unit some 7000 strong. It saw considerable action in 1942, and was attached to Army Group Centre as the 'Experimental Formation Centre'. However, in accordance with Hitler's orders that no Russian unit in German service should be larger than a battalion, the unit was broken up by Field Marshal von Kluge and its battalions assigned to reinforce German units. This, together with the order that they should be re-equipped with German uniforms and weapons, caused considerable dissension in the ranks, and after numerous desertions and several near mutinies, the unit was disbanded.

Many other volunteer battalions, companies and squadrons were formed. The majority of them, composed of volunteers of Russian nationality, were later incorporated into the Russian Army of Liberation

Below: Azerbaijani volunteers served in both the SS and the German Army. Most of the original *Osttruppen* volunteers were transferred to the SS in 1944, but many remained under Army control, serving in France and Poland.

– the name given to all Russian volunteer formations which recognized General Vlasov as their leader.

The Germans also formed a number of *Ost-Legionen* (eastern legions), largely from POWs held in the *Generalgouvernement* in Poland and organized by ethnicity. The legions were not tactical formations, but were created as administrative centres where national units, mostly battalions, were organized and trained. The region of the Caucasus in particular was home to several of the ethnic groups fighting on the side of the Germans. In order to promote better unit cohesion and loyalty, the German Army attempted to divide some of the Caucasian peoples into units according to their religion.

In 1942, in addition to the various *Ost-Legionen*, the German Army used the staff of the disbanded 162nd *Infanterie-Division* to supervise the training of Turkic-manned eastern battalions in the territory of the *Generalgouvernement*. The division was itself reactivated on 21 May 1943 as the new 162nd *Infanterie-Division (turk.)*. The original German 162nd *Infanterie-Division* had been destroyed at Stalingrad. A second division of eastern troops, the 1st *Kosaken-Division*, was also formed during 1943, by using several pre-existing Cossack cavalry regiments organized under brigade-level command staffs. On 13 December 1942 the position of *Inspekteur der*

Opposite: An officer inspects members of a *Turkverband*, one of the early *Osttruppen* units formed on the Eastern Front in 1941. 'Turk' units were manned by Asiatic volunteers from the Caucasus and Central Asia.

Eastern legions

By the end of 1942, the following eastern legions had been created:
• *Armenische Legion:* established by an order of 30 December 1941, but not actually created until 4 July 1942 in the *Generalgouvernement*, to serve units composed of Armenians.
• *Aserbeidschanische Legion:* this unit was created on 22 July 1942 by renaming the original *Kaukasisch-Mohammedanische Legion* to serve (Muslim) Azerbaijani formations. This legion was converted into the staff of *Infanterie-Regiment* 314 of the 162nd *Infanterie-Division (turk)* on 1 June 1943.
• *Georgische Legion:* established by an order dated 30 December 1941, but not actually formed until 24 February 1942 in the *Generalgouvernement*, to serve Georgian units.
• *Kaukasisch-Mohammedanische Legion:* formed 24 March 1942 in the *Generalgouvernement* from parts of the *Turkestanisch-Kaukasisch-Mohammedanische Legion*. Renamed *Aserbeidschanische Legion* on 22 July 1942.
• *Nordkaukasische Legion:* formed 5 August 1942 at *Truppenübungsplatz Rembertow* in the *General-*

gouvernement to serve (Orthodox Christian) North Caucasian units.
• *Turkestanisch-Kaukasisch-Mohammedanische Legion:* formed on 13 January 1942 out of *Abwehr-Unternehmen Tiger* B, a special forces unit operated by *Amt Ausland/Abwehr* of the OKW, composed of Germans from *Brandenburg-Regiment z.b.V.* 800 and Caucasian volunteers from the POW camps. On 24 March 1942 the legion was broken up into three separate elements: *verstärkt Turkestanisches Infanterie-Bataillon* 450, the *Kaukasisch-Mohammedanische Legion*, and the *Turkestanische Legion*.
• *Turkestanische Legion:* formed 24 March 1942 in the *Generalgouvernement* from parts of the *Turkestanisch-Kaukasisch-Mohammedanische Legion*, to serve Turkoman units
• *Wolgatatarische Legion:* formed in January 1942 in the *Generalgouvernement* to serve Volga-Tartar and Volga-Finn units.

Other ethnic groups from the Soviet Union, such as the Cossacks and Kalmyks, did not have their own ethnic legions, although they did form a significant number of volunteer combat units.

Osttruppen im OKH was created within the German Army high command. The eastern troop command staff was designated *General der Osttruppen* in early 1943, and was renamed *General der Freiwillige-Verbände* on 1 January 1944. In May 1943 there were 10 regiments, 170 battalions, 221 companies and 11 platoons/sections of *Osttruppen* operating under the authority of the *General der Osttruppen*.

Police units

Even before the German Army was forming its *Ost-Bataillone*, the SS and *Ordnungspolizei* were forming their own 'native' units in the Baltic and the Ukraine, mainly for police and security duties. The *Schutzmannschaft* (*Schuma*) battalions were police units under control of the local HSSPF (*Höhere SS und Polizei Führer* – Higher SS and Police

Commander), and were given designations based on the duties they were intended to perform: '*Wach-*' for installation and depot guard duty; '*Ersatz-*' or '*Stamm-*' for replacement or training service respectively; '*Pionier-*' for units mainly made up from engineers and '*Front-*' for front-line combat duty.

In addition to the *Schuma* battalions, the SS and *Ordnungspolizei* used Byelorussian, Ukrainian, Latvian and Estonian volunteers to form several police rifle regiments for front-line and anti-partisan service. In May 1943 the *Schuma* designation, in use since early 1942, was dropped in favour of '*Polizei-*'. At the same

Below: Russian auxiliaries race through a burning village on the southern Russian steppe. Many volunteers from the Ukraine and southern Russia were more than willing to carry out atrocities on behalf of the Germans.

time, the police regiments which were formed from mainly non-German personnel became '*Polizei-Schützen-*' regiments.

The native police battalions continued to serve in anti-partisan and front-line combat roles to the end of the war, but by 1944 more and more of their personnel were being drafted unwillingly into the 'volunteer' *Waffen*-SS divisions such as the 14th *Waffen-Grenadier Division der SS (ukranishe Nr. 1),* 15th *Waffen-Grenadier Division der SS (lettische Nr. 1)* and 20th *Waffen-Grenadier Division der SS (estnische Nr. 1).*

Cossack volunteers

Possibly the largest group of former Soviet citizens to fight for the Germans was the Cossack nation, who wanted to use the Germans to help build their own independent state, Kazakia. German commanders had great sympathy for the Cossacks, as their bravery and their hatred of the Soviets produced quick results for the Germans. As early as mid-1942, a Cossack cavalry

Above: The largest contingent of volunteers fighting for the Germans was provided by the Cossacks. They had a long and proud warrior tradition, and saw service with the *Wehrmacht* as a means to an end: the establishment of the independent state of Kazakia.

formation existed in Mohylev, under the command of a former Soviet major, Kononov, who had crossed over to the Germans at the first opportunity with the greater part of his regiment. In the summer of 1942 the German armies entered territories inhabited by the Cossacks. During the civil war which followed the Bolshevik revolution, they had formed six federated republics: the Cossacks of the Don, of the Kuban, of Terek, of Orenburg, of the Ural, and of Astrakhan.

After the communist victory these had been liquidated by the Bolsheviks with extreme cruelty. The Cossacks, therefore, greeted the Germans as liberators. The entire populations of towns, villages and settlements went out to meet the German troops with flowers and gifts of all kinds, singing their national anthems. Cossack formations of the Red Army came over to the Germans almost to a man. Thousands of Cossacks in POW camps offered their services in the fight against the Soviets. The scattered remnants of the Kalmyk tribe, numbering no more 80,000 men, women and children, formed and equipped 16 cavalry squadrons which cleared the steppes of the remaining Soviet units, showing no mercy in return for years of terror at the hands of the NKVD.

In the summer of 1943, the 1st Cossack Division was formed under the command of General von Pannwitz. It had six cavalry regiments. Shortly afterwards the division was expanded into the XV SS Cossack Cavalry Corps, which numbered some 50,000 men. This was part of Himmler's plan to take over all foreign formations from the Army. Two further Cossack brigades and 12 Cossack reserve regiments were formed, and a number of smaller units were attached to German formations.

In all, Cossack troops on the German side numbered about 250,000 men. The Germans used the Cossacks to fight Soviet partisans, to cover the rear of their armies, and sometimes for action at the front. Later on, some Cossack formations were moved to France and Yugoslavia. The Cossack command objected, on the ground that the Cossacks should fight only against the Soviets, but in vain.

Vlasov and the Russian liberation movement

The success of some of the former Soviet troops fighting on the side of the *Wehrmacht*, together with

Below: Andrey Vlasov (right) was a charismatic Soviet military leader who after his capture in 1942 was persuaded by a faction in the German General Staff to switch sides. However, Vlasov was never given the freedom he needed to build up a true Russian liberation army.

Left: **Formed early in 1944, the** *Mussulmanischen SS-Division Neu-Turkistan* **took part in the brutal suppression of the Warsaw Rising, serving alongside the murderous thugs who made up the** *SS-Sturmbrigade Dirlewanger.*

Seventh and Twentieth Soviet Armies, and later deputy commander of the Volkhov front, was captured.

Vlasov was the son of a Russian smallholder from Nizhni Novgorod. Originally a theological student, in 1919 he was conscripted into the Red Army and saw service against the 'Whites' in the Ukraine, the Caucasus and the Crimea. Joining the Communist Party in 1930, he rose swiftly through the ranks of the Red Army, serving in China as military adviser to Chiang Kai-Shek in 1938. In the early stages of the war with Germany he commanded a division, escaping the encirclement of Kiev and playing a major part in the defence of Moscow. He was captured in July 1942 after the Germans had encircled a large part of the Volkhov front in the previous month. Taken to a camp for *prominente,* or important prisoners, he was persuaded by the Germans to switch sides, mainly because of his distaste for Stalin and the communist

the counter-productive effect of harsh German policies in the occupied territories, convinced a faction in the German Government and *Wehrmacht* high command that the only way to guarantee German success in the East would be to create a genuine Russian liberation movement, but Hitler's opposition to any such movement meant that they had little success.

However, a small group of civil servants and officers continued in their efforts. They gained a glimmer of hope when on 12 July 1942 General Andrey Andreyevich Vlasov, former commander of the Thirty-

system. Vlasov argued that Germany should create a Russian provisional government and a Russian army of liberation to be under his command.

In September 1942, while still in the POW camp, General Vlasov wrote a leaflet for the Propaganda Section of the *Wehrmacht*, WPrIV. In it he called on the officers of the Red Army and the Russian intelligentsia to overthrow Stalin, whom he blamed for all the disasters which had befallen Russia. Hundreds of thousands of copies of the leaflet were dropped over Soviet lines by the *Luftwaffe*. Within days, thousands

of deserters from the Red Army were coming over to the Germans. Most asked to serve under General Vlasov and wanted to fight against the Soviets. But Hitler was not amused. The last thing he wanted was a powerful Russian liberation movement. He wanted European Russia for the German race. At the *Führer's* command, Field Marshal Keitel forbade everybody, up to and including the General Staff, to present any kind of memorandum or report on the subject of General Vlasov and Russian formations.

The Russian National Committee

In spite of this prohibition, in December 1942 the German promoters of the Russian anti-Soviet movement decided to sponsor the Russian National Committee, headquartered at Smolensk, with General Vlasov as chairman. Vlasov's personal charm, his talents and his ability to inspire confidence made him the obvious choice. However, opposition from non-Russian anti-communists together with inefficient dissemination of the new committee's manifesto meant that it had little effect on Soviet citizens living in the occupied areas. Nevertheless, in March 1943 the commanders of Army Groups Centre and North invited General Vlasov, on their own initiative, to go on a tour of their areas and deliver speeches to prisoners of war, Soviet volunteers and the local population.

In the second half of April Field Marshal Keitel demanded to know who had allowed General Vlasov to issue a political proclamation; he also threatened grave consequences if it proved true that General Vlasov was appearing in public, and was being called 'the future leader of the Russians'. Keitel issued an order on behalf of the *Führer* which stated that: 'Vlasov is only a prisoner of war. His shameless speeches have infuriated the *Führer*, who has forbidden

> **'The Führer *has forbidden mentioning the name Vlasov in his presence ... If in future Vlasov appears anywhere in public, he will be arrested and handed over to the Gestapo.'***
>
> **Order issued by Keitel**

mentioning the name Vlasov in his presence. Vlasov is immediately to be sent back to the POW camp, and will be kept under special surveillance. If, in future, Vlasov appears anywhere in public he will be arrested and handed over to the Gestapo.'

Soon all army groups and some of the armies reported that the publication of a political declaration and a change of attitude towards the anti-Soviet volunteers were a necessity, otherwise the occupation of the Eastern territories would prove to be an impossible task. Vlasov abandoned his previous stand of the 'one and undivided Russia', consented to the principle of self-determination of the non-Russian peoples and agreed that Russia, in a peace settlement, would renounce her claims to the Ukraine and the Caucasus.

Hitler once more intervened. On 8 June, he declared that the Liberation Army was a dangerous folly. He would never consent to its organization. The setting-up of any states in the occupied territories was out of the question. Instead of forming volunteer units, Russians would be sent to Germany to work in coal mines, replacing Germans. He accepted that Vlasov might be needed for propaganda work at the front, but any other activity would not be permitted. Hitler's *diktat* reduced the Russian National Committee and its proposed Liberation Army to a propaganda tool, controlled by Germans and working through Russian-language newspapers and pamphlets. Even so, the committee and the Liberation Army became symbols of the Russian nation's fight against Soviet tyranny.

'Treacherous' behaviour

By the summer of 1943, it is estimated that anything from 800,000 to one million Russians were serving the German Army in the East. However, the success of the Soviet autumn offensives that year were blamed on the treacherous behaviour of the Russian volunteer formations on the front line. Hitler was enraged, and ordered that all eastern formations be immediately disbanded, and that 80,000 of their men, as a first

Opposite: Members of the Georgian Legion undergo training in the summer of 1943. Although they have been issued with German uniforms, they are armed with captured Soviet Degtyarev DP light machine guns.

contingent, immediately be sent to France to dig coal. After three days Hitler modified his order when it became clear that such an action would leave a massive hole in the *Wehrmacht*'s manpower on the Eastern Front. Only formations from the broken sector of the front were disbanded. Some days later, Hitler appeared to have calmed down, and he ordered that rather than disband, the *Osttruppen* were to be sent to other

Below: The complex ethnic mix of the Soviet Union ensured that there would always be a sizeable number of minority peoples willing to fight against the Russians, even if that meant accepting having to fight under the control of the German *Wehrmacht*.

theatres of operations. By the end of 1943 several hundred thousand eastern volunteers had been transferred to France, Italy and the Balkans.

One exception to Hitler's policy came with the formation of a Ukrainian SS division, 14th *Waffen-Grenadier Division der SS (galizische Nr. 1)*. Part of Himmler's expansion of the SS, the division was formed on the understanding that it would only be used to fight the Soviets. It suffered heavy losses in June 1944 during the massive Soviet summer offensive, and was reformed as the 1st Ukrainian Division in the autumn. However, Himmler was not a complete convert, nor did he realize the scale of Russian involvement in the *Wehrmacht*.

In October 1944, the General of Eastern Troops informed the *Reichsführer*-SS that in June 1944 there were more than 800,000 eastern volunteers serving in the German Army, with a further 100,000 in the *Kriegsmarine* and *Luftwaffe*. Himmler simply could not believe it. Nor could Hitler. As late as the end of March 1945, he could still exclaim at a staff conference: 'We just don't know what is floating around. I have just heard for the first time, to my amazement, that a Ukrainian SS Division has suddenly appeared. I don't know a thing about this.'

The enforced captivity of the Russian National Committee, and of General Vlasov, continued in spite of many efforts on the part of the German sympathizers of the anti-Soviet movement. By the middle of 1944, the Russian Army of Liberation was still not a true military organization. Units which bore its name were mostly commanded by German officers and were dispersed all over Europe; General Vlasov and the Russian National Committee had no influence whatsoever, and were not recognized by the German Government.

KONR formed

However, Soviet advances in the East persuaded Himmler, previously a confirmed opponent of the ROA (*Russkaya Osvoboditelnaya Armiya*), to change his mind. After a meeting with Vlasov, *Reichsführer-SS* Himmler proposed that a new committee be created – the KONR (*Komitet Osvobozhdeniya Narodov Rossii*, or Committee for the Liberation of the Peoples of Russia) – along with a KONR army under General Vlasov's command. The committee and army were to embrace all Soviet citizens living under German rule, in order to unite their political and military activities in the fight against Bolshevism.

Initially, five divisions were to be organized from the millions of Russian prisoners and forced labourers who had been brought to Germany. These would gradually be reinforced by ROA units currently serving all over Europe. The KONR met strong opposition from the non-Russians, who felt that it was mainly a Russian enterprise and controlled by Russians whom they did

Above: Waffen-SS instructors teach Ukrainian volunteers how to use a 50mm (2in) 50-PM 30 light mortar. The Ukraine had suffered dreadfully under Stalin, and large numbers enlisted with the Germans. Others, however, fought against both the Germans and the Soviets.

not trust. The formation of the KONR army also met with difficulties. The German Army did not want to give up its *Ost-Bataillonen*, and delayed their transfer. German industrialists objected to the raid on their slave labour force for personnel. As a result, only two divisions were formed. The first units were operational by February 1945.

After a series of actions against the Soviets, the 1st Division retreated on its own initiative back towards Prague, reaching the city on 2 May. In the city, Czech nationalists had risen against the Nazis, but were in danger of being wiped out. Since most of the nationalists were also anti-Soviet, the Red Army had stopped to allow the SS to do their work for them, as

Above: Volunteers from Josef Stalin's homeland, Georgia, on parade. The Georgian Legion consisted of at least 12 infantry battalions, and the 822nd Georgian Infantry Battalion served on the Atlantic Wall during the Allied invasion of Normandy.

they had at Warsaw. The Czechs appealed to Vlasov's men for aid. Vlasov despised the SS, so he attacked his former allies, routing them and preserving the Czech city.

Vlasov and the rest of his force, desperate to escape the vengeful Red Army, retreated westwards to surrender to the British and the Americans. During the flight, however, many were shot by Soviet troops, the majority were captured by the Red Army, and others were handed over by the Americans. Some 17,000 of

Vlasov's men are said to have been deported to Russia, where many were executed and the remainder imprisoned in the *Gulag* for life. Their fate was shared by most of the members of the Cossack Corps (handed over to the Russians by the British to whom they had surrendered), by the 162nd Turkoman Division and by most other members of the *Osttruppen*. Among their number was General Vlasov.

On 2 August 1946 the first mention of the Vlasov movement appeared in the Soviet press. The last page of *Pravda* announced the death by hanging of the following: Vlasov, Malyshkin, Zhilenkov, Trukhin, Zakutny, Blagoveshchenski, Meandrov, Maltsev, Bunyachenko, Zverev, Korbukov and Shatov. 'All accused admitted their guilt in the charges made against them ... The sentence has been executed.'

LATVIA

DATE OF OCCUPATION: JULY 1941
NUMBER OF VOLUNTEERS: 80,000
MAIN SS UNITS INCLUDING VOLUNTEERS: 15th Waffen-Grenadier Division der SS (lettische Nr. 1); 19th Lettische SS-Freiwilligen Division

As with the other Baltic States, Latvia fought for its independence from the Soviet Union after World War I, and came under pressure from both Germany and the USSR during the 1930s. In common with Lithuania and Estonia, Latvia was forced to accept a Soviet garrison in 1940, and in 1941 the country itself was absorbed by Stalin's Russia. The Soviets took Latvia's small army into the Red Army, and political opponents and nationalists quickly came

to the attention of the NKVD. Many were arrested and executed, while others were transported to labour camps in Russia. The German attack on Russia in 1941 saw the *Wehrmacht*'s Army Group North smashing through the Baltic States in its drive towards Leningrad. German intelligence had previously initiated ties with Latvian nationalist organizations to promote a mutiny in Latvian units of the Red Army. Riga was besieged by the beginning of July, and by the 10th the entire country was in German hands.

Below: Latvian volunteers in the *Waffen*-SS are seen manning an artillery piece in the summer of 1943. At that time the 1st SS Motorized Brigade, by now a largely Latvian formation, was in intense action around Smolensk.

Above: Women and children are ordered to strip prior to execution. Baltic police units were used to support German anti-partisan operations in 1942 and 1943 – operations which were often little more than massacres of unarmed civilians accused of 'harbouring bandits'.

Latvian nationalists

The Germans were seen as liberators by many Latvians, and initially had the full support of Latvian right-wing nationalists. Although a minority in Latvia, these groups had been an important factor in the nation's politics from the early 1920s. The *Aizsargi,* or 'Guards', was created in 1919. A paramilitary organization along the lines of the SA, it had been used by K. Ulmanis, the Peasants' Union Party leader, in a military coup which took place in May 1934.

Once he established his dictatorial state, Ulmanis made the *Aizsargi* a part of the police. Another nationalist group, the Lettish National Club, was banned soon after being formed in the early 1920s. However, its members were the core for a new extreme

nationalist group, the 'Fiery Cross', formed in 1927. It was renamed the *Perkonkrust,* or 'Thunder Cross', Lettish People's Association in 1933. Although membership never rose above 5000, the Thunder Cross advocated the disenfranchisement and persecution of non-Letts, particularly the Jews. Ulmanis and his government were Latvian nationalists, who immediately enacted laws against all minorities in the state, closing German, Russian and other minority language schools and declaring non-Latvian-speaking organizations to be illegal.

Assisting the *Einsatzgruppen*

Former members of Latvian nationalist organizations resumed their activities right after the Red Army withdrawal, and offered their willing assistance to the SD's *Einsatzgruppen* who instituted the massive Nazi slaughter of Jews in the wake of the advancing *Wehrmacht.* Former *Aizsargi* and *Perkonkrust* members, together with former Latvian Army and police members, formed voluntary 'self-defence squadrons' in the summer of 1941. These were used by the *Gestapo* and the SD for searches, arrests, raids and mass shootings of Jews, communists, Soviet activists and sympathizers. Tens of thousands of Jews and communists were slaughtered in the autumn of 1941 at places like Riga, Daugavpils and Liepaja. However, the Latvian irregulars were soon to expand their areas of operations.

Partisan activity quickly forced the *Wehrmacht* to set up units to provide rear-area security all along the Eastern Front. To free German soldiers for front-line duty, as many of these as possible were to be formed from local volunteers. On 25 August 1941, Army Group North formally authorized the formation of volunteer battalions of Baltic citizens.

In autumn 1941 regular police battalions were organized out of the irregular self-defence squadrons, and in October of that year the first Latvian police battalion went into action just over the Russian border

in the area of Pskov. Over the next three years over 40 Latvian police battalions were formed, ranging in size from 200 to 600 men. Latvian battalions saw action in Latvia itself, but were also deployed in the Ukraine, in Byelorussia and as far away as the Caucasus. Some battalions gained an unsavoury reputation for atrocity as they supported the *Einsatzgruppen* in their attempts to eliminate the Jews.

Heavy losses incurred by the German Army during the Red Army's winter counter-offensive (1941–42) in the environs of Moscow forced OKW to attach many of the Latvian police units to the German Army as reserve units. Later they were used to fill gaps in the front line, but were most actively involved in the fierce

Below: *Reichsführer*-**SS Heinrich Himmler visits Latvian SS artillery units on the Narva River. The Latvian SS divisions were to be heavily involved in the fierce fighting which took place in this area in 1944.**

partisan war. By 1942, German manpower resources were being stretched to breaking point. German troops were in action from North Africa to Norway and from the Bay of Biscay to the Caucasus. The legion programme was an SS attempt to increase numbers by calling for non-German volunteers to fight the communists. Volunteers came from all over Europe, but the largest legion by far was the Latvian Legion.

Latvian SS

The first large unit of the new Latvian Legion was formed at the Leningrad front from three police battalions, later reinforced by three further battalions. Initially known as the 2nd *SS-Infanterie-Brigade (mot)*, it was redesignated as the 2nd Lettish *Freiwilligen* SS Brigade. It was to be expanded as the 19th *Waffen-Grenadier Division der SS (lettische Nr. 2)* in the summer of 1944. In the meantime, the first Latvian division, the *Lettische SS-Freiwilligen Division*, had been authorized in September 1943. Renamed the 15th *Waffen-Grenadier Division der SS* (*lettische Nr. 1*) soon after, it was formed from the new recruits in Latvia. Only partially trained, the division was transported to the front at the end of November 1943. Some regiments had not even received winter clothing. Dispersed for further training among the German 83rd and 205th Infantry Divisions, the Latvians were treated with contempt, and many of their new German-issued weapons were taken by their 'allies'. In German eyes, it was a waste of resources giving modern weapons to people who could only serve as cannon fodder.

Opposite: **A Latvian volunteer in full winter gear, 1943. Latvian SS units fought hard at the end of the war. In spite of early doubts, Himmler stated that the Latvians and other Balts were essential to the defence of the Eastern Front.**

Conscription introduced

Appearances can be deceiving, however. Although the Letts served in greater numbers than any other nationality, probably less than 20 per cent were volunteers. Initially, German authorities organized genuine volunteer recruitment campaigns, but when desired results were not obtained, further steps had to be taken. At the end of 1942, the German Labour Administration notified those Letts born between 1919 and 1924 to report for registration on 26 February 1943.

The draftees were supposed to be given a choice between serving with the legion, serving with the German *Wehrmacht* as auxiliaries, or working in important war industries – which in other words meant being transported to Germany to work as forced labour. They had to sign a declaration that they were volunteering, and those who refused were sent to the Salaspils concentration camp. Draftees wore SS uniforms, but since they were neither fully Aryan nor true volunteers, they were not considered to be true SS men. Rather than serving in SS divisions, the Latvian units (and other similar non-Germanic formations) were designated 'divisions of the SS'. The two SS divisions were not the only Latvian forces fighting in the front. Police regiments and battalions were being used in front-line combat on top of their rear-area security duties. Additionally, tens of thousands of Latvian auxiliaries had been pressed into service by the German units to which they were attached. Although attempts were made to transfer these auxiliaries to the Latvian Legion, German commanders in the field refused; one German commander replied that 48 per cent of his men were Latvians and to comply with the request would fatally weaken his division. Ultimately both the Latvian police battalions and the grenadier divisions were considered part of the legion. As a result, the Latvian Legion, with a peak strength in excess of 87,000 men, was more than 10 times as large as any of the other volunteer legions.

When the Soviets pushed the Germans back in the last year of the war, Courland in western Latvia remained in Axis hands, and the Latvian 19th SS Division fought fiercely in the defence of its homeland. Part of the 15th SS Division, forced back by the Soviets, retreated westwards to try to surrender to the Americans or the British. Cut off by advancing Soviet armies, the unit found itself in Berlin, where it unwillingly played its part in the defence of Hitler's bunker in the last days of the war. It later surrendered to the Americans at Güterglück near the Elbe River. In all, more than 150,000 Latvians served more or less willingly with the German forces during World War II.

ROMANIA

DATE OF OCCUPATION: ALLY
NUMBER OF VOLUNTEERS: 50,000
MAIN SS UNITS INCLUDING VOLUNTEERS: 7th SS-Freiwilligen Gebirgs Division *Prinz Eugen*; 8th SS-Kavallerie Division *Florian Geyer*

As in many other countries of Eastern Europe, Romania had a large ethnic German population, though many of these *Volksdeutsche* were indistinguishable from their Romanian neighbours. Concentrated in the Banat region (which straddles the Romanian and Serbian border) and in Transylvania, there were over 500,000 Romanians who claimed German descent.

Recruiting the *Volksdeutsche*

When Gottlob Berger, head of the SS recruiting office, sought to find manpower to expand the SS late in 1940, he looked to the more 'Aryan' of the *Volksdeutsche* as well as to the Nordic countries for volunteers. In the winter of 1940 and 1941, the SS launched a recruitment drive in Transylvania, successfully reaching its target of 1000 volunteers who were trained and then sent as replacements to the elite SS-*Reich* Division, which later became the 2nd SS-*Panzer Division Das Reich*. The Romanians, who were Germany's allies in the Axis pact, were not pleased with the SS poaching on their patch. In fact, under Romanian law it was illegal for Romanian nationals to serve in foreign armies, so further recruits were invited to visit Germany where they could join the SS as individuals.

The next SS recruitment drive took place early in 1942 with the formation of the *SS-Freiwilligen Gebirgs Division*, later known as the 7th *SS-Freiwilligen Gebirgs Division Prinz Eugen*. Volunteers in this instance mainly came from the Banat, as well as from Serbia and Croatia. Formed as a mountain division, *Prinz Eugen* was equipped with obsolete and captured equipment such as Czech machine guns and French light tanks. Its first commander was SS *Brigadeführer*

und Generalmajor der Waffen-SS Artur Phleps. Phleps had served in the Imperial Austrian Army, and had commanded a mountain corps in the Romanian Army until 1941. Despite its poor equipment, the *Prinz Eugen* Division was one of the most effective counter-insurgency units the Germans fielded in Yugoslavia during the war, and was greatly feared by the partisans. However, that reputation was gained primarily by brutality and utter ruthlessness. The conflict in Yugoslavia combined guerrilla war with civil and tribal warfare, and neither side was prone to giving quarter.

Although Germany was still on the offensive in 1942, it was becoming increasingly difficult to find enough manpower to replace combat losses on the Eastern Front. Berlin put pressure on the government of Marshal Antonescu, and the Romanians eventually gave permission for Germany to actively recruit among Romanian *Volksdeutsche*. By 1943, over 60,000 had joined the *Waffen*-SS. They did not serve in individual Romanian formations, but large numbers served in the 8th *SS-Kavallerie Division Florian Geyer*, the 11th *SS-Freiwilligen Panzergrenadier Division Nordland*, and in the newly formed 17th *SS-Panzergrenadier Division Goetz von Berlichingen* and the 18th *SS-Freiwilligen Panzergrenadier Division Horst Wessel*.

However, not all of the Romanian *Volksdeutsche* served in SS fighting units. In August 1942, an agreement between the Romanian governor of Transnistria and the SS authorized the *Volksdeutsche* to organize a *Selbschutz*, or self-defence, force, eventually growing to be 8000 strong. As with other *Selbschutz* forces elsewhere in Eastern Europe, its main role was intended to be to fight partisans, but in reality its main use was as an anti-Jewish force. In addition to killing Jews, the force also liaised with and profited from German companies moving in to take over Jewish businesses.

Waning enthusiasm

Ethnic Romanians did not join German units in any numbers until the last year of the war. Romanians began losing enthusiasm for the conflict in 1943 after the tide began to turn against the Axis. The military dictatorship which had run the country was overthrown by a coup in August 1944. A fascist government in exile led by Horia Sima was set up in Vienna, and the SS initiated plans to create a Romanian National Army. Troops for the new force would come from POWs taken after Romania switched sides, from members of the fascist Iron Guard which had fled Romania after the coup and from regular Romanian soldiers who were opposed to the idea of a communist regime. Two regiments of two battalions each were operational early in 1945. *Waffen-SS Grenadier Regiment Rumänische Nr. 1* saw action in Pomerania, north of Stettin, where it was almost

completely destroyed. The second regiment was made into an anti-tank unit, *Waffen-SS Panzer Zerstörer Regiment Rumänische Nr. 2*. A third regiment never got beyond training.

Romanians also provided the personnel for several small special operations units at the end of the war. Seventy volunteers trained near Vienna and joined a Brandenburg unit, the *Brandenburg Streifkorps Karpaten*. After further training in guerrilla warfare at Korneuburg, they were to be dropped behind Soviet lines to perform intelligence gathering and sabotage. Another 175 Romanian men transferred from other SS divisions for training at Stockerau. These were intended to join Otto Skorzeny's commandos in the largely mythical 'Alpine Redoubt' tasked with supporting the Sixth SS Panzer Army's offensive at Balaton in Hungary.

In the event, the expected breakthrough failed, and the *Jägdeinsatz Rumanien* retreated through Austria into the Alps, eventually surrendering to the Americans a month after the end of the war.

Below: An SS *Reiter* (cavalry trooper) of the SS Cavalry Division *Florian Geyer* moves through a burning village in the Balkans. Romanian *Volksdeutsche* served with this formation, which acquired a brutal reputation in the partisan war in Yugoslavia.

ESTONIA

DATE OF OCCUPATION: JULY 1941
NUMBER OF VOLUNTEERS: 25,000
MAIN SS UNITS INCLUDING VOLUNTEERS: Estnische SS-Legion;
20th Waffen-Grenadier Division der SS (estnische Nr. 1)

The origins of the involvement of Baltic soldiers in the war in the East can be found in the difficult position in which the three states of Estonia, Latvia and Lithuania found themselves in 1939 – trapped between Nazi Germany to the west and communist Russia to the east. The rapid destruction of Poland in 1939 and the partition of the country between Germany and the USSR came as a severe shock to the Estonian Government, particularly when it became clear that Adolf Hitler was going to give the USSR a free hand in the Baltic.

At the end of September, the Soviets demanded that Estonia allow Soviet troops to be based on its territory, and 35,000 Red Army troops had arrived by 18 October. For the moment, the Soviets demanded little more – they were fully involved in preparing for the invasion of Finland. However, by June 1940, with the *Wehrmacht* triumphant in the West, the Soviets presented an ultimatum. The Estonian Government must resign, a new government acceptable to Moscow must be formed, and Soviet military forces must be allowed to occupy the country.

Soviet occupation

In spite of considerable anti-Soviet sentiment among the Estonian population, the government caved in on 17 June, and within days the Red Army was on the move. Lessons learned in fighting the Finns meant that they moved in strength: 160,000 men were supported by over 500 tanks and were also able to call on more than 1100 aircraft deployed to cover the occupation of all three Baltic States. To prevent any escape by sea the coast was blockaded by the Soviet Baltic Fleet. Along with the armies were the NKVD security units, who had instructions to prepare for nearly 60,000 political and military detainees. Among the first victims of the

Russians were the 12,000 ethnic Germans living in Estonia. Over 2000 were executed over the next 12 months, and most of the rest were deported to Germany, while 35,000 ethnic Estonians were conscripted to work as forced labourers in Russia. The Estonian Army was absorbed into the Red Army as the 22nd Territorial Rifle Corps (though the 16,000 Estonians were outnumbered by 20,000 Russians). Most Estonian officers were imprisoned or executed. By June 1941 Estonian numbers in the unit had dropped to 5500, and most deserted to the Germans after the launch of Operation *Barbarossa*.

When the Germans launched their invasion on 22 June 1941, Army Group North, attacking out of East Prussia, had Leningrad as its objective. But to reach the cradle of the communist revolution, it would have to force its way through the Baltic States. Within two weeks, Field Marshal Ritter von Leeb's forces had driven through Lithuania to reach Riga, Latvia's capital, and were approaching the Estonian border. The German Eighteenth Army began crossing the Estonian border over a wide front on 7 July. Over the next six weeks, the Germans smashed Soviet forces in the region, and the capital Tallinn was taken by the end of August. The Germans were assisted in their task by approximately 12,000 Estonian irregulars, who were known as the 'Forest Brothers'. These became the nucleus of an Estonian 'Home Guard', which had reached a strength of 25,000 men by 1 September.

Security units

Soon after the occupation of Estonia, the Germans began to allow the formation of Estonian units, variously called security, police or defence battalions or companies. Their primary purpose was to provide security in German rear areas, which came to mean fighting partisans. Volunteers were plentiful, and by March 1942 there were 16 Estonian battalions and companies with 10,000 men on active service in Russia. Eventually more than 50 such units were to be formed, with as many as 25,000 Estonians under arms.

Above: Detached from the *Estnische SS-Freiwilligen Brigade* in 1943, the *Estnisches SS-Freiwilligen Bataillon Narva* was assigned to the crack SS Panzer Grenadier Regiment *Nordland*, part of the *Wiking* Division.

Their experience of Soviet oppression at first hand meant that the Baltic States were seen by the SS as potentially valuable recruiting grounds for foreign volunteer legions to take part in the 'crusade' against communism. On 28 August 1942 the *Waffen-SS* announced the intended formation of the *Estniches Freiwilligen SS Legion*.

Estonian SS units formed

By the end of the year, 1280 men were under training at Debica in Poland as the 1st *Estnisches SS-Freiwilligen Grenadier Regiment*. In March 1943, one battalion was detached as the *Estnisches SS-Freiwilligen Bataillon*

Narva, replacing the disbanded Finnish battalion as the third battalion of the *Nordland* Regiment of the *Wiking* Division.

At the same time continuing manpower shortages led to reinforcements being conscripted in Estonia, some 12,000 men being called into service. Of these, 5300 were sent to the legion battalions training at Debica, which were reinforced and organized as the

Right: Haralt Nugiseks, *Waffen-Unterscharführer der SS* and recipient of the Knight's Cross on 9 April 1944. Nugiseks, an Estonian volunteer, was an NCO in the 1st *SS-Volunteer-Grenadier-Regiment 46*, which was part of the 20th *Waffen-Grenadier Division der SS (estnische Nr. 1).*

3rd *SS-Freiwilligen Brigade*. The remaining conscripts were sent to German Army units. Five thousand more Estonians were mobilized in the winter of 1943–44. They were used in the expansion of the Estonian SS brigade into a full division, which was authorized on 24 January 1944. The 20th *SS-Freiwilligen Division* was renamed in June 1944, becoming the 20th *Waffen-Grenadier Division der SS (estnisches Nr. 1)*.

On 1 February, as the advancing Soviet armies approached the Narva River, another 45,000 Estonians were called up. Some 20,000 were used to form six new *Schutzmannschaft* and *Polizei Front* battalions. About 60,000 men were serving in these border guard units by the end of February, with a further 10,000 in the Estonian SS division. A further 37,000 men were deployed as home guard battalions, while 3000 teenagers served in anti-aircraft defence units. By the autumn of 1944 more than 100,000 Estonians were in German service.

Fighting as part of Field Marshal Walter Model's Army Group North, the Estonian units spent most of February fighting to destroy Soviet bridgeheads across the Narva River. Their success enraged the Soviet high command, which threw nine full corps against the Axis forces in March and April. In one of the largest (and least known) battles of the war, seven Axis divisions fought the Russians to a standstill. Soviet casualties exceeded 120,000, while the Germans and their Estonian and other European allies lost 20,000 men killed or wounded.

The end

After a period of regrouping, the Soviets threw two armies of 205,000 men against five understrength German divisions with just 27,000 men. Unable to stand up to such overwhelming strength, the Axis forces retreated through a series of defensive lines when the Soviets attacked on 24 July. Further attacks came south of Lake Peipus in August, Russian tanks smashing through the lightly armed Estonian border regiments and battalions. However, the attack was blunted by the arrival of German panzers.

Finland's armistice with the Russians in September 1944 left the entire north of Estonia open to attack, and OKW decided to evacuate. With the retreating Germans went 43,000 Estonian soldiers and 24,000 civilians. The Estonian battles probably cost the Soviets something under 200,000 dead; the Germans probably lost between 40,000 and 50,000.

Over 80,000 Estonians fled the country in 1944, mostly to Sweden or Germany. More than 6500 Estonian citizens were executed by the Germans, including 929 Jews and 243 gypsies.

HUNGARY

DATE OF OCCUPATION: ALLY

NUMBER OF VOLUNTEERS: 20,000

MAIN SS UNITS INCLUDING VOLUNTEERS: 25th Waffen-Grenadier Division der SS *Hunyadi*; 26th Waffen-Grenadier Division der SS *Hungaria*

At the beginning of the twentieth century, Hungary was a large, ethnically diverse nation with a population of more than 18 million. Some two million of those were ethnic Germans, or *Volksdeutsche*. After the fall of the Hapsburg Empire at the end of World War I, Admiral Miklós Horthy, the one-time *aide-de-camp* of Emperor Franz Josef, was appointed regent to the vacant Hungarian throne. In common with all the losing states of the Great War, Hungary suffered major territorial losses, the country losing a third of its area under the terms of the Treaty of Trianon. The Trianon treaty had the same kind of effect on the Hungarians as the Treaty of Versailles had on the Germans. The country had lost a third of its territory, and three million Hungarians suddenly became minority citizens in neighbouring and traditionally hostile countries. Between the wars, Hungary grew economically, but the lost territories remained a painful subject. Any party which promised to regain Hungarian territory was likely to succeed.

After the Great Depression, the government of Prime Minister Gyula Gombos signed a trade agreement with Germany which began to pull Hungary into the Axis camp. After Germany's annexation of Czechoslovakia, Hungary got back some of its lost territory. In 1940 the Germans gave back parts of Poland which had been conquered the previous year, and in 1941 the Hungarians received part of Yugoslavia. The membership of the Axis alliance and the apparent German generosity in handing back former Hungarian territory meant that the Hungarian Government felt honour-bound to join the war. After taking part in the invasion of Yugoslavia, the Hungarians provided an army to fight with the Germans in the invasion of Russia in June 1941.

The experience was not kind to the Hungarians, especially after the Hungarian Second Army was wiped out in the Don Bend after the fall of Stalingrad. The Hungarian Government was also coming under pressure from the Germans, who wanted a free hand to conscript the two million or more Hungarian *Volksdeutsche*. The Germans were also pressuring the Hungarians to give up their large Jewish population for 'resettlement'. In a 1943 meeting with Hungarian prime minister Miklos Kallay, Hitler leaned on the Hungarians to allow the recruitment of 80,000 ethnic Germans. Soon afterwards, German teams were moving through Hungary drafting *Volksdeutsche*. *Volksdeutsche* had already been volunteering individually in some numbers since the beginning of

the war, and many of the new SS divisions formed after 1942 had Hungarian troops in their number. The Nazis recruited Hungarian Germans by bringing them into Germany for youth camps, summer schools and sports programmes, where they were indoctrinated with propaganda. The German Army encouraged those who had Magyarized their names to change them back to their Germanic form.

However, the new draft was not voluntary, and anti-German feeling, already high after severe losses on the Eastern Front, grew more intense.

First SS units

After it became clear that the Germans were on the retreat in Russia, Admiral Horthy and Prime Minister Kallay sought to negotiate a separate armistice for Hungary with the Western Allies. To keep Hungary (and its vital oil reserves) in the Axis fold, the Germans occupied the country on 19 March 1944. Horthy was permitted to remain regent, but Kallay was replaced by General Dome Sztojay, head of the Hungarian Arrow Cross fascists and fanatically pro-German. Under the new regime, more than 500,000 Jews were rounded up and deported to the death camp at Auschwitz, a move which had been resisted by the previous government. Sztojay's appointment freed the SS to recruit actively among the Hungarian population.

The first Hungarian SS unit was *SS-Kampfgruppe Deák*, raised by SS-*Oberführer* László Deák. Consisting of 1000 men in three companies, the *Kampfgruppe* was raised on 15 August 1944, from Hungarian Army and police volunteers. Declared operational in September, the unit went into action in the Banat soon afterwards. Absorbed into the 25th *Waffen-Grenadier Division der SS Hunyadi (ungarische Nr. 1)* early

'World War II brought heavy losses to Hungary: during the Battle of Stalingrad and the offensive on the Don, 40,000 soldiers of the Second Hungarian Army were killed and 70,000 were captured by the Red Army.'

in November 1944, the *Kampfgruppe* was later used to form the 61st *Waffen-Grenadier Regiment der SS (ungarische Nr. 1)*.

In October 1944, *Kampfgruppe Ney* was formed by Hungarian SS-*Obersturmbannführer* Dr Károly Ney. Established in Budapest from former Hungarian Army soldiers – members of the KABSZ, or Eastern Front Comrades' Federation – the unit's recruitment was organized under the auspices of the *SS-Ersatz Kommando/Ungarn* (SS Replacement Command/Hungary) at Budapest. Weapons, uniforms and equipment were provided by the 22nd *SS-Freiwilligen Kavallerie Division Maria Theresa*, with which it was to serve as a security company. By the end of October the unit had grown to battalion size. Two months later it had grown to regimental size, and battalions were detached to serve with 3rd *SS-Panzer Division Totenkopf*, and with 5th *SS-Panzer Division Wiking*. In the last months of the war it saw extensive combat.

At about the same time, the 800-man complement of the Hungarian *Honvéd* Mountain Training Battalion transferred to the SS, swearing allegiance to Adolf Hitler under the designation of the 1st *Ungarische SS-Schibataillon*. Transferred to Neuhammer Camp in Germany for training, it was almost disbanded and absorbed into the newly forming 25th *Waffen-Grenadier Division der SS Hunyadi*. However, the SS *Führungshauptamt* changed its mind, and on 1 December it was reinstated. Equipped with the latest small arms, heavy machine guns and anti-tank weapons, the Ski Battalion saw continuous action against the Russians in the last five months of the war.

Towards the end of October 1944, the SS and police commander in Hungary asked the Hungarian Government to provide the manpower for two SS divisions. The Hungarians agreed – on condition that they would only fight in Hungary, and only against the Russians. In November 1944 Himmler ordered that the 25th *Waffen-Grenadier Division der SS Hunyadi* be raised. By the end of November, strength had been

Opposite: *Standartenführer* **Gustav Lombard, commander of the** *Florian Geyer* **SS Division, is awarded the Knight's Cross, March 1943. The previous year, 9000 Hungarian** *Volksdeutsche* **had been assigned to the division.**

Above: SS troops retreat west through Hungary towards the Austrian border. Most prefered to surrender to American forces; every member of the SS knew his likely unpleasant fate should he ever fall into Soviet hands.

raised to 16,700 men, most being former members of the 13th *Honvéd* Light Infantry Division. Transferred to the Neuhammer training ground in Germany, the division was followed by many of the families of its members, fearful of the approaching Red Army. By December divisional strength was over 22,000 men – but its total weaponry came to just 50 machine guns and 2000 rifles. More equipment arrived over the next month, but the approaching Russians meant that the training ground had to be abandoned early in February 1945. The division, little more than a rabble, retreated to Austria where it surrendered to the Americans.

The second SS division raised in Hungary was the 26th *Waffen-Grenadier Division der SS Hungaria*. Its formation was ordered at the end of November 1944, based around a battalion of former Hungarian Army mountain troops which had been redesignated as the 26th *Waffen-Schibataillon der SS*. By Christmas 1944, some 8000 men had been mustered, the majority – about 5000 – being civilian recruits or draftees with no prior military experience. In January 1945 around 15,000 men were transferred to Poland for training. Short of supplies and food but issued with weapons, the troops clashed with Polish partisans before the massive Soviet winter offensive forced the still untrained division to make a headlong retreat towards southern Germany.

On 8 January, a Hungarian assault unit was formed by merging the remnants of two ski battalions. The 1st *Ungarische SS-Sturmjäger Regiment* was assigned to the IV SS Panzer Corps and saw action with the 5th *SS-Panzer Division Wiking* and the German Army's 3rd Panzer Division. Fought to a standstill and without ammunition or supplies, the regiment split up into small battlegroups which retreated into Austria.

The German Army was finally driven out of Hungary by the Soviets in April 1945. The war cost the lives of half a million Hungarians, and 40 per cent of the nation's material resources were destroyed. The provisions of the Treaty of Trianon were reinstated and Hungary was forced to pay a large indemnity.

CROATIA

DATE OF OCCUPATION: APRIL 1941
NUMBER OF VOLUNTEERS: 20,000
MAIN SS UNITS INCLUDING VOLUNTEERS: 13th Waffen-Gebirgs Division der SS *Handschar* (kroatische Nr. 1); 23rd Waffen-Gebirgs Division der SS *Kama* (kroatische Nr. 2)

Germany's assault on Yugoslavia, launched on 6 April 1941, was the first step in Adolf Hitler's determination to take his revenge on a state which had stood out against Nazi political pressure. Yugoslavia was an artificial state, formed out of fragments of the Austro-Hungarian and Ottoman Empires. Internal rivalries between Serbs and Croats,

Orthodox Christians and Catholics, Muslims and Christians, and communists and nationalists made breaking the nation into its constituent parts a relatively easy task. Croatia, largely Catholic, had designs on parts of Serbia and Bosnia-Herzegovina. It already had a pro-German nationalist/fascist party in the shape of the *Ustase*, led by Ante Pavelic. Following the German victory, Yugoslavia was dismembered and

Below: The German puppet state of Croatia provided two infantry divisions to fight under German Army control on the Eastern Front, but as the partisan war in Yugoslavia grew, the units had more than enough work to do at home.

Left: An SS man talks with local civilians in Split, Croatia. *Waffen*-SS units were heavily involved in the partisan war in the Balkans, and two nominally Muslim divisions were raised on Heinrich Himmler's orders to play their part in the conflict.

Chetniks, fought with either side depending on circumstances. The Croatian *Ustase* set up a concentration camp system every bit as harsh as their German mentors. Pavelić and the *Ustase* now launched a genocidal campaign against the Serbian and Jewish populations under his control throughout Croatia and Bosnia-Herzegovina. *Ustase* thugs slaughtered tens of thousands of Serbs in Croatia, often forcing them into their Orthodox churches and burning them alive. Other Serbs were given the choice of conversion to Roman Catholicism or death. On 17 April, Croatia declared war on the British, thus making Croatia a formal Axis partner. Following the German invasion of the USSR, Pavelić and his government offered the services

divided among the victors – Germany, Italy, Hungary and Bulgaria. Croatia was granted independence as an Axis puppet state under Pavelić. As a reward for supporting the Axis, Hitler ceded Bosnia-Herzegovina to Croatia.

The Germans might have thought that they had conquered the Balkans, but nobody had told the locals. The transfer of Germany's élite combat troops to the Russian Front was the signal for the start of one of the most brutal, most bitterly fought partisan campaigns the world has ever seen. Part of the problem was that it was several wars in one. The Croat puppet state was heavily involved, as were large numbers of German troops. Fascists from Croatia were on the side of the Germans, while Tito's communist guerrillas were on the other. The Serbian royalist forces, called

of Croatian troops to the *Wehrmacht*. Hitler and the German high command agreed to the offer, requesting that ground troops be recruited and sent to join the 'battle of freedom-loving nations against Communism', with air and naval units following once they could be trained to an adequate level. On 2 July, Pavelić called for volunteers, hoping for around 4000 to make up an infantry regiment. But in less than a fortnight, nearly 10,000 Croats had stepped forward, and it was easy for the Germans to select the best volunteers to make up a large infantry regiment.

Kroatischen Infanterie-Regiment 369

Established on 16 July 1941, the volunteer regiment was given the German Army title of *Verstarken Kroatischen Infanterie-Regiment 369*, or 369th

Reinforced Croatian Infantry Regiment. The regiment had 3895 officers, NCOs and men. The unit was issued with German uniforms and used German rank insignia. The only national insignia was a red and white chequered armshield surmounted with the title *Hrvatska* (Croatia), and a similar helmet badge. A training and replacement battalion was also set up at Stokerau in Austria. After three weeks of training and equipping at Dollersheim in Germany, the regiment entrained for Dongena in Bessarabia, from where it began a 35-day, 750km (466 mile) forced march to reach the front lines at Budniskaja in the Ukraine. Assigned to the 100th *Jäger* Division early in October, the regiment went into action on the 13th of that month. Over the next year the regiment fought in all of the German campaigns in the Ukraine. The first major reinforcements arrived on 26 August 1942, and the regiment was withdrawn to rest and refit.

Debacle at Stalingrad

At the end of September, the Croatian regiment received orders to join the German Sixth Army, then fighting through the suburbs of Stalingrad. The 369th Regiment was the only non-German *Wehrmacht* unit to take part in the battle through the city. Losses were heavy – by 13 October it was down to 983 men in one weak battalion and two weak companies. Losses grew even worse as the Croats took part in the ferocious, no-quarter, hand-to-hand fighting around the *Krasny Oktyabr* (Red October) tractor factory. By 3 November, numbers had dropped to under 200, with nine machine guns and six anti-tank guns. Although some reinforcements arrived from Stokerau, these were not enough to take the regiment up to even battalion strength. On 16 January 1943, the Soviets launched a major attack on the Croatian position. On 23 January, 18 wounded Croats were flown out of Stalingrad – the last to leave alive. The rest of the regiment's surviving members were killed in battle, or sent as prisoners on the long death march to Siberia after Stalingrad's fall.

Those lucky enough to have been sent back wounded in the previous months were used as a core around which a new Croatian formation would be built. Its origins dated back to 1941, following the success of the 369th Regiment in German service. The

Wehrmacht decided to raise a Croatian division, which began to form on 21 August 1942. Training battalion personnel and about 1000 former members of the 369th Regiment were joined by fresh volunteers from Croatia. The division took the German Army title 369.*Infanterie-Division (kroat.)*, but was more commonly known by its members as the *Vrazja*, or 'Devil's', Division.

Partisan war

Instead of heading for the Eastern Front, however, it was sent back home to Croatia, where the partisan war had become a major factor in German planning. In January 1943 it was decided that the situation in Croatia was becoming critical due to the communist partisan uprisings in the region, and the division was instead to be used in the Balkans rather than on the Eastern Front. Upon arrival in Croatia, the division had approximately 14,000 men in its ranks. Over the next year, the division was heavily engaged in northern Bosnia, taking part in a number of major anti-partisan battles. Tens of thousands of partisans were killed, but losses on the Axis side were also heavy, and the operations were unable to destroy the guerrilla movement. Late in January 1945, the partisans launched a major offensive against Mostar, and in February the 369th was forced to make a fighting retreat through Croatia towards Austria. On 11 May 1945, the 1000 or so survivors surrendered to the British, who promptly handed them back to the partisans. Most were executed immediately.

In January 1943, the German Army formed a second Croatian division at Dollersheim in Germany. Intended to fight in the partisan war in the Balkans, it had a German officer and NCO cadre. Designated the 373.*Infanterie-Division (kroat.)*, it was known as the *Tigar*, or 'Tiger', Division by its members. Sent to northern Bosnia in the summer of 1943, it was deployed in an operational area between the Adriatic coast of Croatia and Sarajevo. Most of its combat operations took place around Banja Luka and Bihac. By December 1944, the 373rd had lost heavily in the defence of Knin, and in January 1945 it retreated towards Bihac, were it became part of the German XV Mountain Corps. At the end of the war survivors surrendered to the partisans west of Sisak.

Above: The Croatian Naval Legion operated with the
Kriegsmarine's **light naval forces in the Black Sea. By 1943,**
however, the legion had been broken up and its members
had been drafted as replacements aboard German vessels in
the Adriatic.

Eight months after the Tiger Division had been
established, the *Wehrmacht* formed a third Croatian
division, again at Dollersheim. Given the title of 392.
Infanterie-Division (kroat.), it was given the nickname
Plava, or 'Blue', Division. As with the 373rd Division,
the officers were mainly Germans, as were the bulk of
the NCOs. The 392nd Division operated from
southern Slovenia along the Adriatic coast as far south
as the city of Knin. The division fought mostly in
northern Croatia, both on the mainland and on the
many islands along the coast. Like the other
German/Croat divisions, the 392nd suffered severely
at partisan hands in the last three months of the war.
On 24 April, the Germans released all Croatian
nationals from service before surrendering to the
partisans north of Fiume (now Rijeka).

Air units

Part of Croatia's initial offer to the Nazis in April 1941
were air and naval volunteer units. Croats who had
formerly served in the Yugoslav Air Force volunteered
for the air legion in large numbers, and on 15 July its
recruits set off for Germany for training. Two fighter
flights were established at Furth and Herzogen
airfields. By September 1941, pilots and groundcrew
had completed training. The unit was issued with
Messerschmitt Bf 109s, and on 6 October arrived at
Poltava, where they became part of *Jagdgeschwader*
(JG) 52.

Over the next two and a half years,
15.*(kroatische)*/JG 52 fought over southern Russia and
the Ukraine. Its one thousandth mission was flown on
21 June 1942, by which time the unit had accounted
for 53 Soviet aircraft. The score had risen to more than
280 when the squadron was recalled to Croatia in the
summer of 1944. Losses incurred were an incredibly
low two planes and five pilots. Equipped with Dornier
Do 17s, the legion's bomber squadron was attached to
Kampfgeschwader (KG) 53. Trained at *Kampfflieger*

Schule 3, in Greifswald, it was sent to the front at the end of October 1941. The bombers were attached to Army Group North, and in just over a year of operations flew nearly 1250 sorties. The squadron was dissolved at the end of 1942, its personnel and aircraft being transferred from the *Luftwaffe* back to the Croatian Air Force.

Himmler's Muslim experiment

During the dismemberment of Yugoslavia following the German invasion of 1941, Croatia claimed the former Austro-Hungarian province of Bosnia-Herzegovina. Something of a melting pot of history, the province was a volatile ethnic and religious mix, including Catholic Croats, Orthodox Serbs as well as Muslims of Croatian, Bosnian and Albanian ancestry. Himmler was fascinated by Islam. He believed that Muslims would make excellent shock troops, since he understood their faith offered them a place in paradise if they gave their lives against an enemy. He also supported the crackpot Nazi theory that Croatians were not Slavs, but were descended from the Aryan Goths. As a result of his beliefs, Himmler advocated the formation of a European Muslim division, which was approved by Hitler on 13 February 1943. It was not approved of by Ante Paveliç, who felt that the SS was poaching on his preserves, but there was little that the Croatian Government could do.

The division began forming on 5 March 1943, and reached its full strength of at least 20,000 men by July. Not all were Muslim volunteers, however. Several thousand *Volksdeutsche* and Catholic Croats were included, and initial Muslim enthusiasm quickly fell off, so numbers had to be made up by conscription.

Originally known as the *Kroatische SS-Freiwilligen Division*, it was turned into a mountain unit and became known as the *Kroatische SS-Freiwilligen Gebirgs Division*. In an attempt to appease the Bosnian members (who did not like Croats), it was renamed the 13th *SS-Freiwilligen Bosnien-Herzogowina Gebirgs Division (Kroatien)*, before eventually receiving its final name of 13th *Waffen-Gebirgs Division der SS Handschar (kroatische Nr.1)* in May 1944.

The name came from the Croat word for a curved scimitar-like sword traditionally associated with Bosnia, the *Handzar* (spelt *Handschar* in German). The division wore regular SS-issue uniforms. The divisional collar patch showed an arm holding a *Handschar* over a swastika. A red and white Croatian shield was worn on the left arm, and the divisional headgear was a traditional Muslim fez. Non-Muslims wore standard SS mountain caps.

In spite of Himmler's belief that Muslims would make good shock troops, the *Handschar* Division had a poor disciplinary record. However, the division could fight – as long as they were in Bosnia, protecting their

The Croatian Naval Legion

The Croatian Naval Legion was formed at the same time as the air legion. The Italians opposed a Croatian naval force operating in the Adriatic, so the naval volunteers became part of the *Kriegsmarine*. The 350-strong Croatian Naval Legion arrived at Varna on the Black Sea on 17 July 1941, and began training on German minesweepers and U-boats. On 30 September 1941 the unit moved to Gensicek in the USSR, where it became operational as the *Kriegsmarine's* 23rd Minesweeping Flotilla. Unable to man their ships over the winter, the sailors dug trenches and fought as infantry to defend the town against a number of Russian attacks. They eventually put to sea in April 1942, and were operational until the end of the year, when they went home to Croatia for rest and recuperation, before returning to Varna in Bulgaria. During their tour of duty in the Crimea, the Sea of Azov and the Black Sea, the Croatians managed to recruit several Ukrainians, former Soviet sailors, some of whom brought their ships with them. In October 1943, the legion was sent to Trieste, where it was broken up and used as drafts to reinforce the crews of *Kriegsmarine* vessels operating in the Adriatic.

homes against communist forces. In spite of the less than outstanding performance of the *Handschar* Division, Himmler persisted in trying to form Muslim fighting units.

In June 1944 Hitler approved the raising of a second Croatian *Waffen*-SS division, which would be given the honour title *Kama* after another type of Turkish sword. The 23rd *Waffen-Gebirgs Division der SS Kama (kroatische Nr. 2)* began to take shape in July and August of 1944. Officer and NCO cadres were German, to which were added several units transferred from the *Handschar* Division. It was sent to the Bachska region (annexed by Hungary in 1941) for training. In September 1944, with the formation's basic training barely complete, the advancing Red Army moved perilously close to the training area. The SS decided to disband the division late in September, and its units began to disperse. The official disbandment took place in October 1944, and most of the divisional elements went to the 31st SS Division. Muslims were ordered to report to the *Handschar* Division, and a large minority deserted on the way.

On 15 July 1943, a German-Croatian police force under German police and SS command was announced. Intended for internal security operations, the force grew rapidly until by the spring of 1944 there were 15 battalions organized into five *Polizei Freiwilligen-Regiments*. A further 15 independent *Polizei-Freiwilligen Kroatien* battalions were raised, eventually combined, nominally, as the *Gendarmerie Division Croatia*. However, they were scattered all over the Balkans and were never gathered into a single unit. A total of 32,000 Croatians served in these German police units.

Some Croatians fought in the Italian Army. On 26 July 1941, the Croatian Army established the 'Light Transport Brigade' which was to serve in the Italian Eighth Army in Russia. It was wiped out on 21 December 1942.

After the destruction of the brigade, the Italian-sponsored 'Croatian Legion', an 1800-man infantry regiment, was established near Lake Garda. With the Italian surrender, its personnel were transferred to the Croatian divisions in the German Army.

SERBIA

DATE OF OCCUPATION: APRIL 1941
NUMBER OF VOLUNTEERS: 10,000
MAIN SS UNITS INCLUDING VOLUNTEERS: Serbisches Freiwilligen Korps

The war in the Balkans was one of the most fiercely fought and merciless campaigns of the war, and it was also one of the most complex. The Croat puppet state was heavily involved, as were large numbers of German troops. At its most simplistic, the Italians, Germans and fascist Croats were on one side, while Tito's communist guerrillas were on the other. The Serbian royalist forces, called *Chetniks*, fought either side depending on circumstances. Croat fought Serb, communist fought royalist, and Muslim fought Christian. The Croatian *Ustase* killed hundreds of thousands of Serbs, Roma and Jews, running a

concentration camp system every bit as harsh as that established by the Germans.

The *Waffen*-SS played a major role in the anti-partisan and pacification campaigns, which were conducted with a medieval level of brutality. This was in part caused by the frustration of not being able to identify the attackers from among the population, but also by a sadistic streak that exists in many people and to which war often gives licence. Most of the local troops who fought under German colours were Croats or Bosnian and Albanian Muslims, but a number of Serbs also fought directly for the Germans.

Serbian Volunteer Command

In September 1941, Dimitri Ljotiae, head of the fascist *Zbor* movement, formed a volunteer body to fight communist partisans. The unit was known initially as

the *Srpska Dobrovoljacki Komanda*, or Serbian Volunteer Command, and most of its fighters were *Zbor* members, but the unit also numbered some nationalist *Chetniks* on its roster. Renamed the *Srpski Dobrovoljacki Korpus* (SDK, or Serbian Volunteer Corps) in 1943, it consisted originally of five 500-man battalions, usually divided into three companies, to which were added an armoured car battalion, a cavalry squadron and an air flight with six light aircraft which were used for reconnaissance.

Equipment was mixed – the armoured car unit operated about 20 obsolete or war-weary vehicles, including pre-war Czech and French light tanks.

SS Serbian Volunteer Corps formed

By the middle of 1944 the SDK had grown to include five 1200-man infantry regiments and an artillery battalion. A sixth regiment, the 2.*gvozdeni puk*, or 2nd

Above: Uniforms gave little indication of loyalties in the Balkans. Serbian SS units wore pre-war royalist uniforms, while *Chetniks* often wore a mixture of German and Yugoslav gear, depending on who they were fighting against.

Iron Regiment, was raised in June, increasing total strength to approximately 9000 men. In November 1944, the unit was taken over by the *Waffen*-SS, and was renamed the *Serbisches Freiwilligen Korps*, or Serbian Volunteer Corps. Although armed by the SS, the unit continued to fight in Royal Yugoslav Army uniforms.

In March 1945, surviving members of the corps retreated into Slovenia with the *Chetnik Shumadia* Division. Retreating further into Austria, the corps surrendered to the British. Most of the corps members were returned to Yugoslavia, where they were executed by the communists.

ALBANIA

DATE OF OCCUPATION: 1943
NUMBER OF VOLUNTEERS: 7000
MAIN SS UNITS INCLUDING VOLUNTEERS: 21st SS Waffen-Gebirgs Division der SS *Skanderbeg* (albanische Nr. 1)

Albania's contribution to Germany's war effort differed somewhat from that of any other nation. Part of the Muslim Ottoman Empire for five centuries, Albania declared its independence in 1912, after the First Balkan War. During the Paris Peace Conference of 1912, a plan to divide the country among its neighbours was defeated by American opposition. The collapse of the Ottoman Empire left the Balkans in chaos, however, and the Albanians asked Italy for assistance in maintaining their country's independence. They got more than assistance, however, once Mussolini's Fascists came to power. Italian interference in Albanian affairs grew over the next decade, in spite of the efforts of King Zog, a Muslim clan chief who came to the throne in 1928 when the country became a monarchy. In 1939, Italian troops occupied Albania, overthrowing the king, and soon afterwards the kingdom was annexed by the Italians.

War declared

Albania became a war front with the Italian attack on Greece in 1941. Germany had to intervene when the Italians became bogged down by dogged Greek resistance, in the process occupying Yugoslavia. The Axis powers planned to dismember Yugoslavia, setting up puppet regimes in Croatia and Serbia. As part of the process they intended to create a 'Greater Albania' by transferring the Kosovo-Metohija region of Serbia, along with territory in southwest Montenegro and southern Serbia (now part of Macedonia), to Albania.

During the occupation of Kosovo-Metohija, the Germans recruited a local paramilitary police force consisting of 1000 Kosovar Albanians and a similar number drawn from the Albanian paramilitary force known as the *Vulnetara*. These assisted the Germans in

the 'ethnic cleansing' which followed, during which tens of thousands of Serbs, Jews, gypsies and other non-Albanians and non-Muslims were arrested, interned, deported or murdered. The Serbs were a particular target for the paramilitaries: Serbian homes and Orthodox Christian churches were looted and destroyed. Albanian nationalists, members of the *Balli Kombetar* (BK, or National Union), were encouraged by the Germans and Italians to think of Albanian Kosovo as part of a Greater Albania.

With the overthrow of Mussolini, communist and nationalist partisans rose against the Fascist regime. Italian military positions and police units were overwhelmed by partisan attacks, and the communists seized most of southern Albania's cities while nationalists seized control of the north. A brief truce between the factions was swiftly broken, and a bitter civil war began – a civil war which was made more complicated by German occupation.

German occupation

In September 1943, following Italy's surrender to the Allies, Germany occupied Albania. *Fallschirmjäger* seized the capital, Tirana, before the guerrillas could, and the German Army marched into the country, swiftly driving the guerrilla forces into the hills. The Germans sent the 100th *Jäger* Division from Greece, the 297th Infantry Division from Serbia and the 1st Mountain Division. However, the Germans were fully occupied defending the coastline, and more troops were needed for operations in the interior. Berlin organized an Albanian government, police and military, and sought to win over the nationalists by supporting the annexation of Kosovo. Large numbers of BK paramilitaries fought on the German side against the communists, though matters were complicated further at the end of 1943 by the rise of a third major guerrilla force in the north. Known as 'Legality', this group wanted to continue the annexation of Kosovo, and was opposed to the communists, the nationalists and the Germans.

studies carried out by Italian Fascists claimed to have proved that the Ghegs, the people who occupied northern Albania and Kosovo-Metohija, were Aryans. The 21st *Waffen-Gebirgs Division der SS Skanderbeg (albanische Nr. 1)* was formed in April 1944. It included 300 Albanian Muslims who had been transferred from the *Handschar* Division, joined by 6500 new Albanian recruits (two-thirds of whom were from Kosovo). To this Albanian core were added German troops and *Kriegsmarine* sailors who no longer had ships to crew. Leadership was provided by a cadre of *Volksdeutsche* officers, NCOs and enlisted men transferred from the 7th *SS-Freiwilligen Gebirgs Division Prinz Eugen*, which at that time was carrying out anti-partisan operations in Bosnia-Herzegovina. The majority of the division's Albanians were Bektashi and Sunni Muslims, but several hundred Albanian Catholics also served.

Unit markings

The SS *Hauptamt* designed a distinctive arm patch for the division, consisting of a black double-headed eagle on a red background, the national symbol of Albania. The division was named after George Kastrioti

One of Himmler's beliefs was the Muslims would make good shock troops. The 13th *Waffen-Gebirgs Division der SS Handschar* was raised from Bosnian Muslims in 1943. However, the division had a poor record – its troops mutinied in training, killing several of their German cadre members. Most had joined the division in order to protect their homes and families from *Ustase/Chetnik* and partisan attacks. The fascist Croat puppet government disapproved of the formation, since they felt that the SS recruitment in Bosnia violated their sovereignty. Needless to say, the division had a patchy combat record.

Nevertheless, Himmler persisted in his attempts to create an Islamic SS unit. Himmler wanted to use Albanian manpower to form two *Waffen*-SS divisions. He was especially keen, on this since anthropological

Skanderbeg (1405–68). Brought up as a hostage in the court of Sultan Murat II, Kastrioti was named Iskander Bey for his prowess in battle. Breaking away from the Turks and becoming a Christian, Skanderbeg led Albania's ultimately unsuccessful fight for independence from the Ottoman Empire.

Albanian recruits wore a white fez-style cap, the national attire of the Ghegs of northern Albania. The SS also issued grey headgear in the same style, with the *Totenkopf* sewn on the front below the Nazi eagle and swastika.

Ethnic cleansing

Ostensibly intended to fight partisans, the division was in fact used to clear Kosovo of 'undesirables', defined as Orthodox Serbs, Jews, gypsies – in fact, anybody who was not Albanian. Many were killed or driven from their homes, while a large number of Kosovo's estimated 500 Jews were deported and died at Belsen. However, although many of *Skanderbeg's* members enthusiastically played their parts in atrocities against Serbs and Jews, a large number proved to be very reluctant recruits. There were as many as 3500 desertions in the unit's first three months of existence.

By the beginning of October, divisional strength had fallen to just 3504 men, and it was disbanded in December. The remaining troops fought as *Kampfgruppe Skanderbeg* before the German cadre was transferred back to *SS-Gebirgsjäger Regiment* 14 of the *Prinz Eugen* Division.

BULGARIA

DATE OF OCCUPATION: ALLY
NUMBER OF VOLUNTEERS: 600?
MAIN SS UNITS INCLUDING VOLUNTEERS: Waffen-Grenadier Regiment der SS (bulgarisches Nr. 1); SS-Panzer Zerstörer Regiment (bulgarisches)

Bulgaria was a full member of the Axis, but it played no real part in the war on the Eastern Front. Bulgaria had been enticed into an active role initially by the return of territory from Romania in 1940. On 1 March 1941, Bulgaria signed on to the Tripartite Treaty. As a result, the Bulgarian Government permitted the Germans to use its naval facilities, air bases and rail network. A day later, German troops bound for Yugoslavia and Greece began staging through the country. Bulgarian troops were primarily used on anti-partisan operations in the occupied Balkans.

Ultimately, seven Bulgarian divisions were employed in Yugoslavia. As a reward, Bulgaria was ceded the Greek territory of Thrace and much of Macedonia. In December 1941, Bulgaria declared war on Britain and the United States – but refused German pressure to participate in the war against Russia. This was because there was considerable pro-Soviet sentiment in Bulgaria, and not exclusively from the communists. In August 1943, the death of Tsar Boris saw power being transferred to a council of regents who were in most respects German puppets, but by 1944 it was obvious that Germany was losing the war and the regime began to look for a way out. In August the rapidly advancing Soviet Army prompted Bulgaria to announce its withdrawal from the war. German troops were asked to leave and Bulgarian troops serving in Greece and Yugoslavia were called home. On 16 September, the Soviet Army entered Sofia. Less than a week before, Bulgaria declared war on Germany and took an active part in operations against the Germans in Yugoslavia, Hungary and Austria.

At the same time several hundred Bulgarians working in Germany, most of whom had been supporters of the old regime, offered their services to the *Wehrmacht*. Up to 600 were accepted and went into training as the *Waffen-Grenadier Regiment der SS (bulgarisches Nr. 1)*. It was hoped that this would form the core of a Bulgarian *Waffen-Grenadier* division, but this was never achieved. The unit participated in some of the final battles of the war, being renamed the *SS-Panzer Zerstörer Regiment (bulgarisches)* in April 1945.

LITHUANIA

DATE OF OCCUPATION: JUNE 1941
NUMBER OF VOLUNTEERS: 50,000 (MAINLY NON-SS POLICE UNITS)
MAIN SS UNITS INCLUDING VOLUNTEERS: NONE

Lithuania, the southernmost of the three Baltic States, had a different relationship with Germany than did Latvia and Estonia. Lithuania shared a frontier with Germany, and had been engaged in a long dispute with the Germans over possession of the port of Memel (Klaipeda in Lithuanian). In the 1930s Lithuanians imprisoned ethnic German Nazis. By

1938, most of these had been released ready to welcome the Germans who seized the port in 1939.

In the wake of the Nazi-Soviet pact which had carved up Poland, the Baltic States were declared to be in the Soviet sphere of influence, and there was little opposition when on 15 June 1940 the Soviets took complete control of Lithuania, including the capital, Vilna (Vilnius), which had been part of Poland until October 1939. Numerous underground groups formed in reaction to the Soviets, one of the most extremely nationalist of which was the *Lietuviu Aktyvistu Frontas* (LAF, or Lithuanian Activist Front).

The Lithuanian Activist Front

Strong supporters of the Nazis, the LAF also were violently anti-Semitic, claiming that the Jews in Lithuania were profiting from the Soviet occupation. Some 150,000 Jews lived in Lithuania between the wars, in a community which had been in existence since the fourteenth century. Another 100,000 were added to the total when Vilnius was returned from Polish control in 1939. Jews had gained some freedoms under the Soviets, but their cultural and economic activities were deemed to be anti-Soviet, and 7000 Jews were arrested and deported to Siberia in June 1941, along with 10,000 other Lithuanians.

Soviet oppression caused real hatred in the Lithuanian population, which

Left: A Lithuanian member of a *Polizei Bataillon*. Although there were no Lithuanian SS formations, some 38 Police Battalions were formed. A few Lithuanian *Volksdeutsche* served in German units, but they joined as individuals.

meant that when the Germans invaded on 22 June 1941, over 100,000 Lithuanians took up arms against the retreating Soviets. Much of Lithuania was liberated even before the arrival of the Germans. Unfortunately, organizations like the LAF were prominent in these guerrilla groups, and they saw no difference between attacking Jews and attacking Russians.

Even before the Germans were in control of the country, Lithuanian nationalists were carrying out anti-Jewish pogroms. These nationalists were soon joined by *Einsatzkommando* 3, and between them the Lithuanians and the Nazis managed to kill the majority of country Jews. City Jews, being more important to the economic life of the country, were herded into ghettos to be dealt with later. By the end of 1941, only 40,000 out of a quarter of a million Jews remained in Lithuania. Some 20,000 had fled abroad, and a similar number had escaped to the Russians. The rest had been liquidated.

Lithuanians served as auxilliaries to the Ordnungspolizei in the occupied areas of the Soviet Union, where they often supported the Einsatzkommandos' murderous 'cleansing' operations.

Police battalions

There was considerable support for the Germans in the early months of the occupation. Large numbers of young men came forward to join the fight against the hated Russians. Many had served with the Soviet 29th Light Infantry Corps – the former Lithuanian Army, which had been absorbed into the Red Army in 1940, and which had deserted *en masse* on the outbreak of war. As in the other Baltic States, the first units to come under German control were the irregular groups who had formed to fight the Soviets.

The first unit to be formed was known as the *Lituanische Hunterschaften*. This provided the basis for the formation of the self-defence units known *Selbschutz-Bataillonen*. Renamed as *Schutzmannschaft-Bataillonen*, or *Schumas*, when they came under German police control, they were reformed into regular *Polizie-Bataillonen* in May 1943. A total of 35 such battalions were formed, usually with a strength of between 500 and 600 men. They were initially used for security duties, but later in the war were used increasingly in combat roles. They were primarily

assigned to rear areas, but as the Soviets drew nearer to Lithuania, they also saw service fighting the Soviets directly.

Lithuanian police battalions served all over the Eastern Front, from the Baltic to the Black Sea. They saw combat at Demyansk, Volkhov, Lake Ilmen, Opotschka and in the Courland. One battalion, the 7th, even managed to break out from Stalingrad, losing half their number in the process. Since they served as auxiliaries to the *Ordnungspolizei* in the occupied areas of the Soviet Union, the Lithuanian police battalions were often used to support the *Einsatzgruppen* of the SD. Rather than working for the Army, units engaged in these murderous actions took their orders from the *Reichsicherheits-hauptamt* (RSHA, or Reich Main Security Office), or from the *Höhere SS-Polizei Führer* (HSSPF) of the *Ostland* regions.

The Lithuanian Defence Corps

Unlike its Estonian and Latvian neighbours, Lithuania never provided Germany with a national SS legion during World War II. This was in part because Himmler considered that the Lithuanians were the least reliable of the Baltic races. Unlike Protestant Latvia and Estonia, who had a long history of relations with Germany, Lithuania was largely Catholic, like the despised Poles with whom the Lithuanians had been allied many times over the centuries. The Lithuanian authorities would not agree to allow any unit to be formed which was not Lithuanian-led, and they also insisted that any such unit must only be used within Lithuania. The Germans finally agreed in February 1944, and a Lithuanian defensive force was formed, though not as part of the SS. It was known as the *Schutzkorps Litauen*, or Lithuanian Defence Corps. On

Opposite: A *Polizei* patrol takes a suspected 'bandit' – the standard propaganda term for a partisan – into custody. Lithuanians served with such units in Poland, Byelorussia and the Ukraine, and they also provided rear-area security in the Baltic region.

Above: SS men enter a Soviet village. Although not part of the *Waffen*-SS, Lithuanian police units sometimes came under SS control when they were thrown into combat in the desperate struggle to hold back the Red Army in the last year of the war.

16 February an appeal went out for volunteers, and although none were too keen to serve the Germans, the Lithuanians were still eager to fight the Russians. Over 19,000 men volunteered, rather than the expected 5000.

Rebellion and desertion

The Germans wanted to use the volunteers to reinforce *Wehrmacht* units, but Lithuanian opposition meant that they were formed into 13 police battalions instead. The *Schutzkorps* began training in March 1944. Less than three weeks later, on 22 March, the Lithuanians were again offended when Field Marshal Walter Model, commander of Army Group North, requested Lithuanian units to protect *Luftwaffe* airfields in Russia.

The last straw came in May, when the Germans announced a general mobilization, and 14 Lithuanian police battalions were placed under *Wehrmacht* command. Near mutiny was followed by massive desertion – 16,000 out of the original 19,000 in the *Schutzkorps*.

The *Schutzkorps* was disbanded and the remaining 3000 men were drafted into *Luftwaffe* Flak batteries. Five armed construction battalions were also formed in 1943, attached to German pioneer units in Army

Group North. These were asked to join the *Waffen*-SS, and something under a half actually joined up as individuals.

Soviet pressure

As the Soviets approached the Baltic States towards the end of 1944, the Germans formed three Lithuanian regiments by grouping three or four Lithuanian police battalions into regimental-sized units known as *Lituanische Freiwilligen Infanterie Regimenter*. Later, as Soviet forces began to enter Lithuania, the Germans formed the Fatherland Defence Force. This was an amalgamation of small groups of retreating Lithuanian

troops organized into two *Kampfgruppen*, under overall German command.

After heavy fighting and crippling losses, the 1000 or so survivors were gathered in East Prussia to form a new unit known as the Lithuanian Engineer Battalion. Caught in the path of the oncoming Soviet juggernaut, the battalion was totally destroyed in February and March 1945.

After World War II ended, tens of thousands of armed Lithuanians remained active, waging a guerrilla war against the Soviet occupation forces well into the 1950s. The last of the Lithuanian partisan forces are thought to have been wiped out in 1956.

POLAND

DATE OF OCCUPATION: SEPTEMBER 1939
NUMBER OF VOLUNTEERS: NONE
MAIN SS UNITS INCLUDING VOLUNTEERS: NONE

Poland suffered more under German occupation than any other country bar the Soviet Union, and proportionately it suffered even more than the Soviets. After the conquest of 1939, Poland was dismembered. The west was annexed directly into the Greater German Reich, the area around Danzig being absorbed into West Prussia and the rest becoming part of *Gau* Posen. The east came under Soviet control under the secret non-aggression pact between Hitler and Stalin. The remaining central portion of the country was controlled by the *Generalgouvernement*, which also took over the Soviet-controlled areas after Operation *Barbarossa* in 1941.

Poland suffered cruelly. One in every six Poles died, mostly as a result of brutal repression by German security forces. The Poles take pride in the fact that they did not collaborate with the Germans – possibly the only occupied country not to do so. However, there were some Polish citizens who volunteered to work for the enemy. The largest group were the *Volksdeutsche*, people of ethnic German descent whose ancestors had lived all over Eastern Europe for centuries. The Nazis

looked on the *Volksdeutsche* as potential citizens of the coming Greater Germany – and as a source of manpower for the expanding *Wehrmacht* and *Waffen*-SS.

Volksdeutsche formations

As early as the first crossing of the border by German troops on 1 September 1939, small groups of *Volksdeutsche* in western Poland (which had been part of Germany until the end of World War I) formed local militia groups. These were later organized into self-protection units known as *Selbschutz*, these being the prototype for similar units set up in the Baltic and elsewhere in occupied Europe after June 1941.

Controlled by the SS, the *Selbschutz* units came under the direct control of the SS-*Hauptamt* and of Heydrich's infamous RSHA. They earned an unsavoury reputation in their few months of existence, and they were disbanded from the end of 1939 through until April 1940. Some 45,000 ethnic German Poles served in the *Selbschutz* units before they were ordered to be disbanded. Many of their members took service in other paramilitary organizations, including the NSKK, the *Generalgouvernement*'s labour office (the *Baudienst*) and in the police forces. Few, if any, Slavic Poles volunteered or were allowed to work as anything but slave labourers.

THE FOREIGN SS DIVISIONS

From its earliest days, the SS was a volunteer organization which saw itself as an elite within the Nazi state. Troops of the first SS divisions were exceptionally fit, and the first foreign recruits were expected to be of the same standard. However, by the middle of the war manpower shortages meant that to fill out newly forming units like the *Prinz Eugen* and the *Florian Geyer* divisions the SS had to accept recruits of a considerably lower standard.

Above: Russian volunteers man an anti-tank gun on the Eastern Front. By this time, in the winter of 1943, foreigners in Army units were being transferred to the SS to help fill out the large numbers of newly created *Waffen*-SS divisions.
Left: Before the war, the SS would only accept mature recruits. However, wartime needs meant that younger volunteers were sought, many of whom went straight from the *Hitler Jugend* after their seventeenth birthdays.

5th SS-Panzer Division *Wiking*

- *Nov 1940 – Jan 1941:* SS-Division (motorisierte) *Germania*   • *Jan 1941 – Nov 1942:* SS-Division (motorisierte) *Wiking*   • *Nov 1942 – Oct 1943:* SS-Panzergrenadier Division *Wiking*   • *Oct 1943 – May 1945:* 5th SS-Panzer Division *Wiking*

Wiking has not been accused of any war crimes, but the infamous Joseph Mengele served (briefly) in the Pioneer Battalion (where he was also awarded the Iron Cross) during his time in the *Waffen*-SS.

Initially authorized in May 1940 as *SS-Division (motorisierte) Germania*, the division was renamed within days, becoming the *SS-Division (motorisierte) Wiking*, to avoid confusion with the *Germania* Regiment of the SS-VT Division. The *Germania* Regiment would form the core of the new division, but it was intended that the bulk of the formation's personnel would be provided by Scandinavian volunteers – hence the name *Wiking*.

Joining the *Germania* Regiment in the division would be the *Nordland* and *Westland* SS Regiments. The first truly international division of the *Waffen*-SS, *Wiking* numbered Dutch, Danes, Norwegians, Finns, Walloons and Flemings among its personnel, together with a smattering of *Volksdeutsche* from the Balkans. However, in spite of the propaganda, which made much of its international nature, the bulk of the division's personnel (as much as 90 per cent) was German. Formation of the division began in the autumn of 1940, and by the time of the German invasion of Russia in June 1941 (Operation *Barbarossa*), *Wiking* was a fully fledged, fully trained SS motorized infantry division.

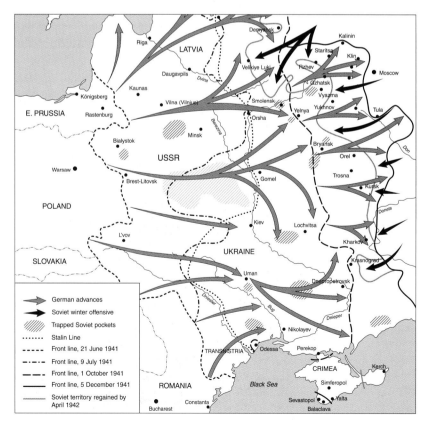

Left: A map showing Operation *Barbarossa* **and the subsequent Soviet counter-offensive of the winter of 1941–42.** *Wiking* **gained its first combat experience as part of Army Group South, attacking through the Ukraine. Following the invasion, the Germans' need for additional manpower led them to recruit foreign volunteers by employing anti-communist propaganda. The glamorous, hard-fighting image of the** *Waffen*-SS **attracted many 'Germanic' volunteers.**

Opposite, right: A Tiger commander of the *Wiking* **Division, April 1944.** *Wiking* **was created as a motorized infantry division, but was successively upgraded into a** *Panzergrenadier* **division and then into a fully fledged panzer division.**

First battles

Wiking first saw action on 29 June 1941. Assigned to Army Group South, it took part in the fighting for Tarnopol in Galicia. In August 1941, the division was at the head of the army group as it fought to establish a bridgehead across the Dnieper River. Continuing the drive, *Wiking* fought its way through Dnepropetrovsk and on to Rostov. When the Germans were pushed out of Rostov by the first truly successful Red Army counter-attack, *Wiking* moved back to the line of the Mius River where it spent the winter months.

Although it suffered heavy losses, it achieved an excellent reputation, even earning the grudging respect of the Soviets in several battle reports for its pugnacious fighting spirit. Soviet commanders were always concerned to learn that their troops were facing the soldiers of the *Wiking* Division. When the Germans launched their major offensive in the summer of 1942, *Wiking* was again one of the spearhead divisions. It fought its way into and through the Caucasus, and would remain in the area until von Kleist's Army Group was forced to pull back after the fall of Stalingrad early in 1943. By this time it had been converted from a motorized infantry division to a *panzergrenadier*, or armoured infantry, division.

Individual elements of the *Wiking* Division were added and removed many times in its existence. As a replacement for the disbanded Finnish battalion of the *Nordland* Regiment, the Estonian *Narwa* Regiment was transferred to *Wiking*. The *Nordland* Regiment itself was detached to help establish another *Waffen*-SS division, providing the nucleus of the new *Nordland* Division.

The Korsun salient

Wiking avoided the cataclysmic battles at Kursk, serving further south with Fourth Panzer Army on the Don, fighting a defensive campaign through the summer and autumn of 1943. In October 1943, the division was again upgraded, being converted from a *panzergrenadier* division to a fully armoured panzer division. In the summer and autumn of 1943, the division fought in defensive operations in the area of Kharkov and the Dnieper River. By the end of 1943, *Wiking* was one of six divisions occupying a 96km (60 mile) salient at Korsun, on the east of the Dnieper.

Hitler had the highly unrealistic belief that the 56,000 men in the salient could thrust in an offensive towards Kiev. He had not reckoned on the Russians. General Konev's 2nd Ukrainian Front punched through the bridgehead lying between Kremenchug, which lay far to the southwest of Kharkov, and Dnepropetrovsk to the east of Kremenchug. Konev's objective was to form a wedge between First Panzer Army and Eighth Army. The latter was no match for the strong Soviet forces and was forced to pull back in the face of the steady advance of the 2nd Ukrainian Front.

In the north, things were no better, with ever more powerful Russian forces throwing the Germans out of Kiev on 6 November after they had established a bridgehead there. Russian pride was further restored with the recapture, after a temporary loss, of the town of Zhitomir on 20 November. Buildings there were reduced to rubble and the streets were littered with the burnt-out hulks of vehicles. Of considerable

compensation were the large supply dumps and foodstuff depots of Fourth Panzer Army which the Germans had established in the high summer of triumph two years before.

For all the efforts of the panzer units and the *Waffen*-SS, the truth was that the Soviet advance had become a flood, with the great winter offensive dealing the decisive blow. Not the least disastrous event was the overwhelming of Army Group Centre when, in mid-December, the Soviets burst out of the salient at Nevel in their progress southwest. Another knockout blow was delivered the following month by the Red Army in the north, forcing Army Group North to give up its encirclement of Leningrad.

The men of *Wiking* were assigned to territory where the prospects were bleak for the Germans. Four divisions were encircled in this flat countryside under snow with the temperature in Kirovograd itself at –20°C (–4°F). On 5 January 1944, Konev's 2nd Ukrainian Front launched its attack and took the city. A breakout was eventually achieved by 3rd Panzer Division with covering fire from the artillery; engineers and *panzergrenadiers* followed while the Russians were pinned down in local fighting. The recapture of Kirovograd still left unfinished business for the Russians. To the north lay the salient around Korsun

and Cherkassy which Hitler was determined to hold and which was defended by six and a half divisions with around 56,000 men. Manstein wanted to open the pocket, but Hitler insisted contact must be established with the beleaguered forces: the Dnieper line would be held, no matter the cost.

The German positions south of the Korsun bulge took the full bombardment. The Russian Fourth Guards and Fifty-Third Armies, soon followed by Fifth Tank Army, struck at the heart of the German line. From the north of the bulge came 1st Ukrainian Front with its massive armoured forces. By 28 January it had joined Konev's 2nd Ukrainian Front, which had advanced from the south. Men of *Wiking* were among the 60,000 trapped there. Being the only panzer unit in the pocket, *Wiking* spearheaded an attempt to break out. At the time, an independent foreign formation, *Wallonien*, was a part of *Wiking*. The division managed to break out, but casualties were heavy, and *Wiking* lost all of its armour and a great deal of other equipment in the process.

The end

The remnants of the division fought on as a *Kampfgruppe*, before being transferred to Poland where it would form the nucleus of a new 5th *SS-Panzer Division Wiking*. Because it was out of the line, it missed the massive Soviet summer offensive, perhaps the most powerful military attack in history, which smashed the German Eastern Front and virtually destroyed Army Group Centre. By the time *Wiking* was again in action, the Soviets had pushed all the way to the Vistula River and to Warsaw.

Along with the 3rd *SS-Panzer Division Totenkopf* and the Army's 19th Panzer Division, *Wiking* fought to stem the Soviet advance, stabilizing the front along the line of the Vistula. *Wiking* was withdrawn from Warsaw in December 1944 and transferred south to relieve 60,000 German soldiers and over 800,000 civilians trapped in the city of Budapest. *Wiking* pushed forward for two weeks, but could not penetrate the massed Soviet armies which were besieging the city. When this operation failed the division was withdrawn into Austria, where it fought in the final battles to defend Vienna in 1945. The division surrendered to the Soviets in May 1945.

Right: Waffen-SS soldiers advance through the smoke and flames rising from a Soviet T-34/76 tank and Zil truck, destroyed during the fighting near Cherkassy in the spring of 1943.

Opposite, left: A *Wiking* officer aims a Kar 98K rifle. On the defensive, *Wiking* remained in the Kharkov area into the winter of 1943. When the Soviets launched their winter offensive, *Wiking* was one of the units cut off in the Cherkassy pocket.

DIVISIONAL INFORMATION

Commanders
SS-Obergruppenführer Felix Steiner
               (Jan 1940 – Jan 1943)
SS-Obergruppenführer Herbert Gille
               (5 Jan 1943 – 8 Jun 1944)
SS-Oberführer Edmund Deisenhofer
               (8 Jun 1944 – 8 Aug 1944)
SS-Standartenführer Rudolf Mühlenkamp
               (8 Aug 1944 – 10 Sep 1944)
SS-Oberführer Karl Ullrich
               (10 Sep 1944 – 5 May 1945)

Order of Battle
Stab der Division
SS-Panzergrenadier-Regiment 9 Germania
SS-Panzergrenadier-Regiment 10 Westland
SS-Panzergrenadier-Regiment Nordland
  (Withdrawn from division in 1943)
Estnisches SS-Freiwilligen-Panzergrenadier-Bataillon
  Narwa (Withdrawn in 1944)
Finnisches Freiwilligen-Bataillon der Waffen-SS

SS-Sturmbrigade Wallonien
SS-Panzer-Regiment 5
SS-Panzerjäger-Abteilung 5
SS-Sturmgeschütz-Abteilung 5
SS-Sturmgeschütz-Batterie 5
SS-Panzer-Artillerie-Regiment 5
SS-Flak-Abteilung 5
SS-Werfer-Abteilung 5
SS-Panzer-Nachrichten-Abteilung 5
SS-Panzer-Aufklärungs-Abteilung 5
SS-Panzer-Pionier-Bataillon 5
SS-Dina 5
SS-Instandsetzungs-Abteilung 5
SS-Wirtschafts-Bataillon 5
SS-Sanitäts-Abteilung 5
SS-Feldlazarett 5
SS-Kriegsberichter-Zug 5
SS-Feldgendarmerie-Trupp 5
SS-Feldersatz-Bataillon 5
I./SS-Panzergrenadier-Regiment 23 Norge
I./SS-Panzergrenadier-Regiment 24 Danmark

6th SS-Gebirgs Division *Nord*

- • *Feb 1941:* SS-Kampfgruppe *Nord*   • *Sep 1941:* SS-Division *Nord*
- • *Sep 1942:* SS-Gebirgs Division *Nord*   • *Oct 1943 – May 1945:* 6th SS-Gebirgs Division *Nord*

Although not a volunteer formation in the classic sense, the 6th SS Division, known as *Nord*, did have a significant foreign volunteer component.

In June 1940, the capitulation of Norway left the border with Finland and the USSR unguarded. To replace the two Norwegian infantry battalions in the area, the Germans decided to deploy SS units rather than regular army formations. The 9th *SS Totenkopf*

Standarte, commanded by *SS-Obersturmbannführer* Ernst Deutsch, was ordered north, with the first unit – *SS Bataillon Reitz*, under the command of *SS-Obersturmbannführer* Wilhelm Reitz – arriving at Kirkenes in the late summer. In February 1941, two further SS regiments arrived in northern Norway: the 6th and 7th *SS Totenkopf Standarten*. Soon afterwards most of the 6th *Standarte* reinforced by elements of the 9th moved forward to defensive positions at Salla in

DIVISIONAL INFORMATION

Commanders

SS-Brigadeführer Karl Herrmann   (28 Feb 1941)
SS-Obergruppenführer Karl-Maria Demelhuber
                                        (15 May 1941)
SS-Obergruppenführer Matthias Kleinheisterkamp
                                        (1 Apr 1942)
SS-Oberführer Hans Scheider   (20 Apr 1942)
SS-Obergruppenführer Matthias Kleinheisterkamp
                                        (14 Jun 1942)
SS-Gruppenführer Lothar Debes   (15 Jan 1943)
SS-Obergruppenführer Friedrich-Wilhelm Krüger
                                        (14 Jun 1943)
SS-Brigadeführer Gustav Lombard   (23 Aug 1943)
SS-Gruppenführer Karl Brenner   (9 Jan 1944)
SS-Standartenführer Franz Schreiber
                                (3 Apr 1945 – 8 May 1945)

Divisional Strength

Jun 1941	10,373
Dec 1942	21,247
Dec 1943	20,129
Jun 1944	19,355
Dec 1944	15,000

Order of Battle

Stab der Division
SS-Gebirgsjäger-Regiment 11 Reinhard Heydrich
SS-Gebirgsjäger-Regiment 12 Michael Gaissmair
SS-Polizei-Grenadier-Bataillon (mot) 506
     (formed from the *SS Skijegerbataljon Norge* after
     the arrival in Oslo late in 1944)
SS-Gebirgs-Artillerie-Regiment 6
SS-Sturmgeschütz-Batterie 6
SS-Infanterie-Regiment (mot) 5
SS-Infanterie-Regiment 9 (until 1943)
SS-Schutzen-Abteilung (mot) 6
SS-Gebirgs-Panzerjäger-Abteilung 6
SS-Flak-Abteilung 6
SS-Gebirgs-Nachrichten-Abteilung (mot) 6
SS-Gebirgs-Aufklärungs-Abteilung (mot) 6
SS-Gebirgs-Pionier-Abteilung 6
SS-Dina 6
SS-Bekleidungs-Instandsetzungs-Kompanie 6
SS-Sanitäts-Kompanie 6
SS-Veterinär-Kompanie 6
SS-Kriegsberichter-Zug 6
SS-Feldgendarmerie-Trupp 6
SS-og Politikompani (two companies of Norwegian
     SS volunteers)

northern Finland. However, the German commander in Norway, General von Falkenhorst, was not impressed with the SS men. Although well equipped, the *Totenkopf Standarten* were not made up of highly trained *Waffen*-SS men but of volunteers transferred from the *Allgemeine*-SS.

With the attack on Russia in June 1941, the units, now brigaded as *SS-Kampfgruppe Nord*, were launched into battle against veteran Soviet troops on the Finnish border at Markajärvi-Salla. The poorly trained SS men made a poor showing, suffering 300 killed and more than 400 wounded in two days. In July and August 1941, units of *Nord* were rested and re-equipped, and their shortcomings were addressed by a period of intensive training. Between July and September *Nord* was gradually moved from the front to the Kiestinki-Uhtua area, 140km (87 miles) to the south. In September 1941, the *Kampfgruppe* acquired an artillery regiment, and further reinforcements were planned to bring the *Kampfgruppe* up to divisional status. Hitler directed that 'a new SS-*Gebirgsbrigade* is

to be formed by volunteering Norwegians and Finns. An Austrian SS-regiment is to be attached, and the remaining units are to be deployed from *Kampfgruppe Nord*'. Although the promised Finnish regiment was not to appear, the new *SS-Division Nord* did take into its ranks the *Freiwilligen-Schikompanie Norwegen,* later enlarged to a battalion. In the meantime, the unit was placed under the temporary command of the veteran Finnish General Siilasvuo – the only time an SS unit was placed under foreign command. As part of the temporary 'Division J', it was assigned to Siilasvuo's III Finnish Army Corps.

In January it was decided that the *Nord* Division should be redesignated as a mountain division in the near future, and plans were set afoot to create new units for the division. These arrived in September

Below: Specializing in mountain and Arctic warfare, the *SS-Division Nord* numbered in its strength the accomplished skiers of the *Freiwilligen-Schikompanie Norwegen*, who were used to mounting long-range Arctic reconnaissance patrols.

Left: Members of the *Nord* Division were mountain troops, classed as *Jäger*, or light infantrymen. As with all such soldiers, they were very fit as well as being highly trained, but they were also lightly equipped.

deployed to hold the line around the Kiestinki area, where it would remain until autumn 1944. It became 6th *SS-Gebirgs Division Nord* on 22 October 1943.

On 2 September 1944, the Finns withdrew from the war. The next day, all German units received the message: '*Birke anschlagen*', or 'Cut the birch'. This was a warning to prepare the evacuation of Finland. Two days later the message '*Birke fällen*' ('Birch has fallen') ordered the evacuation to begin. During August and September the Germans had activated two temporary units called *Kampfgruppe West* and *Ost* to secure their southern flank. Units from *Nord* together with *Divisions-Gruppe Kräutler* formed the bulk of these two groups. At the end of September, the two *Kampfgruppen* fought several short engagements with their erstwhile Finnish allies, but the retreat was not slowed to any great degree.

Nord reached Norway in October 1944. At the end of the year it was transferred to Germany, where it took part in the abortive offensive mounted south of the Ardennes designed as a diversion for the main Ardennes offensive. *Nord* fought mainly against US forces, and the survivors surrendered to the Americans in May 1945.

1942, and the division was redesignated *SS-Gebirgs Division Nord*. By now detached from 'Division J', *Nord* was assigned to fight alongside the Army's 7th Mountain Division in the new German XVIII Mountain Corps, which had arrived in Finland during the winter of 1941 and spring of 1942. *Nord* was

---

7th SS-Freiwilligen Gebirgs Division *Prinz Eugen*

• *Mar 1942:* Freiwilligen-Gebirgs Division   • *Apr 1942:* SS-Freiwilligen Division *Prinz Eugen*   • *Oct 1942:* SS-Freiwilligen Gebirgs Division *Prinz Eugen*   • *Oct 1943 – May 1945:* 7th SS-Freiwilligen Gebirgs Division *Prinz Eugen*

The 7th *SS-Freiwilligen Gebirgs Division Prinz Eugen* was created for partisan operations in the Balkans, and the bulk of its strength consisted of *Volksdeutsche* volunteers and conscripts from Romania, Hungary and Yugoslavia.

Named after the great eighteenth-century commander Prince Eugene of Savoy, *Prinz Eugen* was equipped with obsolete and captured equipment such as Czech machine guns and French light tanks. It was one of the most effective counter-insurgency units the Germans

fielded in Yugoslavia during the war and was greatly feared by the partisans. However, that reputation was gained primarily by brutality and utter ruthlessness.

The origins of the *Prinz Eugen* Division can be found in Himmler's desire to form entire SS units from the massive manpower resource that was the large *Volksdeutsche* community living outside Germany's borders. Many *Volksdeutsche* were already serving in the *Wehrmacht*, but primarily as individual volunteers. Gottlob Berger, head of the SS recruiting office,

Right: Mountain troopers from the *SS-Division Prinz Eugen* prepare weapons to be loaded onto a pack mule. In the Balkans this was often the most effective means of moving supplies across the rugged terrain.

proposed to form a new SS division early in 1942. It was to be made up of volunteers from the large *Volksdeutsche* community living in Serbia, Croatia and the Banat.

The new *Freiwilligen-Gebirgs Division* was initially established in March 1942. At its core were two Croatian units, an SS *Selbstschutz* (a locally recruited SS protection force) and a unit known as the *Einsatz-Staffel Prinz Eugen*. Early hopes that there would be a flood of volunteers to make up the numbers proved unrealistic. The SS was forced to introduce conscription from among the *Volkdeutsche* community to reach a target divisional strength of 21,500 members. This did not please the Paveliç government in Croatia, who felt that their German allies were poaching Croatian manpower.

Anti-partisan warfare

The new SS division was intended from the start for use in anti-partisan warfare in the Balkans. In October 1942, the division saw its first major action in the south of Serbia, in mountainous terrain east of the Ibar River, near the Montenegro border. By now it had been reclassified as a mountain division, and its designation had been changed to *SS-Freiwilligen Gebirgs Division Prinz Eugen*. Late in 1942, *Prinz Eugen* was transferred to the Zagreb-Karlovac area, where it was one of the units taking part in the massive anti-partisan operation known as Operation 'White'. This was one of a series of major anti-partisan operations in the region, whose primary aim was to destroy the communist resistance movement led by Tito. Although some partisans were killed, the operation was in the main a failure, since the bulk of Tito's forces managed to evade the German offensive.

In 1943, *Prinz Eugen* was assigned to the *Wehrmacht*'s Army Group E. In May of that year the division took part in another major anti-partisan campaign, known as Operation 'Black'. Later in the year elements of the division were sent to Bosnia, operating to the north of Sarajevo. After that, it was

deployed around Mostar where it would continue to play its part in the fiercely fought, no-quarter partisan war for the next year. In the summer of 1943 *Prinz Eugen* was sent to the Dalmatian coast, where in September it disarmed Italian units in the region after the Badoglio government signed an armistice with the Allies. It was then used to occupy former Italian positions on Brac, Hvar and Korcula Islands and on the Peljesac Peninsula. In October 1943 *Prinz Eugen* officially became the 7th *SS-Freiwilligen Gebirgs Division Prinz Eugen*. In December, the division once more moved inland, where operations against Tito's forces, as before, proved to be less than effective.

In January 1944, the division was transferred to the area around Split and Dubrovnik for training, recuperation and re-equipment. In March it was back in Bosnia, where it again took up the fight against Tito's partisans, with a major battle being fought at Drvar in May. The Red Army's summer offensive was unleashed in June 1944, and the Soviet steamroller threatened to smash through the Axis forces without stopping. In August *Prinz Eugen* was transferred north

Left: A *Sturmbannführer* **(Major) of the** *Prinz Eugen* **Division poses proudly for a portrait photograph. Most of the officers and cadre were German, though large numbers of Eastern European** *Volksdeutsche* **served in the unit.**

to Bulgaria, where it suffered great losses fighting against the Red Army. The Soviet advance threatened to cut off Army Group E in Greece, so in September *Prinz Eugen* and other *Waffen*-SS units were moved south to Macedonia. There they were ordered to hold open a corridor to allow 350,000 German soldiers to escape from possible encirclement by the advancing Soviets. Once again, *Prinz Eugen* was badly mauled, but the operation succeeded in its main aim. Once the trapped German troops had escaped through the Macedonian corridor, the division was free to retreat from Cacak to Brcko and over the Drina.

In January 1945, the division fought partisans near Otok, and later was sent to the area of Vukovar where it fought again against advancing Soviet forces and Tito's partisans. From February to April 1945, the division was in action against the partisans and the Soviets, finally ending the war in Slovenia and being taken by the Yugoslav government.

DIVISIONAL INFORMATION

Commanders
SS-Obergruppenführer Artur Phleps   (30 Jan 1942)
SS-Brigadeführer Karl Reichsritter von Oberkamp
                                     (15 May 1943)
SS-Brigadeführer Otto Kumm   (30 Jan 1944)
SS-Brigadeführer August Schmidthuber (20 Jan 1945)

Divisional Strength
Dec 1942   19,835
Dec 1943   21,120
Jun 1944   18,835
Dec 1944   20,000

Order of Battle
SS-Freiwilligen-Gebirgsjäger-Regiment 13 Artur Phleps
SS-Freiwilligen-Gebirgsjäger-Regiment 14 Skanderbeg
SS-Freiwilligen-Gebirgs-Artillerie-Regiment 7

SS-Sturmgeschütz-Abteilung 7
SS-Panzerjäger-Abteilung 7
SS-Flak-Abteilung 7
SS-Pionier-Bataillon 7
SS-Gebirgs-Aufklärungs 7
SS-Feldersatz-Abteilung 7
SS-Kavallerie-Schwadronen
SS-Gebirgs-Nachrichten-Abteilung 7
SS-Freiwilligen-Gebirgs-Aufklärungs-Abteilung (mot) 7
SS-Panzer-Aufklärungs-Zug
SS-Radfahr-Abteilung
SS-Kradschützen-Bataillon 7
SS-Nachschub-Kompanie 7
SS-Werkstattkompanie
SS-Sanitäts-Abteilung 7
SS-Freiwilligen-Gebirgs-Veterinär-Kompanie
SS-Freiwilligen-Gebirgs-Kriegsberichter-Zug

8th SS-Kavallerie Division *Florian Geyer*

- *Jul 1941:* SS-Kavallerie Brigade/SS-Reiter Brigade   • *Jun 1942:* SS-Kavallerie Division
- *Oct 1942:* 8th SS-Kavallerie Division   • *Mar 1944 – Feb 1945:* 8th SS-Kavallerie Division *Florian Geyer*

The *Florian Geyer* Division was one of several SS units that started out as purely German-based formations but which during the course of the war increasingly numbered non-Germans, or *Volksdeutsche,* among its units. It was named after Florian Geyer (1490–1525), a Franconian knight. Geyer was a supporter of Martin Luther and led the German Peasants' War of 1522–25.

The origins of the *Florian Geyer* Division date back to the original SS cavalry units. The cavalry components of the SS *Totenkopf Standarten*, or regiments, were formed in the winter of 1939. In the summer of 1941, they were combined as an *SS-Kavallerie Regiment* under the aegis of the *Kommandostab* RFSS. The cavalry so gathered were formed into an official unit in August 1941, known variously as the *SS-Kavallerie Brigade* or the *SS-Reiter Brigade*. It was commanded by Hermann Fegelein, and therefore it was often referred to as the *Fegelein Brigade* or *Kampfgruppe Fegelein*. Fegelein began his career in Middle Franconia as a groom and then became a jockey.

A chance contact with a horse fancier who was a Nazi led him into the party. Fegelein's knowledge of horses led the *Waffen*-SS to select him as the commanding officer of the *SS-Kavallerie* units, becoming commander of the new brigade on its formation in 1941. He was

wounded in September 1943 south of Kharkov and posted to the *Führer*'s HQ as Himmler's official SS liaison officer.

Anti-partisan operations

In June 1942 the *SS-Kavallerie Brigade* was upgraded to divisional status with the addition of 9000 Hungarian *Volksdeutsche* volunteers. Their primary function was security, being used behind the front lines to mop up bypassed Soviet Army units. Gradually, their main function became the waging of an extremely ruthless anti-partisan campaign. One month later the division went into action with the Ninth Army, part of Army Group Centre.

It was used to destroy pockets of Soviet resistance around the Vyazma-Bryansk-Rzhev salient. It continued to fight under Ninth Army control until

Right: The *Wehrmacht* used horses and horse transport throughout the war. Here, members of the *SS-Kavallerie Brigade* ride down a dusty Russian road in the summer of 1941. The brigade would eventually be expanded to become the *8th SS-Kavallerie Division Florian Geyer*.

Above: The pro-German Hungarian defence minister Marshal Károly Beregfy (wearing glasses) visits the *Florian Geyer* Division at Budapest late in 1944. By February 1945 the division had been wiped out by the Red Army.

December 1942, when most of the division was sent south to Army Group South. In the Don Basin it was assigned to the Second Panzer Army as *Kampfgruppe Fegelein*. In January and February 1943 the division was again under the control of Ninth Army, where it saw extensive combat south of Orel. In March it was part of XXXXVII Panzer Corps. In April 1943 it was withdrawn to Bobruyal for refitting.

Croatia

In May 1943 the *SS-Kavallerie Division* began the anti-partisan operations which it would fight until the end of the war. Successful in this brutal form of combat, the division was again transferred to Army Group South in July 1943. It was ordered to Croatia, where it would be used in the Brod area for combat against Tito's communist partisans.

As a mounted unit the division was effective against the partisans since on horseback it could operate more rapidly over terrain impassable to vehicles than could partisans on foot. The division saw a considerable

amount of action at Bespalowka and Bol-Gomolscha before being withdrawn for rest and refitting.

On 23 October, the unit was redesignated as 8th *SS-Kavallerie Division*. At the end of the year the division had over 9300 men on strength, the bulk being Hungarian *Volksdeutsche*.

In January and February 1944, the division continued anti-partisan operations. In March, the divisional units were dispersed, being used for further anti-partisan operations in the Balkans, Hungary and Poland. On 12 March the division received the honour title *Florian Geyer,* becoming the 8th *SS-Kavallerie Division Florian Geyer*. On 19 March, elements of *Florian Geyer* became part of *Kampfgruppe Streckenbach* under *SS-Gruppenführer* Bruno Streckenbach. The unit was transferred north from

Osijek, Yugoslavia, to Budapest. In April, one of the division's regiments – *SS-Kavallerie Regiment 17* – was sent to Kisber, Hungary, for rest and refitting. From there it would form the nucleus of 22nd *SS-Freiwilligen Kavallerie Division Maria Theresa*.

Budapest

In November 1944 the division became part of the Budapest garrison. By December, the Red Army had reached the shores of Lake Balaton, Hungary. By Christmas Eve, Budapest had been surrounded by 250,000 Soviet troops from the 2nd and 3rd Ukrainian Fronts. In the ensuing siege, 800,000 civilians were trapped in the city. SS units were pulled back to Buda on the west bank of the Danube. After several weeks of bitter fighting, the Buda pocket had been reduced to a semi-circle about 1000m (1093 yards) across.

On 11 February 1945, the remnants of the division attempted a last-ditch breakout along with what was left of the 22nd *SS-Freiwilligen Kavallerie Division Maria Theresa* and the 33rd *Waffen-Kavallerie Division der SS*. Budapest fell the next day. The division was annihilated. Only 170 survivors managed to reach German lines. The divisional commander, *SS-Brigadeführer* Joachim Rumohr, committed suicide; the remaining survivors were transferred to the 37th SS Cavalry Division.

Hermann Fegelein, the unit's original commander, did not long survive the division. Having become one of Hitler's inner circle, he had married Margarete Braun, Eva Braun's sister, on 3 June 1944. Fegelein was in the *Führerbunker* in Berlin in the last days of the Reich. As Berlin fell, he tried to escape with a mistress who may have been an Allied spy. He was captured by the *Gestapo*, and Hitler had him shot for desertion.

DIVISIONAL INFORMATION

Commanders

SS-Brigadeführer Gustav Lombard	(Mar 1942)
SS-Gruppenführer Hermann Fegelein	(Apr 1942)
SS-Obergruppenführer Willi Bittrich	(Aug 1942)
SS-Brigadeführer Fritz Freitag	(15 Feb 1943)
SS-Brigadeführer Gustav Lombard	(20 Apr 1943)
SS-Gruppenführer Hermann Fegelein	(14 May 1943)
SS-Gruppenführer Bruno Streckenbach	(13 Sep 1943)
SS-Gruppenführer Hermann Fegelein	(22 Jan 1943)
SS-Gruppenführer Bruno Streckenbach	(1 Jan 1944)
SS-Brigadeführer Gustav Lombard	(14 Apr 1944)
SS-Brigadeführer Joachim Rumohr	(1 Jul 1944 – 11 Feb 1945)

Divisional Strength

Dec 1942	10,879
Dec 1943	9326
Jun 1944	12,895
Dec 1944	13,000
Feb 1945	170

Order of Battle

SS-Kavallerie-Regiment 15
SS-Kavallerie-Regiment 16
SS-Kavallerie-Regiment 17
SS-Kavallerie-Regiment 18
SS-Artillerie-Regiment 8
SS-Panzerjäger-Abteilung 8
SS-Aufklärungs-Abteilung 8
SS-Nachrichten-Abteilung 8
SS-Pionier-Bataillon 8
SS-Flak-Abteilung 8
SS-Feldersatz-Bataillon 8
SS-Sturmgeschütz-Abteilung 8
SS-Radfahr-Aufklärungs-Abteilung 8
SS-Ski-Bataillon
SS-Verwaltungsstruppen 8
SS-Sanitäts-Abteilung 8
SS-Veterinär-Kompanie 8
SS-Feldpostamt
SS-Kriegsberichter-Zug (mot) 8
SS-Feldgendarmerie-Trupp 8
SS-Krankenkraftwagenzug

11th SS-Freiwilligen Panzergrenadier Division *Nordland*

- *Feb 1943:* Kampfverband *Waraeger* • *Feb 1943:* Germanische-Freiwilligen Division
- *Apr 1943:* SS-Panzergrenadier Division 11 (Germanische) • *Jul 1943:* SS-Panzergrenadier Freiwilligen
Division *Nordland* • *Oct 1943 – May 1945:* 11th SS-Freiwilligen Panzergrenadier Division *Nordland*

The 11th *SS-Freiwilligen Panzergrenadier Division Nordland* had its origins in an OKW order to activate a new SS panzer corps in early 1943. This new corps was to be designated III *(Germanische) SS-Panzerkorps*, and it was to include as many Germanic volunteers as possible.

Nordland was to include the SS *Wiking* Division, together with a new German-Scandinavian division yet to be formed. The corps headquarters was activated

Below: Cold and weary, *Waffen*-SS men occupy a hastily dug trench near the city of Narva in Estonia. In the city, the *Nordland* and *Nederland* Divisions of the SS were fighting a bloody street battle with the Red Army.

on 30 March 1943, but it proved impossible to withdraw *Wiking* from the Eastern Front and the plan to field the new corps was delayed.

However, plans to create the new SS volunteer division went ahead. Himmler wanted to give the new division the name *Waraeger* in reference to the Swedish Viking Varangian Guard, which saw service as the bodyguard of the Byzantine emperors in the Dark Ages. Hitler, more practical than his mystical SS henchman, considered the name too obscure and decided that the name of the veteran volunteer regiment *Nordland* deserved to be honoured, and ordered the division to be so named in July 1943. *Nordland* was to differ from the prototype volunteer

Right: An *Obersturmbann-führer* (Lieutenant-Colonel) from the *Nordland* division on the Narva front. The battles against the Soviet forces in the Baltic area saw foreign SS units from all over Europe participating in fierce action.

division *Wiking* in its makeup. Although much had been made of the multi-national nature of the elite *Wiking* Division by Nazi propaganda, in truth the bulk of its strength and nearly all of its senior NCOs and officers were German. In the new division, the Germans hoped to utilize a far greater proportion of foreign volunteers, especially in the more senior ranks. Much use was made of the remnants of the disbanded Germanic legions in staffing the division, and it certainly carried the widest range of nationalities to be found in any *Waffen*-SS division. By the end of the war, troops from Denmark, Estonia, Finland, France, the Netherlands, Norway, Sweden, Switzerland and even a handful of British volunteers had either served in the division or been attached to it. The principle combat units were made up of combat veterans of the *Legion Norwegen* and the *Freikorps Danmark*. The ranks were filled out with *Volksdeutsche* and with *Reichsdeutsche*. The first division commander was *SS-Brigadeführer und Generalmajor der Waffen-SS* Friedrich 'Fritz' von Scholz, who had been commander of the *Nordland* Regiment of *Wiking*.

The Battle of Narva

After completing training, *Nordland* and III (*Germanische*) *SS-Panzerkorps* were posted to Croatia to gain combat experience in the war against Tito's

communist partisans. Going into action on 28 August, *Nordland* fought several vicious actions against an equally cut-throat enemy. Just before *Nordland* was reassigned, on 12 November 1943, it was upgraded to full *panzergrenadier* status. Along with III (*Germanische*) *SS-Panzerkorps Nordland* it began transferring to the Eastern Front on 25 November and was fully deployed with Army Group North by 22 December 1943.

The division arrived in the Leningrad sector to take part in the unsuccessful German attempt to fight off a massive Soviet breakout from the Oranienbaum pocket, a breakout which succeeded in relieving the 900-day siege of Leningrad. Over the next three months of continuous combat the Germans were driven back over the Narva. In fact, so many volunteer units saw action at Narva that it became known as the 'Battle of the European SS'.

Although the Germans had been forced to retreat, the long period of combat had also exhausted the

Above: *SS-Gruppenführer* **Friedrich 'Fritz' Scholz, Elder von Rarancze, commander of the** *Nordland* **Division, makes a tour of inspection. On 28 July 1944, Scholz died of wounds received in the Narva battles.**

Soviets. The impetus had run out of the Red Army's advance and the battle for Narva became a battle of snipers. During this period the battered first battalions of both the *Norge* and *Danmark* Regiments were withdrawn to Germany for rest and rebuilding. They would never again be assigned to *Nordland*. After being brought up to strength, in December 1944 both battalions were assigned to the *Wiking* Division. Early in 1945 they were transferred south for the failed attempt to relieve Budapest.

Back on the Baltic front, Soviet pressure began to increase in early June 1944 and it soon became apparent that a major Soviet thrust was in the making. Then, on 22 June, the third anniversary of Operation *Barbarossa*, Operation *Bagration* was launched against Army Group Centre. This was the long-awaited Soviet summer offensive and it tore a 400km (249 mile) wide gap in the German lines, annihilating the entire German army group in the process. The rapid Soviet advance threatened to isolate the hundreds of thousands of German troops in the Baltic States. To avoid being cut off, the Germans began planning for the withdrawal from the Narva bridgehead to the Tannenberg Line. Through July and August, the troops of III (*Germanische*) *SS-Panzerkorps* took part in some of the most vicious fighting ever seen on the Eastern Front.

The Battle for Berlin

On 14 September 1944 the German forces in Estonia were ordered to fall back into Latvia. By the morning of the 22nd *Nordland* had taken up positions 30km (18.6 miles) to the northeast of Riga, the Latvian capital. By the evening, *Nordland* had been relocated to the southeast of the city. Its arrival prevented the encirclement of the German Eighteenth Army by Soviet forces. As the Red Army's advance continued, *Nordland* slowly withdrew into the Courland pocket, fighting doggedly all the way, from where it was evacuated to Germany in early 1945. At this time III (*Germanische*) *SS-Panzerkorps* included *Kampfgruppen* from the 27th *SS-Freiwilligen Grenadier Division Langemarck*, 28th *SS-Freiwilligen Grenadier Division Wallonien*, elements of 10th *SS-Panzer Division Frundsburg*, and *Nordland*, and was subordinated to the newly created Eleventh Panzer Army, commanded by *SS-Obergruppenführer* Steiner.

By 21 February the conclusion was reached that no more useful gains could be made against an increasingly powerful enemy without undue casualties so Steiner ordered a general withdrawal back to the north bank of the Ihna. Between 23 and 28 February III (*Germanische*) *SS-Panzerkorps* made a slow withdrawal to the area around Stargard and Stettin on the northern Oder River.

It saw heavy fighting around Danzig, Stettin and Stargard, before becoming part of the force defending Berlin. At 20:00 on 30 April the *Norge* and *Danmark Kampfgruppe* commander, *SS-Sturmbannführer*

Ternedde, was given the news of Hitler's death. Ternedde was ordered to take the survivors and break out of the ruined city. In the event, very few of them made it to safety.

Others were caught up in the last few hours of the defence of the *Reichstag* and other government buildings. By 1 May 1945 the Soviets had overcome the last defenders of the *Reichstag*, and organized resistance in the ruined city had ceased. As night fell on 2 May the few survivors of *Nordland* and the rest of the exhausted Berlin garrison, some 130,000, marched into Soviet captivity.

Unit markings

Soldiers of the division wore a special collar patch showing a so-called curved swastika (*Sonderrad*). The members of *SS-Panzergrenadier-Regiment 23* wore the title *Norge*. Members of the *SS-Panzergrenadier-Regiment 24* wore the title *Danmark*. Members of *SS-Panzer-Abteilung 11* were given the title *Herman von Salza*. All other members of the division wore the cuff title *Nordland*. Generally speaking, soldiers of the division also wore their own particular national insignia as an arm patch.

DIVISIONAL INFORMATION

Commanders

SS-Brigadeführer Franz Augsberger	(22 Mar 1943)
SS-Gruppenführer Fritz von Scholz	(1 May 1943)
SS-Brigadeführer Joachim Ziegler	(27 Jul 1944)
SS-Brigadeführer Gustav Krukenberg	(25 Apr 1945)

Divisional Strength

Dec 1943	11,393
Jun 1944	11,749
Dec 1944	9000

Order of Battle

SS-Panzergrenadier-Regiment 23 Norge
SS-Panzergrenadier-Regiment 24 Danmark
SS-Panzer-Abteilung11 Herman von Salza
SS-Panzer-Artillerie-Regiment 11

SS-Panzer-Aufklärungs-Abteilung 11
SS-Sturmgeschütz-Abteilung 11
SS-Panzerjäger-Abteilung 11
SS-Nachrichtung-Abteilung 11
SS-Pionier-Bataillon 11
SS-Nachrichtung-Abteilung-Truppen 11
SS-Nachschub-Truppen 11
SS-Instandsetzungs-Abteilung 11
SS-Wirtschafts-Abteilung 11
SS-Kriegsberichter-Zug 11
SS-Feldgendarmerie-Trupp 11
SS-Feldersatz-Bataillon 11
SS-Bewährungs-Kompanie 11
SS-Sanitäts-Abteilung 11
SS-Werfer-Bataillon 521
SS-Jäger-Regiment 11

13th Waffen-Gebirgs Division der SS *Handschar* (kroatische Nr. 1)

- *Mar 1943:* Kroatische SS-Freiwilligen Division   • *Jul 1943:* Kroatische SS-Freiwilligen Gebirgs Division
- *Oct 1943:* SS-Freiwilligen Bosnien-Herzegowina Gebirgs Division (Kroatien)   • *13th* SS-Freiwilligen Bosnien-Herzegowina Gebirgs Division (Kroatien)   • *May 1944 – May 1945:* 13th Waffen-Gebirgs Division der SS *Handschar*

When Croatia proclaimed its independence on 10 April 1941, part of the land it claimed was the former Austro-Hungarian province of Bosnia-Herzegovina. The province was a volatile ethnic and religious mix, including large numbers of Catholic Croats, Orthodox Serbs and Muslims.

It was these Muslim inhabitants of Bosnia that Himmler and the SS would target in their recruitment of a Croatian SS Division. Hitler approved the formation of the division on 13 February 1943, and grudging approval was given by the Croatian leader, Ante Paveliç, on 5 March 1943. The division was at full strength, in excess of 20,000 men, by the summer of 1943, though not all were volunteers. Nearly 3000 of the recruits were Catholic Croats. The uniform worn by the division was regular SS issue, with a divisional collar patch showing an arm holding a scimitar, over a Swastika. On the left arm was a red and white chequerboard shield, the Croatian colours. Standard headgear for Muslim members of the division was a fez, in field grey (normal service) or red (walking out), with the SS eagle and death's head emblazoned on it. Non-Muslim members were allowed to wear the normal SS *Feldmutze*. The oval

DIVISIONAL INFORMATION

Commanders

SS-Oberführer Herbert von Obwurzer (1 Apr 1943)

SS-Gruppenführer Karl-Gustav Sauberzweig
(9 Aug 1943)

SS-Brigadeführer Desiderius Hampel (Jun 1943)

Divisional Strength

Dec 1943	21,065
Jun 1944	19,136
Dec 1944	12,793

Order of Battle

SS-Waffen-Gebirgsjäger-Regiment 27

SS-Waffen-Gebirgsjäger-Regiment 28

SS-Waffen-Artillerie-Regiment 13

SS-Panzerjäger-Abteilung 13

SS-Aufklärungs-Abteilung (mot) 13

Waffen-Gebirgs-Pionier-Abteilung der SS 13

Waffen-Gebirgs-Nachrichten-Abteilung der SS 13

Waffen-Flak-Abteilung der SS 13

SS-Nachrichten-Abteilung 13

Kroatische SS-Radfahr-Bataillon

Kroatische SS-Kradschützen-Bataillon

SS-Divisionsnachschubtruppen 13

Versorgungs-Regiment-Stab 13

SS-Verwaltungs-Bataillon 13

SS-Sanitäts-Abteilung 13

SS-Krankenkraftwagenzug

SS-Freiwilligen-Gebirgs-Veterinär-Kompanie 13

SS-Feldpostamt 13

SS-Kriegsberichter-Zug 13

SS-Feldgendarmerie-Trupp 13

SS-Feldersatz-Bataillon 13

SS-Kraftfahr-Lehr-Abteilung 13

Opposite: The commander of the Croatian Army, General Stanzer, inspects an anti-tank gun of a new Bosnian Muslim regiment. When the SS began raising similar units, it allowed members to retain the traditional fez headgear.

Edelweiss patch signifying mountain troops was worn on the right arm.

Mutiny

The division departed for training in occupied France, all personnel having arrived there by September 1943. While at Villefranche, it became the only SS division to mutiny, the rising being incited by communist partisans who had infiltrated the recruitment process. Several German officers were killed during the mutiny, though most of the troops did not take part. Fourteen soldiers were executed.

By February 1944, after further training at Neuhammer in Germany, the division was declared operational. It was transferred back to Bosnia for active service against the partisans. Its area of operation was northeastern Bosnia and western Serbia. The division participated in several anti-partisan campaigns, including Operations *Wegweiser*, *Save*, *Osterei*,

Maibaum and *Maiglockchen*. Some successes were achieved, and overall the *Handschar* proved itself as a competent anti-guerrilla unit, as long as its men were fighting their hereditary enemies. Atrocities were committed, but atrocity was not unusual in the Balkans, and the *Handschar* was no worse than many other SS divisions.

In more conventional action against the Soviets it was far less effective. With the penetration of the Red Army up to the Croatian borders in late 1944, the division was transferred to southern Hungary and became involved in front-line fighting. Desertions plagued the division from this point on, as many of the Muslims decided to return to Bosnia to protect their homes and families.

The 9000 German personnel of the division were used as an SS battlegroup, known as *Kampfgruppe Henke*. This fought in southern Hungary, joining combat against the Russians near the Yugoslav border. On 7 May 1945, the remnants of the division surrendered to the British in Austria. All remaining Muslim volunteers were handed over to Tito's forces after the capitulation and most were executed at Maibor on the Drava.

14th Waffen-Grenadier Division der SS (ukrainische Nr. 1)

• *Apr 1943:* SS-Freiwilligen Division *Galizien* • *Summer 1943:* SS-Schützen Division *Galizien* • *Oct 1943:* SS-Freiwilligen Division *Galizien* • *Jun 1944:* 14th Galizische SS-Freiwilligen Division • *Nov 1944:* 14th Waffen-Grenadier Division der SS (ukrainische Nr. 1) • *Apr 1944 – Apr 1945:* 1st Ukrainische Division der Ukrainischen National-Armee

The 14th *Waffen-Grenadier Division der SS* was authorized as the *SS-Freiwilligen Division Galizien* in April 1943, the name being changed briefly to *SS-Schützen Division Galizien*. Volunteers were largely from the western Ukraine.

The historical name of the area was Galicia, and the title was applied to the new division, possibly to avoid alerting Hitler that the SS was forming a division from the despised Slavs. Training of the troops began at the *Truppenübungsplatz der SS* Heidelager in Debica in

September 1943 before the division was moved to Silesia in April 1944 for further training. The recruits were mainly *Volksdeutsche* and Ukrainians from the area around Lemberg. On 22 October 1943 the division name was changed back to *SS-Freiwilligen Division Galizien*.

First combat

It was sent to the front at Brody in the Ukraine in June 1944. Inadequately armed, poorly trained, and with troops lacking in motivation, it was no match for the powerful Soviet assault which was launched as part of the Red Army's massive summer offensive. The division was quickly encircled and smashed, with only about 3000 of its 15,000 members managing to reach the German lines.

It was soon rebuilt as the 14th *Waffen-Grenadier Division der SS*. After the completion of basic training at *Truppenübungsplatz* Neuhammer, it was sent into Slovakia at the end of August, where it was used to help suppress the Slovak National Uprising. From there the division was deployed into northern Yugoslavia to fight partisans. In January 1945 it was again redesignated, now being known as the 14th *Waffen-Grenadier Division der SS (ukrainische Nr. 1)*. In January 1945 it

Left: A Ukrainian volunteer in the 14th *Galizische SS-Freiwilligen Division* poses with his Soviet-manufactured Degtyarev DP light machine gun. The 'Galician' designation was chosen partly to avoid alerting Hitler that Slavs were being recruited into the SS.

DIVISIONAL INFORMATION

Commanders

SS-Gruppenführer Walther Schimana	(30 Jun 1943)
SS-Brigadeführer Fritz Freitag	(20 Nov 1943)
SS-Brigadeführer Sylvester Stadler	(22 Apr 1944)
SS-Brigadeführer Nikolaus Heilmann	(Jul 1944)
SS-Brigadeführer Fritz Freitag	(5 Sep 1944)
SS-Brigadeführer Pavlo Schandruk	(24 Apr 1945)

Divisional Strength

Dec 1943	12,634
Jun 1944	15,299
Dec 1944	22,000

Order of Battle

Waffen-Grenadier-Regiment der SS 29
Waffen-Grenadier-Regiment der SS 30
Waffen-Grenadier-Regiment der SS 31
Waffen-Artillerie-Regiment der SS 14
SS-Waffen-Füsilier-Bataillon 14
SS-Waffen-Panzerjäger-Kompanie 14
SS-Freiwilligen-Panzerjäger-Kompanie 14
SS-Freiwilligen-Flak-Abteilung 14
Waffen-Nachrichten-Abteilung der SS 14
SS-Radfahr-Bataillon 14
Waffen-Pionier-Bataillon der SS 14
SS-Versorgungs-Kompanie 14
SS-Divisionsnachschubtruppen 14
SS-Sanitäts-Abteilung 14
SS-Veterinär-Kompanie 14
SS-Feldpostamt 14
SS-Kriegsberichter-Zug 14
SS-Feldgendarmerie-Trupp 14
SS-Feldersatz-Bataillon 14

was transferred to Pressburg (now Bratislava in Slovakia) where it took part in anti-partisan operations in the Untersteiermark (now Slovenia).

In April 1945, the unit was officially transferred to the newly forming Ukrainian National Army as the 1st *Ukrainische Division der Ukrainischen National-Armee*. Although still strong numerically, the division was short of weaponry and supplies. Retreating into the Austrian Alps north of Klagenfurt, the division surrendered to the Americans between the towns of Tamsweg and Judenberg.

Since 1945, there has been a good deal of controversy about the record of the division. Supporters claim that they were exceptional soldiers, who were not involved in the concentration camps and did not commit war crimes. To others, however, they were a sinister legion of bloodthirsty murderers. As always in such cases, the truth probably lies somewhere between the two extremes.

Right: A volunteer from the Ukraine prepares a meal in a dugout. He is wearing the Galician Division's unique collar patch, a lion rampant, reflecting the blue and gold lion rampant worn on the divisional armshield.

15th Waffen-Grenadier Division der SS (lettische Nr. 1)

• *Feb 1943:* Lettische SS-Freiwilligen Division   • *Oct 1943:* 15th Lettische SS-Freiwilligen Division
• *Jun 1944 – May 1945:* 15th Waffen-Grenadier Division der SS (lettische Nr. 1)

The origins of the 15th *Waffen-Grenadier Division der SS (lettische Nr. 1)* date back to 1943, when the *Lettische SS-Freiwilligen Legion* was upgraded to divisional status. The legion had been formed in the spring of 1943, when three infantry regiments were raised.

Along with the Latvian SS Volunteer Brigade (formerly 2nd SS Infantry Brigade) the Latvian Legion served under the VI SS Volunteer Corps. In November 1943, the Latvian Legion saw action at Novo-Sokolniki, northern Russia, as part of the Sixteenth Army, Army Group North. The legion was taken out of combat in October 1943 to become the kernel of a new volunteer division, the 1st Division of the SS Latvian Legion (renamed 15th *Lettische SS-Freiwilligen Division*). The division later became the 15th *Waffen-Grenadier Division der SS (lettische Nr. 1)* and it was assigned to the XXXXIII Corps of the German Sixteenth Army.

A fighting withdrawal

The Soviet winter offensive which was launched at the end of December continued until February 1944. The fighting was furious, and both sides suffered heavy casualties. The 15th *Lettische SS-Freiwilligen Division* was assigned to the VI SS Corps, where it fought alongside the 19th Latvian SS Division which had been formed around the 2nd SS Infantry Brigade (the Latvian SS Volunteer Brigade). In March 1944 both Latvian divisions fought to control strategic points along the Velikiye River. Although the VI SS Corps faced 11 Russian Army divisions, the Soviet offensive was contained at great cost.

The launch of the great Soviet summer offensive in June 1944 saw the 15th SS Division being forced back from its defensive positions along the line of the Sanukha River. A month later, the Latvian division was fighting yet another attack, near Ostrova in Estonia.

DIVISIONAL INFORMATION

Commanders
SS-Brigadeführer Peter Hansen   (25 Feb 1943)
SS-Gruppenführer Carl Graf von Pückler-Burghauss
                                                    (May 1943)
SS-Brigadeführer Nikolas Heilmann   (17 Feb 1944)
SS-Brigadeführer Herbert von Obwurzer (21 Jul 1944)
SS-Oberführer Arthur Ax   (26 Jan 1945)
SS-Oberführer Karl Burk   (15 Feb 1945)

Divisional Strength
Dec 1943   20,291
Jun 1944   18,413
Dec 1944   16,870

Order of Battle
Waffen-Grenadier-Regiment der SS 32
Waffen-Grenadier-Regiment der SS 33

Waffen-Grenadier-Regiment der SS 34
Waffen-Artillerie-Regiment der SS 15
Waffen-Füsilier-Bataillon der SS 15
Waffen-Flak-Abteilung der SS 15
Waffen-Nachrichtung-Abteilung der SS 15
Waffen-Pionier (motorisierte) der SS 15
Waffen-Panzerjäger-Abteilung der SS 15
SS-Sanitäts-Abteilung 15
SS-Nachschub-Truppen 15
SS-Feldpostamt 15
SS-Veterinär-Kompanie 15
SS-Wirtschafts-Bataillon 15
SS-Bau-Regiment 1 der 15. SS-Division
SS-Bau-Regiment 2 der 15. SS-Division
SS-Feldersatz-Bataillon 15
SS-Waffen-Feldgendarmerie-Trupp 15
SS-Kriegsberichter-Trupp

Right: A Latvian SS man sends up a signal from a Walther LP flare gun. The first Latvian SS division, the 15th, fought long and hard against the Soviets as part of Army Group North; some stragglers were still in action as Berlin fell in May 1945.

The power of the offensive meant that the Latvians could pull back only at the cost of two regiments all but wiped out. Surviving infantry-men and the divisional artillery were transferred to the 19th SS Division while NCO and officer cadres were shipped to the *Truppenübungsplatz der SS* West Prussia. In September, conscripts from Latvia and engineers from the SS Training and Replacement Battalions at Dresden were used to reform the 15th *Waffen-Grenadier Division der SS (lettische Nr. 1)*.

Final act

Although training was far from complete, in January 1945 the division was ordered to positions along the Oder–Vistula Canal. By end of February, the Red Army had broken through to the Baltic at Kolberg, cutting off large German forces including the 15th SS Division. As part of *Kampfgruppe Tettau*, the division broke through the Soviet lines to reach German-held territory, its 33rd Grenadier Regiment acting as rearguard. Survivors were sent to the town of Neubrandenburg, north of Berlin, for refitting.

As the Soviets pushed on towards the German capital, a battle group drawn from the 32nd and 33rd Regiments was dispatched towards Berlin to help in the defence of the city. On 24 April 1945, after fighting off Russian attacks in the south of the city, the *Kampfgruppe* began to withdraw westwards to surrender to the Americans. A week later, the rest of the division also moved west from Neubrandenburg and reached the American lines near Schwerin, where it too surrendered.

18th SS-Freiwilligen Panzergrenadier Division *Horst Wessel*

- *Jan 1944:* 18th SS-Panzergrenadier Division
- *Jan 1944 – May 1945:* 18th SS-Freiwilligen Panzergrenadier Division *Horst Wessel*

In January 1944, Hitler ordered Himmler to raise a *Waffen*-SS division from a cadre of SA reservists. In fact, the 18th *SS-Freiwilligen Panzergrenadier Division Horst Wessel* was cobbled together from a *Totenkopf Standarte* motorized brigade and 1st *SS-Infanterie-Brigade,* together with elements from the 6th *SS-Gebirgs Division Nord* and numerous Hungarian and Yugoslav *Volksdeutsche.*

The division was named after one of the Nazi Party's heroes, portrayed in National Socialist mythology as a young Berlin stormtrooper who was killed in a streetfight with communists before the Nazis came to power. In fact, although Horst Wessel was indeed an SA man killed by a communist, he was actually a street thug and pimp who was killed in a fight over who would benefit from the income of Wessel's prostitute girlfriend.

The division was assembled at the Stablack training aree in East Prussia. In January 1944 it was transferred to Zagreb in Croatia. From there it was deployed to the Agram area on the Hungarian-Yugoslav border where it went into action against Tito's partisans. In March the division was moved into Hungary alongside the *Florian Geyer* SS Cavalry Division where it was used as a threat to control the Hungarian Government, at that time showing signs of trying to find a way out of the war.

In July, the bulk of the division was sent to form a *Kampfgruppe* under XXIV Panzer Corps in the Ukraine. The unit took under its command elements of the 8th *SS-Sturmbrigade Frankreich,* formed after the dissolution of the *Légion des Volontaires Français.*

Slovakia and Budapest

Under intense Soviet pressure the *Horst Wessel Kampfgruppe* retreated through Podhajce and Lipica to the Dniester River, then back through Baliezne, Podrozne and Siechow. One unit was detached in August, and for the next three months it was used in the crushing of the Slovak National Uprising. In

DIVISIONAL INFORMATION

Commanders

SS-Brigadeführer Wilhelm Trabandt	(25 Jan 1944)
SS-Gruppenführer Josef Fitzthum	(3 Jan 1945)
SS-Oberführer Georg Bochmann	(10 Jan 1945)
SS-Standartenführer Heinrich Petersen	(Mar 1945)

Divisional Strength

Jun 1944	8530
Dec 1944	11,000

Order of Battle

SS-Panzergrenadier-Regiment 39
SS-Panzergrenadier-Regiment 40
SS-Artillerie-Regiment 18
SS-Panzerjäger-Abteilung 18
SS-Panzer-Aufklärungs-Abteilung 18
SS-Panzer-Abteilung 18
SS-Sturmgeschütz-Abteilung 18
SS-Panzerjäger-Abteilung 18
SS-Flak-Abteilung 18
SS-Nachrichten-Abteilung 18
SS-Pionier-Bataillon 18
SS-Verwaltungstruppen-Abteilung 18
SS-Wirtschafts-Bataillon 18
SS-Nachschub-Truppen 18
SS-Instandsetzungs-Abteilung 18
SS-Feldgendarmerie-Abteilung 18
SS-Feldersatz-Bataillon 18
SS-Sanitäts-Abteilung 18

September the rest of the division was moved into Hungary, where it fought the advancing Soviets in the area around Jasz and Ladany.

At the end of the war *Horst Wessel* was used in the abortive attempt to break the Soviet siege of Budapest. Then it was split into two *Kampfgruppen*. One was used around Karlsbrunn and Ratibor before surrendering to the Red Army at Mährisch-Ostrau. The other *Kampfgruppe* moved to Zobten in April,

Above: SS troops on the outskirts of Budapest. In common with many SS units, the *Horst Wessel* Division saw its last major action in the abortive German attempt to relieve the besieged defenders of the Hungarian capital.

where it came under the control of VIII Army Corps. There was no serious fighting in the area, and after the final German surrender the unit tried to move westwards to surrender to the Americans.

19th Waffen-Grenadier Division der SS (lettisches Nr. 2)

- *April 1941:* SS-Brigade (mot) 2 • *May 1943:* Lettische SS-Freiwilligen Brigade
- *Oct 1943:* 2nd Lettische SS-Freiwilligen Brigade • *Jan 1944:* 19th Lettische SS-Freiwilligen Division
- *May 1944 – April 1945:* 19th Waffen-Grenadier Division der SS (lettisches Nr. 2)

The 19th *Waffen-Grenadier Division der SS* was the second division of Latvian volunteers raised by the *Waffen*-SS. Like its sister unit the 15th *Waffen-Grenadier Division der SS*, German troops formed the nucleus of the formation, the *SS-Brigade (mot) 2* also providing the bulk of the NCO and officer cadre.

Numbers were made up by the addition of Latvians who had been serving in the SS *Schutzmannschaft* battalions. Although not formed until May 1944, the division found itself in combat less than a month later when the Soviet summer offensive got under way. Over the next six months it formed part of the heavily outnumbered German force in the Baltic States which managed to hold back the assault of vastly superior Red Army forces.

Battle of Narva

The division fought at the Battle of Narva along with many other Germanic and volunteer SS units. It was later trapped in the Courland pocket as the German forces in the Baltic States retreated from the advancing Soviet juggernaut. Little has been documented about the division's record in the last months of the war, but there are rumours that some divisional units may have mutinied at the end of 1944.

Unlike other volunteer *Waffen*-SS divisions the Latvian divisions were known for their fighting ability and for their commitment to the Nazi cause. In 1945, after being smashed by the advancing Soviet Army, the remaining elements of the two Latvian SS divisions regrouped under the command of *Waffen-Standartenführer* Villus Janums for the defence of Berlin. They later surrendered to the Americans at Güterglück near the Elbe River.

Opposite: A Latvian machine-gunner with the tools of his trade: an MG42 general-purpose machine gun and fifty-round belts of 7.62mm (0.3in) ammunition.

DIVISIONAL INFORMATION

Commanders

SS-Brigadeführer Heinrich Schuldt   (7 Jan 1944)
SS-Standartenführer Friedrich-Wilhelm Bock
                                                          (15 Mar 1944)
SS-Gruppenführer Bruno Streckenbach (15 Apr 1944)

Divisional Strength

Dec 1943	8033
Jun 1944	10,592
Dec 1944	9396

Order of Battle

Waffen-Grenadier-Regiment der SS 42 Voldemar Veiss
Waffen-Grenadier-Regiment der SS 43 Heinrich Schuldt
Waffen-Grenadier-Regiment der SS 44 (lettische Nr. 6)
Waffen-Artillerie-Regiment 19
SS-Füsilier-Bataillon 19
SS-Panzerjäger-Abteilung 19
SS-Flak-Abteilung 19
SS-Pionier-Bataillon 19
SS-Nachschub-Truppen 19
SS-Sanitäts-Abteilung 19
SS-Feldpostamt 19
SS-Veterinär-Kompanie 19
SS-Wirtschafts-Bataillon 19
SS-Nachrichten-Abteilung 19

20th Waffen-Grenadier Division der SS (estnische Nr. 1)

• *Oct 1942:* Estnische SS-Legion • *May 1943:* Estnische SS-Freiwilligen Brigade • *Oct 1943:* 3rd Estnische SS-Freiwilligen Brigade • Jan 1944: 20th Estnische SS-Freiwilligen Division • *May 1944 – May 1945:* 20th Waffen-Grenadier Division der SS (estnische Nr. 1)

The 20th *Waffen-Grenadier Division der SS (estnische Nr. 1)* was formed from the 3rd *Estnische SS-Freiwilligen Brigade*, and directly descended from the Estonian Legion, authorized by Adolf Hitler in August 1942.

The regiment-sized legion took some time to organize, becoming operational in the spring of 1943. Formed as a motorized infantry regiment, the legion was referred to in German orders as the 1st *Estnische SS-*

Freiwilligen Grenadier Regiment. It quickly grew to brigade size, however. The 20th *Estnische SS-Freiwilligen Division* was formed in January 1944. Difficulties in forming the division while its component units were fully engaged in action at the front meant that formation took longer than expected.

On 14 May 1944 it was 5000 men under strength, and Himmler ordered it up to full strength by 15 June. It was not, in fact, completely up to strength until July

1944. Units of the division were in action during the three-month campaign known as the Battle of the Narva, which took place early in 1944. The remnants of the division were later evacuated from Estonia along with the rest of the German forces. The division was reconstructed at *Truppenübungsplatz* Neuhammer from October 1944.

New division

By now it had been given the title 20th *Waffen-Grenadier Division der SS (estnische Nr. 1)*; in Estonian it was known as the 20th *SS-Relvagrenadieride Diviis (Eesti Esimene)*. In February 1945 the formation was so weakened that it had to be referred to as a battle group (SS-*Kampfgruppe*), possibly named *Augsberger* after its commander. The unit continued fighting in Silesia and later Czechoslovakia until the end of the war when parts surrendered to the Western Allies while the main body of the division surrendered to the Russians north of Prague.

Opposite: Estonian SS volunteers aboard a captured Soviet T-34 tank. The Germans captured so much Soviet materiel in 1941 and 1942 that entire units were equipped with Soviet weapons, armour, artillery and vehicles.

DIVISIONAL INFORMATION

Commanders
SS-Brigadeführer Franz Augsberger
(24 Jan 1944 – 19 Mar 1945)
SS-Brigadeführer Berthold Maack
(20 Mar 1945 – 8 May 1945)

Divisional Strength
Jun 1944	13,423
Dec 1944	15,382

Order of Battle
Waffen-Grenadier-Regiment der SS 45 Estland
(*estnische Nr. 1*)
Waffen-Grenadier-Regiment der SS 46 (estnische Nr. 2)
Waffen-Grenadier-Regiment der SS 47(estnische Nr. 3)
Waffen-Artillerie-Regiment der SS 20
SS-Waffen-Füsilier-Bataillon 20
SS-Waffen-Pionier-Bataillon 20
SS-Feldersatz-Bataillon 20
SS-Waffen-Nachrichten-Abteilung 20
SS-Ausbildungs-und-Ersatz-Regiment 20

21st Waffen-Gebirgs Division der SS *Skanderbeg* (albanische Nr. 1)
(Apr 1944 – May 1945)

On 17 April 1944, Himmler approved the formation of an Albanian *Waffen*-SS division. It was named *Skanderbeg* after Iskander Bey, a fifteenth-century Kosovan hero.

The governments of Albania, of Albanian Kosovo and of Bosnia submitted the names of 11,398 recruits. Of these, 9275 were adjudged to be suitable for drafting. Of this number, 6491 ethnic Albanians were actually drafted into the *Waffen*-SS. A reinforced battalion of approximately 300 ethnic Albanians serving in the Bosnian Muslim 13th *Waffen-Gebirgs Division der SS Handschar* were transferred to the newly forming division. To this Albanian core were added veteran German troops from Austria and *Volksdeutsche* officers,

NCOS, and enlisted men, together with a number of *Kriegsmarine* sailors. The total strength of the Albanian *Waffen*-SS division would be 8500–9000 men.

The *Skanderbeg* Division did not have a good reputation. Intended to fight partisans, in its earliest days it was used to massacre Orthodox Serb civilians in Kosovo-Metohija. Over 10,000 Serbian families were forced to flee Kosovo. Albanian colonists and settlers from northern Albania took over their lands and homes. The goal of many members of the *Skanderbeg* Division was not to fight for the Germans: rather it was to advance Albanian nationalism by deporting and killing the non-Albanian populations of Western Macedonia, creating an ethnically pure and homogenous region of

Greater Albania, free of Serbs, Jews and Roma (gypsies). *Skanderbeg* targeted all of these groups when the division occupied Tetovo and Skopje and other towns and cities in Western Macedonia.

However, the Red Army was advancing in ever-increasing strength. In October 1944, *Skanderbeg* occupied Skopje, the capital of Macedonia. By November 1944, the Germans were withdrawing their forces from the Aegean islands and from Greece. Called on to fight in something other than their own private war, many of the division's members deserted. The remnants of the division were reorganized into *Regimentgruppe 21.SS-Gebirgs Skanderbeg* which was concentrated at Skopje. The *Kampfgruppe Skanderbeg*, with the *Prinz Eugen* Division, defended the Vardar River valley in Macedonia to allow Alexander Löhr's Army Group E to retreat from Greece and the Aegean.

By January 1945, remnants of the *Skanderbeg* Division retreated to Kosovska Mitrovica in Kosovo and then to Brcko in Bosnia-Herzegovina. They reached Austria in May, 1945, when Germany surrendered, following the collapse of the regime.

Above: The *Skanderbeg* Division committed numerous atrocities in Kosovo, aimed at driving the Serbs out of what the Albanian Muslims considered their historical territory.

DIVISIONAL INFORMATION

Commanders
SS-Brigadeführer Josef Fitzhum   (April 1944)
SS-Oberführer August Schmidthuber   (1 May 1944)

Order of Battle
Waffen-Gebirgs-Regiment der SS 50
Waffen-Gebirgs-Regiment der SS 51
Waffen-Gebirgs-Artillerie-Regiment 21
SS-Aufklärungs-Abteilung 21
SS-Panzerjäger-Abteilung 21
SS-Gebirgs-Pionier-Bataillon 21
SS-Versorgungs-Abteilung 21
SS-Nachrichten-Abteilung 21
SS-Sanitäts-Abteilung 21

22nd SS-Freiwilligen Kavallerie Division *Maria Theresa*

(May 1944 – Feb 1945)

The *Maria Theresa* Division was formed in May 1944. Assembled at Kisber, Hungary, it was based on a nucleus provided by the 17th *SS-Kavallerie Regiment* transferred from the 8th *SS-Kavallerie Division Florian Geyer*.

The bulk of the strength of the division was provided by Hungarian *Volksdeutsche*, who had originally been drafted by the Hungarian Army but had been transferred to the *Waffen*-SS following an agreement between the German and Hungarian Governments. The symbol of the division was a cornflower, adopted as it was the favourite flower of the Empress Maria Theresa of Austria, after whom the division had been named.

In September 1944 a detachment from *Maria Theresa,* consisting of *SS-Kavallerie Regiment 52*, was assigned to a *Kampfgruppe* commanded by *SS-Haupt-*

sturmführer Toni Ameiser. *Kampfgruppe Ameiser* was deployed to Romania where it was intended to reinforce the *Wehrmacht*'s LVII Panzer Corps. It was unable to reach its designated positions because of the advance of the Red Army, and after fighting alongside Hungarian troops it was encircled by the Soviets.

One section of the *Kampfgruppe*, commanded by *SS-Hauptsturmführer* Harry Vandieken, fought its way to the Harmas River, swimming across to safety on the German-held bank. The second part of the *Kampfgruppe*, commanded by Ameiser, remained in the

Below: SS cavalrymen await a Soviet attack on the Eastern Front. The second SS cavalry division to be formed, *Maria Theresa* lasted less than a year before being wiped out during the battles for Budapest early in 1945.

trap for a month, eventually fighting its way through to the German lines south of Budapest on 30 October.

The rest of the division was still in training when it was sent to reinforce Budapest in November 1944. It was still in the city when the Red Army closed a ring of iron around the Hungarian capital, and it was destroyed along with most of the rest of the German defenders.

Only 170 men managed to make it through the Soviet lines to safety. The survivors, along with those parts of the *Maria Theresa* Division which had not been sent into Budapest, were used as the core of the newly formed 37th *SS-Freiwilligen Kavallerie Division Lützow*. What was left of the divisional flak units were transferred to 32nd *SS-Freiwilligen Grenadier Division 30 Januar*.

DIVISIONAL INFORMATION

Commanders		
SS-Brigadeführer August Zehender	(21 Apr 1944)	

Divisional Strength

Jun 1944	4914
Dec 1944	8000

Order of Battle

SS-Kavallerie-Regiment 52
SS-Kavallerie-Regiment 53
SS-Kavallerie-Regiment 54
SS-Kavallerie-Regiment 17
SS-Artillerie-Regiment 22
SS-Panzer-Aufklärungs-Abteilung 22
SS-Panzerjäger-Abteilung 22
SS-Pionier-Bataillon 22
SS-Nachrichten-Abteilung 22
SS-Divisionsnachschubtruppen 22
SS-Verwaltungstruppen-Abteilung 22
SS-Sanitäts-Abteilung 22

23rd Waffen-Gebirgs Division der SS *Kama* (kroatische Nr. 2)

- *June 1944 – October 1944:* Waffen-Gebirgs Division
- *October 1944:* 23rd Waffen-Gebirgs Division der SS *Kama* (kroatische Nr.2)

Approval was given for the raising of a second Croatian *Waffen-SS* division on 17 June 1944. The 23rd *Waffen-Gebirgs Division der SS Kama (kroatische Nr. 2)* was recruited from Croatian volunteers – including both *Volksdeutsche* and anti-communist Croats – and Bosnian Muslims.

In common with many volunteer divisions, the unit was stiffened by a cadre of German senior NCOs and officers. Further strength was supplied by its sister formation, the *Handschar* Division, which provided its reconnaissance battalion and a number of Croat officers and NCOs.

Like the *Handschar*, the unit was named after a traditional weapon from the region – in this case, a short Turkish sword or long fighting knife known as a *kama*. *Kama* never reached anything like its planned strength. At its peak, in September 1944, it had a total of 3793 men in training to play their part in the anti-partisan war. That training was taking place at Backa in Hungary, far enough from the main areas of partisan action as to be safe from attack. They were not safe from the Red Army, however, which by the end of September was advancing perilously close to the divisional training grounds in southern Hungary. The SS wanted the division to be ready for combat by the end of September, but as the troops had not completed basic training this was never a realistic prospect.

On 1 October 1944, as the Red Army advanced into Hungary, the SS decided to disband the unit, transferring already formed units as replacements to other divisions. Most of the division's personnel were used to form the 31st *SS-Freiwilligen Grenadier*

Division. The Muslims of *Kama* were transferred to the *Handschar* Division. Most reported for duty, but a large minority deserted *en route*. The divisional number 23 was assigned to the newly forming *Nederland Panzergrenadier Division*.

Above: Himmler's persistent attempts to form Muslim SS divisions did not pay off. The fez-wearing SS men of the *Handschar* and *Kama* Divisions were effective when fighting for their homes, but were otherwise almost completely unreliable.

DIVISIONAL INFORMATION

Commanders
SS-Standartenführer Helmuth Raithel   (1 Jul 1944)
SS-Oberführer Gustav Lombard   (28 Sep 1944)

Divisional Strength
Jun 1944   2199
Sep 1944   3793

Order of Battle
Waffen-Gebirgsjäger-Regiment der SS 55 (kroatische Nr. 3)
Waffen-Gebirgsjäger-Regiment der SS 56 (kroatische Nr. 4)

Waffen-Gebirgs-Artillerie-Regiment der SS 23
SS-Aufklärungs-Abteilung 23
SS-Flak-Abteilung 23
SS-Panzerjäger-Abteilung 23
SS-Nachschub-Abteilung 23
SS-Pionier-Bataillon 23
SS-Nachrichten-Abteilung 23
SS-Feldlazarett 23
SS-Feldersatz-Bataillon 23
SS-Sanitäts-Abteilung 23
SS-Verwaltungs-Abteilung 23

23rd SS-Freiwilligen Panzergrenadier Division *Nederland*

• *Jul 1941:* SS-Freiwilligen Verband *Niederlande*   • *Aug 1941:* SS-Freiwilligen Legion *Niederlande*   • *Oct 1943:*
4th SS-Freiwilligen Panzergrenadier Brigade *Nederland*   • *Oct 1944:* SS-Freiwilligen Panzergrenadier Brigade
Nederland   • *Feb 1945 – May 1945:* 23rd SS-Freiwilligen Panzergrenadier Division *Nederland* (niederlandische Nr. 1)

The 23rd *SS-Freiwilligen Panzergrenadier Division Nederland* consisted of Dutch volunteers and was formed on 10 February 1945, when *SS-Freiwilligen Panzergrenadier Brigade Nederland* was upgraded to divisional status.

The *Nederland* Brigade had been in action in the Baltic States since the end of 1943, and had shared in the retreat from Leningrad to the Narva line and back to the Courland pocket. Along with the rest of III *SS-Korps*, *Nederland* was evacuated by sea to Stettin, where they were to form part of the defensive line on the Oder. The SS had originally intended for the Dutch soldiers to be assigned to the *Nordland*

Division but after protests from the Dutch Nazi party, the NSB, it was decided that they would form their own division. *Nederland* was given the number 23 when the *Kama* Division was disbanded. The 23rd *SS-Freiwilligen Panzergrenadier Division Nederland* had little more than 1000 effective combatants when it fought its last battles on the Eastern Front.

Below: The first parade of the SS-*Freiwilligen Legion Niederlande* took place in the historic Rittersaal Square in The Hague. The legion would eventually provide the nucleus for a *Panzergrenadier* brigade and then for a *Panzergrenadier* division.

DIVISIONAL INFORMATION

Commander *SS-Brigadeführer* Jürgen Wagner

Divisional Strength Dec 1944 6000

Order of Battle
SS-Freiwilligen-Panzergrenadier-Regiment 48
SS-Freiwilligen-Panzergrenadier-Regiment 49
SS-Artillerie-Regiment 23
SS-Nachrichten-Abteilung 23
SS-Panzerjäger-Abteilung 23
SS-Pionier-Bataillon 23
SS-Flak-Abteilung 23

Nederland, together with the SS divisions *Nordland*, *Wallonien* and *Langemarck*, was responsible for the defence of the Oder front between the towns of Stettin and Neustadt. In April 1945 *Nederland* was split up. The *General Seyffardt* Regiment headed south. It was destroyed near Hammerstein while fighting alongside the 15th *Waffen-Grenadier Division der SS*. The 13 soldiers who were captured were executed by the Russians.

At the end of April the *De Ruyter* Regiment, which had remained on the Oder front, withdrew to the west, around the north of Berlin. On 3 May 1945, near the village of Parchim, the regiment destroyed an attacking Red Army tank unit, and then its members heard more tanks approaching. These were American, and the regiment was happy to surrender to them.

24th Waffen-Gebirgs Division der SS (*Karstjäger*)

• *1942:* SS-Karstwehr-Bataillon • *Aug 1944:* 24th Waffen-Gebirgs (*Karstjäger*) Division der SS • *Dec 1944:* Waffen-Gebirgs Brigade der SS (*Karstjäger*) • *10 Feb 1945 – May 1945:* 24th Waffen-Gebirgs Division der SS (*Karstjäger*)

The *SS-Karstwehr-Bataillon* had been fighting partisans in northern Italy and the Dolomites since 1942. On 1 August 1944, it was upgraded to become the 24th *Waffen-Gebirgs (Karstjäger) Division der SS*, though it was never more than brigade-sized.

Since it was impossible to build the *SS-Karstwehr-Bataillon* into a true division, in December 1944 it was redesignated as the *Waffen-Gebirgs Brigade der SS (Karstjäger)*. However, it was redesignated as a division on 10 February 1945. Originally under the control of the HSSPF *Adriatisches Meer* (Higher SS and Police Commander Adriatic), it was manned mainly by Italian volunteers, but it also included volunteers from Slovenia, Croatia, Serbia and the Ukraine. *Karstjäger* mainly fought partisans in Istria, with considerable success, but at the end of the war it found itself in action with the Western Allies advancing through Italy. On 8 May 1945 *Karstjäger* surrendered to the British.

DIVISIONAL INFORMATION

Commanders
SS-Obersturmbannführer Karl Marx (Aug 1944)
SS-Sturmbannführer Werner Hahn (5 Dec 1944)
SS-Oberführer Adolf Wagner (10 Feb 1945)

Divisional Strength
June 1944 1831
Dec 1944 3000

Order of Battle
Waffen-Gebirgsjäger-Regiment der SS 59
Waffen-Gebirgsjäger-Regiment der SS 60
Waffen-Gebirgs-Artillerie-Regiment 24
SS-Panzerkompanie
SS-Gebirgsbatterie
SS-Gebirgs-Sanitäts-Kompanie 24
SS-Gebirgs-Nachrichten-Kompanie 24
SS-Gebirgs-Pionier-Kompanie 24

25th Waffen-Grenadier Division der SS *Hunyadi* (ungarische Nr. 1)

• *Oct 1944:* 25th SS-Freiwilligen Grenadier Division   • *Nov 1944:* 25th Waffen-Grenadier Division der SS *Hunyadi* (ungarische Nr. 1)

The 25th *Waffen-Grenadier Division der SS Hunyadi (ungarische Nr. 1)* consisted of Hungarian volunteers. Authorized in October and set up in November 1944, it included 1000 Hungarians from *Kampfgruppe Deák*, who were used to form the 61st SS-*Grenadier Regiment*.

Waffen-Schi-Bataillon der SS 25 was raised from Hungarian Army mountain troops. Some divisional troops were transferred from *Waffen*-SS training schools, but the bulk of the troops were provided by Hungarian recruiting depots.

Training camp

Transferred to the Neuhammer Training Ground in Germany, the division was still far from operational when the Red Army entered Silesia. With over 22,000 men in the camp, together with many wives and families, Neuhammer was seriously overcrowded, and it was a relief when orders were given that the division should retreat to Bavaria. The division surrendered to the Americans after a brief firefight at Salzkammergut in Austria.

DIVISIONAL INFORMATION

Commanders
SS-Standartenführer Thomas Müller   (Nov 1944)
SS-Gruppenführer Josef Grassy   (Late Nov 1944)

Divisional Strength
Dec 1944   15,000

Order of Battle
Waffen-Grenadier-Regiment der SS 61
Waffen-Grenadier-Regiment der SS 62
Waffen-Grenadier-Regiment der SS 63
Waffen-Artillerie-Regiment der SS 25
Waffen-Schi-Bataillon 25
SS-Divisions-Füsilier-Bataillon 25
SS-Panzerjäger-Abteilung 25
SS-Veterinär-Kompanie 25
SS-Feldersatz-Bataillon 25
SS-Versorgungs Regiment 25

Left: German and Hungarian soldiers retreat from the city of Budapest, having narrowly avoided being caught in the vast Soviet encirclement in the spring of 1945. All German attempts to break the siege would ultimately fail.

26th Waffen-Grenadier Division der SS *Hungaria* (ungarische Nr. 2)
(Dec 1944 – May 1945)

The 26th *Waffen-Grenadier Division der SS Hungaria (ungarische Nr. 2)* was formed under the authority of the Hungarian defence minister, at the request of Himmler. *Waffen-Schi-Bataillon der SS 26* from the Hungarian Army was ordered to join the new division.

Late in December 1944, 5000 civilian draftees brought the strength up to 8000. By January divisional strength was up to more than 16,000, and the formation had been moved to Siederatz in Poland for training. Weapons were issued early in January – just in time to allow foraging parties to fight off attacks by Polish partisans.

Forced to retreat by the Soviet winter offensive (minus mortars and machine guns, which had been taken by the German Ninth Army), the partially trained division reached the Oder after suffering over 2500 casualties. Plans to refit at Neuhammer were dashed when on 8 February the Soviets attacked the training ground. The more experienced members of the division served as a rearguard while the rest of the formation retreated westwards. As part of XVII *Waffen-Armee Korps der SS (Ungarisches)* the *Hungaria* Division retreated into Austria, where it surrendered to the Western Allies at Attersee. Many of the division's surviving troops were turned over to the Soviets, and were destined for the *Gulag* or the firing squad.

Below: The last great battles of the *Waffen*-SS were fought in Hungary, from where the Sixth SS Panzer Army was driven back into Austria. By this time, the majority of SS troops were foreign-born.

DIVISIONAL INFORMATION

Commanders		Order of Battle
SS-Sturmbannführer Rolf Tiemann	(Nov 1944)	*Waffen-Grenadier-Regiment der SS 64*
SS-Oberführer Zoltan Pisky	(Nov 1944)	*Waffen-Grenadier-Regiment der SS 65*
SS-Oberführer László Déak	(Jan 1945)	*Waffen-Grenadier-Regiment der SS 85*
SS-Oberführer Berthold Maack	(29 Jan 1945)	*Waffen-Artillerie-Regiment der SS 26*
SS-Gruppenführer Josef Grassy	(21 Mar 1945)	*SS-Waffen-Panzerjäger-Abteilung 26*
		SS-Waffen-Artillerie-Regiment 26
Divisional Strength		*SS-Waffen-Flak-Abteilung 26*
Dec 1944	8000	*SS-Waffen-Schi-Bataillon 26*
Jan 1945	c.15,000	*SS-Waffen-Pionier-Bataillon 26*
		SS-Waffen-Nachrichten-Abteilung 26
		SS-Waffen-Versorgungs-Regiment 26
		SS-Waffen-Ausbildungs-und-Ersatz-Regiment 26

27th SS-Freiwilligen Grenadier Division *Langemarck* (flämische Nr. 1)

• *Jul 1941:* SS-Freiwilligen Legion *Flandern* • *May 1943:* SS-Sturmbrigade *Langemarck* • *Oct 1943:* 6th SS-Freiwilligen Sturmbrigade *Langemarck* • *Oct 1944 – Apr 1945:* 27th SS-Freiwilligen Grenadier Division *Langemarck* (flämische Nr. 1)

The division was formed on 19 October 1944, when the 6th *SS-Freiwilligen Sturmbrigade Langemarck* was upgraded to divisional status. The *Langemarck* Division, named after a village near Ypres which saw some of the bloodiest fighting in World War I, was descended directly from the SS Flanders Legion, the original Flemish volunteer unit in the *Waffen*-SS.

The Flemish Legion had been less than impressive in its early actions on the Eastern Front, but experience had shown that the volunteers from Flanders could fight, and fight hard. Although the legion had been withdrawn from combat by the beginning of 1943, it was expanded to form the *Sturmbrigade Langemarck* by the addition of fresh recruits from Flanders, a Finnish battalion and some German artillery and support units.

The *Sturmbrigade* was attached to the *Das Reich* Division in the Ukraine, before being sent to the Leningrad front as part of Felix Steiner's III *SS-Germanische Panzerkorps*. The *Langemarck* Brigade took part in the fighting retreat from the Baltic, and played its part in the long sequence of fierce battles on the Narva. In the autumn of 1944, the brigade was

Opposite: An SS sharpshooter takes aim with an advanced Gewehr-43 self-loading rifle. On the Oder front in February 1945, even the possession of improved weapons could do little against the sheer weight of numbers of the Red Army.

refitting on the Lüneburg Heath when it was upgraded to become the 27th *SS-Freiwilligen Grenadier Division Langemarck (flämische Nr. 1)*, though it never really approached divisional size.

At the end of 1944, the 27th Division was assigned to the 3rd SS Panzer Corps, part of the Eleventh Army. On 15 February, the Eleventh SS Army launched a counter-attack, known as Operation *Sonnenwende*. Three corps were nominally involved, but only the 3rd SS Panzer Corps (*Nordland* and *Langemarck* Divisions) were ready. They attacked southwards towards Arnswalde, about 30km (18.6 miles) southeast of Stargard. The operation was finally brought to a close in the face of more and more powerful Red Army attacks.

Most of the division surrendered at Mecklenburg, though a small battlegroup took part in the last-dich defence of Berlin.

DIVISIONAL INFORMATION

Commanders

SS-Obersturmbannführer Conrad Schellong
                                    (19 October 1944)
SS-Oberführer Thomas Müller
                                    (Late October 1944)

Divisional Strength

Dec 1944   7000

Order of Battle

SS-Panzergrenadier-Regiment 66
SS-Panzergrenadier-Regiment 67

SS-Panzergrenadier-Regiment 68
SS-Artillerie-Regiment 27
SS-Panzerjäger-Abteilung 27
SS-Nachrichten-Abteilung 27
SS-Pionier-Bataillon 27
SS-Div. Versorgungs Regiment 27
SS-Feldersatz-Bataillon 27
SS-Sanitäts-Abteilung 27
Verwaltungs-Kompanie
Propaganda-Kompanie
Kampfgruppe Schellong

28th SS-Freiwilligen Grenadier Division *Wallonien*

- *1941:* Wallonisches-Infanterie-Bataillon 373 (Heer) • *Jun 1943:* SS-Sturmbrigade *Wallonie* • *Oct 1943:* 5th SS-Freiwilligen Sturmbrigade *Wallonien* • *Oct 1944 – May 1945:* 28th SS-Freiwilligen Grenadier Division *Wallonien*

The 28th *SS-Freiwilligen Grenadier Division Wallonien* was formed when 5th *SS-Freiwilligen Sturmbrigade Wallonien* was upgraded to divisional size (in name only; it was never to have the strength of an early-war division).

Walloon (French-speaking) Belgian volunteers had originally served in *Wallonisches-Infanterie-Bataillon 373* of the German Army, but with the disbandment of most of the European legions in 1943, many of its members were transferred to the *Waffen*-SS.

The new *Sturmbrigade*, consisting mainly of Belgian volunteers but including some Frenchmen and Spaniards, fought on the Dnieper bend and was trapped in the Cherkassy pocket while serving with the *Wiking* Division. The unit's commander, *Obersturmbannführer* Lucien Lippert, was killed at Nowo-Buda on 15 February 1944 and he was replaced by *Hauptsturmführer* Léon Degrelle. The Walloons escaped from the pocket with 632 men of the

approximately 2000 who had originally been trapped by the Red Army. Degrelle became a hero to the Nazi propaganda machine, and he was appointed commander of the new 28th *SS-Freiwilligen Grenadier Division Wallonien* in October 1944. While still being formed in Hanover and Brunswick, the unit was ordered to be converted to a 'Type 45' division (reduced in size from three to two regiments, with the regiments themselves reduced to two battalions each).

In February 1945 the division was assigned to III *SS (Germanisches) Korps* in Pomerania, where it fought until the end of the war. Some divisional units managed to retreat to Denmark; most of the rest surrendered to the Soviets in Brandenburg in May 1945.

Below: Léon Degrelle (foreground) and survivors of the Walloon *Sturmbrigade* after their escape from Cherkassy. The rebuilt unit formed the basis of the 28th SS Division, placed under Degrelle's command in October 1944.

DIVISIONAL INFORMATION

Commanders

SS-Standartenführer Léon Degrelle
(19 Oct 1944 – Apr 1945)

Divisional Strength

Dec 1944   4000

Order of Battle

SS-Panzergrenadier-Regiment 69
SS-Panzergrenadier-Regiment 70
SS-Artillerie-Regiment 28

SS-Panzerjäger-Abteilung 28
SS-Panzeraufklärungs-Abteilung 28
SS-Nachrichten-Abteilung 28
SS-Pionier-Bataillon 28
SS-Nachschub-Kompanie 28
SS-Flak-Kompanie 28
SS-Verwaltungskompanie 28
SS-Sanitäts-Kompanie 28
SS-Veterinär-Kompanie 28
SS-Ersatz-Bataillon 28
Kampfgruppe Capelle

29th Waffen-Grenadier Division der SS (russische Nr. 1)

The 29th *Waffen-Grenadier Division der SS (russische Nr. 1)* was to be formed from *Waffen-Sturm-Brigade RONA*. This unit, descended from one of the first Soviet formations to fight for the Germans, had possibly the worst reputation of any SS unit.

Manned by thugs and murderers, the *RONA* Brigade had gained an unsavoury reputation during the partisan war, and its members committed numberless atrocities during the suppression of the Warsaw Rising – so many, in fact, that even the SS were appalled. The unit's commander, Bronislav Kaminski, was killed – most likely by the *Gestapo* – in August 1944.

In December 1944 the *RONA* was absorbed by General Vlasov's ROA. Vlasov ordered Colonel Sergei K. Bunyachenko to form the first ROA division, using the Kaminski Brigade as its core. When Bunyachenko saw the men from *RONA* he shouted to the German liaison officer: 'So that's what you're giving me, bandits, robbers and thieves! You'll let me have what you can no longer use!'. The division was disbanded before its formation got under way, and the number 29 was given to *Waffen-Grenadier Division der SS (italienische Nr. 1)*.

Right: Bronislav Kaminski (right), receives orders from SS-*Gruppenführer* Heinz Reinefarth, the SS commander detailed to suppress the Warsaw Uprising, August 1944.

DIVISIONAL INFORMATION

Commanders

Waffen-Brigadeführer der SS Bronislav Kaminski
(17 Jun 1944)
SS-Brigadeführer Christoph Diehm
(19 Aug 1944)

29th Waffen-Grenadier Division der SS (italienische Nr. 1)

• *Nov 1943:* Italienische-Freiwilligen-Legion • *Late 1943:* 1st Sturmbrigade Italienische Freiwilligen Legion • *Sept 1944:* Waffen-Grenadier Brigade der SS • *Mar – May 1945:* 29th Waffen-Grenadier Division der SS (italienische Nr. 1)

The 29th *Waffen-Grenadier Division der SS (italienische Nr. 1)* was descended from the Italian volunteer legion formed by Italian fascists after the fall of Mussolini and the Italian armistice with the Allies.

It came into existence in September 1944, when the *Waffen-Grenadier Brigade der SS (italienische Nr. 1)* was upgraded to a division.

The formation was given the number 29 when *Waffen-Grenadier Division der SS (russische Nr. 1)* was disbanded before ever being formed. The Italian SS division never reached full divisional strength, though it came closer than many of the other foreign SS divisions formed late in the war. It was primarily used on anti-partisan operations in northern Italy, but at the end of the war it saw some action against the British and the Americans.

Some parts of the Italian division surrendered to the Allies; those members of divisional units foolish enough to surrender to the Italian resistance were mostly executed.

DIVISIONAL INFORMATION

Commanders
SS-Oberführer Constantin Heldmann
(10 Feb 1945)
SS-Oberführer Erwin Tzschoppe
(Late Feb/early Mar 1945)

Divisional Strength
Dec 1944   15,000

Order of Battle
Waffen-Grenadier-Regiment der SS 81
Waffen-Grenadier-Regiment der SS 82
Waffen-Artillerie-Regiment der SS 29
Füsilier-Bataillon 29
Panzerjäger-Abteilung 29
SS-Pionier-Kompanie 29
SS-Nachrichten-Kompanie 29

30th Waffen-Grenadier Division der SS (russische Nr. 2)

(Aug – Dec 1944)

The 30th *Waffen-Grenadier Division der SS (russische Nr. 2)* was formed in August 1944 in Poland from *Schutzmannschaft-Brigade Siegling.* This in turn had been assembled from several small Russian volunteer formations withdrawn from the front following the Soviet summer offensive.

Germans provided the officer cadre for the unit. Most of the rest of the division was Russian, though it also counted Byelorussians, Ukrainians, Armenians, Tartars, Poles and at least one Czech among its number.

Never considered reliable, the division suffered from many desertions, and at the end of August troops of two infantry battalions mutinied, killing a number of German officers and NCOs. The second battalion of the 1st Regiment was disbanded, and 2300 men regarded as unreliable were transferred to construction units. The division transferred to France over the last two weeks in August, where it immediately came under attack by the French resistance.

Combat losses

Some divisional units avoided action, though others did engage the resistance fighters with enthusiasm. Strength dropped rapidly through combat losses and

DIVISIONAL INFORMATION

Commanders
SS-Obersturmbannführer Hans Siegling
(18 Aug 1944)

Divisional Strength
Dec 1944   4400

Order of Battle
Waffen-Grenadier-Regiment der SS 75
Waffen-Grenadier-Regiment der SS 76

Waffen-Grenadier-Regiment der SS 77
SS-Artillerie-Abteilung 30
SS-Aufklärungs-Abteilung 30
SS-Füsilier-Kompanie
SS-Pionier-Kompanie
SS-Nachrichten-Kompanie
SS-Sanitäts-Kompanie
SS-Panzerspäh-Kompanie
SS-Feldersatz-Bataillon

desertions. Over the next months it joined in the general retreat of the *Wehrmacht*, eventually being assigned to guard bridges on the Rhine.

Losing many men in battles with the French First Army, the division was driven to the Swiss border, where it was disbanded in December 1944. Officers were transferred to the *Nibelungen* Division, the last SS 'Division' of the war; reliable Russian troops were used

Above: A mixed force of Germans and Russian auxiliaries move through Kovel in 1942. A large number of varied Soviet volunteer units were combined, eventually becoming the 30th *Waffen-Grenadier Division der SS*.

in *Waffen-Grenadier Division der SS (weissruthenische Nr. 1)*, while the unreliable volunteers were sent to Vlasov's *Russkaya Osvoboditelnaya Armiya* (ROA).

30th Waffen-Grenadier Division der SS (weissruthenische Nr. 1)

• *Jul/Aug 1944:* Schutzmannschaft-Brigade *Siegling* • *Dec 1944:* Waffen-Grenadier Brigade der SS (weissruthenische) • *Mar 1945:* 30th Waffen-Grenadier Division der SS (weissruthenische Nr. 1)

Authorized in February 1945, with wholly unrealistic plans to complete formation by June 1945, the 30th *Waffen-Grenadier Division der SS (weissruthenische Nr. 1)* was an expansion of the *Waffen-Grenadier Brigade der SS (weissruthenische)*.

The formation began gathering its troops at Grafenwohr on 9 March 1945. Why the SS felt it necessary to convert an understrength brigade which had already been downgraded from divisional status – it had originally been the 30th *Waffen-Grenadier Division der SS (russische Nr. 2)* which had been broken up in December 1944 – is a matter for conjecture. The unit was far too weak and poorly equipped to be able to function as a division.

The unit never reached any great size, and saw no action. Like its predecessor, the White Russian division was disbanded very shortly after its formation began. The German cadre were assigned to the newly formed 38th *SS-Grenadier Division Nibelungen*.

DIVISIONAL INFORMATION

Commanders
SS-Obersturmbannführer Hans Siegling
(10 Feb 1945)

Order of Battle
Waffen-Grenadier-Regiment der SS 75
Artillerie-Abteilung
Panzerjäger-Abteilung
Reiter-Schwadron

Below: Russian volunteers in service with the *Wehrmacht* go into action. Those who survived two years of warfare in the East found themselves forced into SS units at the end of the war, few of which were of any value militarily.

31st SS-Freiwilligen Grenadier Division

(Oct 1944 – May 1945)

Orders for the formation of the 31th *SS-Freiwilligen Grenadier Division* were issued in October 1944, and by the beginning of December 1944 some 11,000 recruits were in training. Many of the recruits were Czech or Slovak *Volksdeutsche*.

The civilian recruits were bolstered by the attachment of parts of the disbanded 23rd *Waffen-Grenadier Division der SS Kama (kroatische Nr. 2)* and by the addition of the *Polizei Regiment Brixen*.

The division fought briefly against the Red Army around its Hungarian training area, but was soon forced to retreat into Germany, where it was intended to complete its formation at Marburg. However, in January 1945, the division was converted into a much reduced-strength 'Type 45' unit. In February it was assigned to Army Group Centre as part of its general reserve.

By war's end, a divisional *Kampfgruppe* was operating around Königgrätz, where survivors surrendered to the Russians. According to some sources this division was to be given the name *Böhmen-Mähren* (Bohemia-Moravia).

DIVISIONAL INFORMATION

Commanders

SS-Brigadeführer Gustav Lombard (1 Oct 1944)
SS-Brigadeführer Wilhelm Trabandt (Apr 1945)

Divisional Strength

Dec 1944 11,000

Order of Battle

SS-Freiwilligen-Grenadier-Regiment 78
SS-Freiwilligen-Grenadier-Regiment 79
SS-Freiwilligen-Grenadier-Regiment 80
SS-Artillerie-Regiment 31
SS-Füsilier-Bataillon 31
SS-Nachrichten-Abteilung 31
SS-Nachschub-Truppen 31
SS-Panzerjäger-Abteilung 31
SS-Pionier-Bataillon 31
SS-Kranken-Transport-Kompanie 31
SS-Veterinär-Kompanie 31
Feldpostamt

33rd Waffen-Kavallerie Division der SS (ungarische Nr. 3)

(Dec 1944 – Jan 1945)

Formed in December 1944, he 33rd *Waffen-Kavallerie Division der SS (ungarische Nr. 3)* was intended to be formed from Hungarian volunteers, mostly from the scattered remnants of Hungarian Army cavalry units. It never reached anything close to divisional size and was destroyed in the fighting near Budapest in January 1945. The number 33 was given to the *Charlemagne* Division.

DIVISIONAL INFORMATION

Commanders

SS-Oberführer László Deák (27 Dec 1944)

33rd Waffen-Grenadier Division der SS *Charlemagne*

- *Mar 1943:* Légion Volontaire Française (Heer)   • *Oct 1943:* Französisches SS-Freiwilligen Grenadier Regiment
- *Nov 1943:* Französisches SS-Freiwilligen Regiment 57   • *Jul 1944:* Französisches-Freiwilligen Sturmbrigade
- *Aug 1944:* Waffen-Grenadier Brigade der SS *Charlemagne* (französische Nr. 1)   • *Feb – May 1945:* 33rd Waffen-Grenadier Division der SS *Charlemagne* (französische Nr. 1)

The 33rd *Waffen-Grenadier Division der SS Charlemagne (französische Nr. 1)* was formed on 2 February 1945 when it was decided to expand *Waffen-Grenadier Brigade der SS Charlemagne (französische Nr. 1)* to full divisional status.

The extra manpower would be provided by volunteers from among the French collaborationists who had fled France ahead of the Allied advances.

The unit was given the number 33 when *Waffen-Kavallerie Division der SS (ungarische Nr. 3)* was destroyed while being formed. As might be expected from the name, the *Charlemagne* Division was a largely French formation, but it also had on its strength transfers from the *Horst Wessel* Division and volunteers from other countries. Some French sources suggest that the division had Swedish, Swiss, Laotian, Vietnamese and even Japanese members.

On deployment to Pomerania on 25 February, the division came under attack just as the trains bearing most of the unit's 7500 troops pulled into Hammerstein. Tanks of the Soviet 1st Byelorussian Front scattered the Frenchmen, who gathered into three *ad hoc* battlegroups. One group under General Krukenberg made it to the Baltic coast, eventually being shipped via Denmark to Mecklenburg. A second group, commanded by General Puaud, ran straight into one of the main axes of the Soviet winter offensive, and was never seen again. The third group took heavy casualties at the railhead before making a fighting retreat westwards to the German lines.

About a third of the 1100 survivors were released from their SS vows of allegiance. The remainder were enough to make up a single *Waffen-Grenadier* regiment. This was among the last units to enter Berlin before the Soviets completed their enclosure of the German capital. Supported by the few remaining *Sturmgeschütze* and Tiger II heavy tanks of *s.SS-Pz. Abt.503* (Heavy SS Panzer Detachment 503), they mounted brief but ferocious counter-attacks at Hasenheide and around Tempelhof Airfield. The Frenchmen then continued to mount rearguard fights along the *Leipzigerstrasse*, in and around the *Luftfahrtsministerium*, and into the *Potsdamerplatz*. On 2 May 1945, after the general order of surrender announced by General Weidling, some 30 surviving Frenchmen went into Soviet captivity near the Potsdamer Station.

Left: The last defenders of Berlin prepare to receive Soviet armour. Among those defenders were *Waffen*-SS men of many nationalities, including the 7500 men of the *Charlemagne* Division. Few would survive the war.

DIVISIONAL INFORMATION

Commanders

SS-Oberführer Edgard Puaud   (Feb 1945)

SS-Brigadeführer Gustav Krukenberg

      (1 Mar 1945)

SS-Standartenführer Walter Zimmermann

      (24 Apr 1945)

Divisional Strength

25 Feb 1945	7500
23 Apr 1945	1100
2 May 1945	30

Order of Battle

SS-Waffen-Grenadier-Regiment 57

SS-Sturm-Bataillon 58

SS-Waffen-Grenadier-Regiment 58

SS-Artillerie-Abteilung 33

SS-Panzerjäger-Abteilung 33

SS-Pionier-Kompanie 33

SS-Nachrichten-Kompanie 33

SS-Feldersatz-Kompanie 33

SS-Nachschub-Bataillon 33

34th SS-Freiwilligen Grenadier Division *Landstorm Nederland*

- *Oct 1943:* Landstorm Nederland   • *Nov 1944:* SS-Freiwilligen Grenadier Brigade *Landstorm Nederland*
- *Feb – May 1945:* 34th SS-Freiwilligen Grenadier Division *Landstorm Nederland*

The 34th *SS-Freiwilligen Grenadier Division Landstorm Nederland* came into existence when *SS-Freiwilligen Grenadier Brigade Landstorm Nederland* was upgraded to a division. A division in name only, since it was smaller than many infantry brigades, it was formed from Dutch stormtroopers, the *Landwacht Nederland* and other Dutch collaborationist organizations.

The division saw little conventional action against Allied forces. Earlier, *Landstorm Nederland* troops fought against the Dutch resistance in northwest Holland, and played a small part in the battle against British paratroopers at Arnhem in September 1944. *Landstorm Nederland* troops even saw combat with fellow Dutchmen, in an encounter with the 'Princess Irene Brigade', a unit of Dutch volunteers serving with the Allies.

The *Landstorm* was renamed *SS-Freiwilligen Brigade Landstorm Nederland* in November 1944, before being nominally made into a division in February 1945. The last strong resistance mounted by *Landstorm Nederland* was against the advancing Canadians around the villages of Oosterbeek and Otterlo in March 1945. The 3000 or so members of the *Landstorm* included

DIVISIONAL INFORMATION

Commanders

SS-Oberführer Martin Kohlroser   (10 Feb 1945)

Order of Battle

SS-Freiwilligen-Grenadier-Regiment 83

SS-Freiwilligen-Grenadier-Regiment 84

SS-Artillerie-Regiment 60

SS-Versorgungs-Regiment 60

SS-Pionier-Kompanie 60

SS-Nachrichten-Abteilung 60

Werkstattkompanie

fanatical Nazis who used terror to persuade the population to acquiesce to their demands. Troops from the 84th Regiment in particular, the former prison camp guards of *SS-Wachbataillon Nordwest*, were happy to shoot Dutch civilians who refused to obey their commands. The *Landstorm* also fought against the Dutch resistance right up to 7 May, when the division was disarmed by the British 49th Infantry Division.

36th Waffen-Grenadier Division der SS

- *15 Jun 1940:* Wilddiebkommando *Oranienburg* • *1941:* SS-Sonderkommando *Dirlewanger*
- *10 Aug 1944:* SS Regiment *Dirlewanger* • *19 Dec 1944*: SS-Sturmbrigade *Dirlewanger*
- *20 Feb 1945:* 36th Waffen-Grenadier Division der SS

The 36th *Waffen-Grenadier Division der SS* was formed in February 1945 when *SS-Sturmbrigade Dirlewanger* was upgraded to a division. With an even worse reputation than the Kaminski Brigade, the 36th *Waffen-Grenadier Division der SS* was the most notorious of *Waffen*-SS units, serving under perhaps the cruellest of all commanders of World War II.

The unit's brutal commander, *Oberführer* Dr Oskar Dirlewanger, was a highly decorated veteran of World War I, but he was also a drunk and a sadist, who had been imprisoned in the 1920s for sexual assaults on children. A protégé of Gottlob Berger, Dirlewanger suggested the creation of a special punishment unit that would allow SS men convicted of crimes to atone for their deeds.

Poachers and thieves

Dirlewanger formed his first unit in 1940 from former Oranienburg concentration camp inmates convicted of poaching. On the Eastern Front, casualties were replaced with Soviet turncoats and criminals.

Sonderkommando Dirlewanger went into action behind the front lines during Operation *Barbarossa*, the Nazi invasion of the Soviet Union. The unit quickly earned a reputation for atrocity in counter-insurgency operations, with a speciality of 'pacifying' an area by slaughtering every man, woman and child. The unit, never large, spent almost all of its career raping, looting and killing in the Soviet Union, but cemented its reputation for barbarity with the murderous part it played in the brutal suppression of the Warsaw Rising in the autumn of 1944.

Reclassified as a 'paper' division in February 1945, the unit was never more than the size of an understrength brigade. Soviet troops all but annihilated the 36th Division in April, and from the middle of the month desertions meant that what was left of the division melted away.

Dirlewanger escaped to surrender in the West, but did not live long. Recognized in June 1945 by Polish troops serving with the French, Dirlewanger was attacked and beaten to death.

DIVISIONAL INFORMATION

Commanders
SS-Oberführer Dr Oskar Dirlewanger
(20 Feb 1945)

Unit Strengths

1 Jul 1940	84
1 Sep 1940	300
4 Feb 1943	700
30 Dec 1943	259
19 Feb 1944	1200
17 Apr 1944	2000
30 Jun 1944	971
15 Aug 1944	648
16 Oct 1944	4000
29 Dec 1944	6000

Order of Battle
Waffen-Grenadier-Regiment der SS 72
Waffen-Grenadier-Regiment der SS 73
Pioneer-Brigade 687 (Heer)
Grenadier-Regiment 1244 (Heer)
Schwere-Panzerjäger-Abteilung 681 (Heer)
Artillerie-Abteilung 36
Füsilier-Kompanie 36
Panzer-Abteilung Stansdorf I

37th SS-Freiwilligen Kavallerie Division *Lützow*

(Feb – May 1945)

The 37th *SS-Freiwilligen Kavallerie Division Lützow* was formed near Marchfeld on the Hungarian–Slovakian border in February 1945. Raw material for the division came from the remnants of the *Florian Geyer* and the *Maria Theresa* Divisions, shattered in the battles around besieged Budapest, which were brought up to strength as far as possible by drafts of Hungarian *Volksdeutsche*.

In March 1945 the division was far from combat-capable. However a *Kampfgruppe* from *Lützow*, consisting of all veteran and battle-ready elements of the division, was sent to Sixth SS Panzer Army. Commanded by *SS-Obersturmbannführer* Karl-Heinz Keitel (son of OKW chief *Generalfeldmarschall* Wilhelm Keitel), the *Kampfgruppe* arrived on 4 April.

Subordinated to I *SS-Panzerkorps Leibstandarte Adolf Hitler*, *Kampfgruppe Keitel* experienced some fierce combat in the retreat from the advancing Soviet Army through Hungary to Austria. In May 1945, a number of units were taken by the Russians, while others moved west to surrender to the advancing Americans.

DIVISIONAL INFORMATION

Commanders
SS-Oberführer Waldemar Fegelein
(26 Feb 1945 – Mar 1945)
SS-Standartenführer Karl Gesele
(Mar 1945 – May 1945)

Order of Battle
SS-Kavallerie Regiment 92
SS-Kavallerie Regiment 93
SS-Kavallerie Regiment 94
SS-Artillerie-Abteilung 37
SS-Aufklärungs-Abteilung 37
SS-Panzerjäger-Abteilung 37
SS-Pionier-Bataillon 37
SS-Nachrichten-Kompanie 37
SS-Sanitäts-Abteilung 37
SS-Nachschub-Truppen 37
Feldersatz-Bataillon 37

Some men from the division took part in a mass breakout from the Altheim POW camp on 13 May after watching the release of regular *Wehrmacht* units while they and other SS men remained in custody.

Left: Members of an SS cavalry unit move along a Hungarian minor road in the Spring of 1945. Although cavalry units were important in the war against the partisans on the Eastern Front, by the time the *Lützow* Division was formed there were few horses available, together with little ammunition and supplies.

THE FOREIGN SS BRIGADES

With the notable exception of the *Wiking* Division, the first SS formations made up from foreign volunteers were regiment-sized legions and brigades. These were not successful in the East, as they were too small to serve independently on a battlefield of the scale encountered in the USSR, and linguistic and national differences meant that when they were brigaded into larger formations they did not match the performance of German units. However, they did provide the basis for more successful SS units that appeared later in the war.

Above: Men of the notorious *Dirlewanger* Brigade in Warsaw in 1944. Originally manned by poachers and convicts, the brigade quickly proved to be little more than than a collection of thugs and murderers.
Opposite: The SS tried to form a British unit using volunteers from POW camps, but the *Britisches Freikorps* was never more than 50 strong.

1st and 2nd SS Motorized Brigades

1st SS Motorized Brigade was originally formed in the summer of 1941 from the 8th and 10th *SS-Totenkopf Standarten*. The *Totenkopf* regiments had been formed on the outbreak of war by calling up *Allgemeine*-SS reservists. As such, they were not part of the *Waffen*-SS, being more closely related to Theodor Eicke's concentration camp guards.

However, by 1941, Himmler had merged the *Totenkopf Standarten* with the *Waffen*-SS. However, they were not front-line soldiers. The SS Brigades were used to follow the *Wehrmacht*'s advance eastwards into Russia, providing rear security and being used to deal with isolated pockets of resistance. From May 1941 to December 1943 1st Brigade was controlled by *Kommandostab Reichsführer-SS*. It fought for almost three years with Army Group Centre, mostly on anti-partisan operations behind the lines. In 1941 and 1942 it was used to provide support and personnel for *Einsatzgruppen* murder squads.

Most of the personnel of this brigade were *Volksdeutsche*, and in April 1943 it took in a sizeable number of Danish recruits form North Schleswig. Later in 1943 Himmler announced that he was going to form a *Volksdeutsche* brigade. This new formation was sent into action but suffered heavy losses during

the fighting for Smolensk and was reduced to the size of a battlegroup.

It was in action in December 1943 around Bobruisk and on the Dnieper as part of the Ninth Army, Army Group Centre, its total strength being 4125 officers, NCOs and men. In January 1944 the brigade was upgraded to become the 18th *SS-Freiwilligen Panzergrenadier Division Horst Wessel*.

2nd SS Motorized Infantry Brigade was formed from the 4th, 5th and 14th *Totenkopf Standarten* at the same time as the 1st Brigade. It was deployed with Army Group North, taking part in the fighting

UNIT INFORMATION

Commanders

SS-Brigadeführer Karl von Treuenfeld
(24 Apr 1941 – July 1941)
SS-Standartenführer Gottfried Klingemann
(5 Jul 1941 – Jan 1943)
SS-Brigadeführer Friedrich von Scholz
(26 Jan 1943 – 30 Apr 1943)
SS-Standartenführer Heinrich Schuldt
(early May 1943 – 18 May 1943)

around Leningrad. This brigade was an international formation that included Dutch, Flemish and Norwegian volunteer legions.

In late 1942, the 19th and 21st Latvian Security Battalions from the Latvian Legion were attached to the brigade. The 18th, 24th and 26th Latvian *Schuma* Battalions serving in Leningrad were used to form the brigade's 2nd SS Volunteer Regiment. On 18 May 1943, these Latvian battalions along with the other three Latvian Legion battalions were incorporated into the 2nd SS (Motorized) Brigade, and converted into the 2nd *Waffen-Grenadier SS Lettische Brigade*. The Dutch, Flemish and Norwegian formations were removed from the 2nd SS Brigade. The 2nd SS Latvian Brigade was deployed with Army Group North.

Estonian SS Legion/Brigade

Immediately after the occupation of Estonia by the Germans, Estonian military units began to be formed to play their part in the war against the hated Russians. Individual *Schutz-*, *Ost-* and *Polizei-* companies and battalions were formed – by March 1942 there were 16 Estonian units with 10,000 men in Russia and 1500 men in a depot battalion at home in Estonia.

Eventually, up to 54 such units were to be formed. Most served along the lines of communication of Army Group North, providing security and fighting partisans.

In August 1942 the SS called for volunteers to form the *Estnische SS-Legion*. By the end of the year over 1200 men had been found acceptable and had been sent to Debica, Poland, for training. The sheer number of volunteers made it possible to expand the unit from a regiment to a brigade, and it was redesignated *Estnische SS-Freiwilligen Brigade* in May 1943. After the *Finnisches Freiwilligen-Bataillon der Waffen-SS* was stood down in March of 1943, the *Estnisches SS-Freiwilligen Bataillon Narwa* was used to replace the Finns as the third battalion within the *SS-Panzergrenadier Regiment Nordland*.

UNIT INFORMATION

Commanders
SS-Obersturmbannführer Franz Augsberger
(20 Oct 1942 – 21 Jan 1944)

Order of Battle (Estnische SS-Legion)
I Bataillon
II Bataillon
III Bataillon
Pionere-Kompanie
Panzerjäger-Kompanie
Artellerie-Kompanie

Order of Battle (Brigade)
SS-Freiwilligen-Regiment 42
SS-Freiwilligen-Regiment 43
SS-Flak-Abteilung 53
SS-Panzerjäger-Abteilung 53
SS-Nachrichten-Kompanie 53
SS-Feldersatz-Bataillon 53
SS-Ausbildungs-und-Ersatz-Regiment 33
SS-Artellerie-Abteilung 53

The Estonians still had sufficient manpower to form a two-regiment brigade, which became 3rd *Estnische SS-Freiwilligen Brigade* in October 1943. It was upgraded to a division by absorbing the other Estonian formations in the German military, and it also added some Estonian police formations. It was designated 20th *Waffen-Grenadier Division der SS (estnische Nr. 1)* in January 1944.

Lettische SS-Freiwilligen Legion
Lettische SS-Freiwilligen Brigade

The *Lettische SS-Freiwilligen Legion* was raised in February 1943. It saw action at Novo-Sokolniki in November 1943, under the command of Sixteenth Army.

In December 1943 it was withdrawn from the front to be expanded to divisional size. It was redesignated 15th *Waffen-Grenadier Division der SS (lettische Nr. 1)*. The *Lettische SS-Freiwilligen Brigade* was formed in late January 1943, using the Latvian battalions from the 2nd SS Brigade.

The existing 18th, 24th and 26th Latvian *Schuma* (or *Schutzmannschaft*) Battalions serving on the Leningrad front were used to form the brigade's 2nd SS Volunteer Regiment. It was redesignated 2.*Lettische SS-Freiwilligen Brigade* in October 1943. The brigade was upgraded to a division and redesignated 19th *Waffen-Grenadier Division der SS (lettisches Nr. 2)* in January 1944.

UNIT INFORMATION

Commanders
SS-Standartenführer Heinrich Schuldt (18 May 1943)
SS-Oberführer Fritz Freitag   (Jul 1943)
SS-Oberführer Heinrich Schuldt   (3 Sep 1943)

Order of Battle (Estnische SS-Legion)
SS-Freiwilligen Grenadier Regiment 39
SS-Freiwilligen Grenadier Regiment 40

Order of Battle (Brigade)
SS-Freiwilligen-Regiment 1
SS-Freiwilligen-Regiment 2
Artillerie-Bat 52
Panzerjäger-Bat 52

Right: Latvian volunteers in a police unit pose for the camera during a mission to hunt down partisans. In January 1943, Latvian security units were combined with the Latvian Legion to form the Latvian SS-Volunteer Brigade.

Finnisches Freiwilligen-Bataillon der Waffen-SS

The *Finnisches Freiwilligen-Bataillon der Waffen-SS* was formed in 1941. Initially known as *SS Freiwilligen-Bataillon Nordost* it was manned by Finnish volunteers who had signed on for a fixed term of two years.

They had also insisted that they would only fight the Soviet Union, and would refuse any orders to fight against the Western Allies. The notoriously independent Finns also refused to take the oath of loyalty to Hitler, and insisted on being commanded by Finnish officers. This demand was mostly met, though some German officers had to be used to make up for shortages. The Finnish battalion did its *Waffen-SS* training at Gross-Born, before being sent to Army Group South at the end of 1941. At the Mius River it was attached to the *Wiking* Division.

It fought in the offensive battles along the Mius River, through the German summer campaign of

---

UNIT INFORMATION

Commanders
SS-Obersturmbannführer Hans Collani

Order of Battle
1. Kompanie	2. Kompanie
3. Kompanie	4. Kompanie (MG)

1942 and continued on to the Caucasus. In May 1943 it was transferred away from the front, as the two-year enlistment period of the volunteers was at an end, and it was disbanded in July 1943. Those who wanted to remain in the *Waffen*-SS joined *SS-Freiwilligen Panzergrenadier Division Nordland* or *SS-Standarte Kurt Eggers*.

SS-Freiwilligen Verband *Danemark*/Freikorps *Danmark*

Freikorps Danmark was founded in 1941 at the request of the Danish Nazi party (the DNSAP) and with the approval of the Danish Government. There was some trouble recruiting officers until it was decided that they would keep their Danish rank (and pension) when they joined the *Waffen*-SS.

The Danish soldiers swore an oath to the commander of the *Wehrmacht* and not the usual oath to Adolf Hitler. Christian Peder Kryssing became the first commander of the unit even though he was not a member (or even supporter) of the DNSAP. Kryssing was soon replaced by Christian Frederick von Schalburg (who at the time was attached to the *Wiking* Division), who finished their training.

First blood

In May 1942 the *Freikorps* was airlifted into the Demyansk salient in northern Russia. They were attached to the *SS-Panzer Division Totenkopf*, then holding a position where the Lovat and Robja Rivers converged. On 27 May the Danes under the

command of *Sturmbannführer* von Schalburg mounted an assault on a Soviet bridgehead. On 2 June 1942, von Schalburg was with an assault group pinned down by enemy fire when he tripped a mine and was badly injured. As his men came to assist they were hit by mortar fire: the commander and two others were killed instantly. The Danes lost 28 men in the failed assault. The replacement commander, von Lettow-Vorbeck, was killed on 11 June at Bolschoje Dubowizy. He was one of more than 70 men killed that day.

At the end of August 1942, after suffering 121 killed and several hundred wounded, the *Freikorps* returned to Denmark with a combat strength of 299 out of the original force of 1200. After taking on new recruits it returned to the Eastern Front in October. The *Freikorps* was withdrawn from the front in March 1943. The unit was disbanded on 20 May and those volunteers who remained in service transferred to *SS-Panzergrenadier Regiment 24 Danmark* of the *Nordland* Division.

UNIT INFORMATION

Commanders

Legion-Obersturmbannführer Christian Peder
   Kryssing   (19 Jul 1941 – 23 Feb 1942)

Legion-Obersturmbannführer Knud Børge-
   Martinsen   (23 Feb 1942 – 1 Mar 1942)

Legion-Obersturmbannführer Christian Frederick
   von Schalburg   (1 Mar 1942 – 2 Jun 1942)

Legion-Obersturmbannführer Knud Børge-
   Martinsen   (2 Jun 1942 – 9 Jun 1942)

SS-Obersturmbannführer Hans von Lettow-Vorbeck
           (9 Jun 1942 – 11 Jun 1942)

SS-Obersturmbannführer Knud Børge-Martinsen
          (11 Jun 1942 – 20 May 1943)

Unit Strength

31 Mar 1942	900
May 1942	1386
Nov 1942	1800

Freiwilligen Legion *Norwegen* (Den Norske Legion)

The *Freiwilligen Legion Norwegen* (*Den Norske Legion*) was formed on 29 June 1941. Volunteers were assured that it would be a Norwegian unit with Norwegian officers, uniforms and language, and that its area of operations would be Finland.

These promises were quickly broken – instead of fighting in Finland, the Norwegians found themselves in Russia, taking part in the bloody stalemate on the Leningrad front.

Coming under the control of the 2nd SS Infantry Brigade, the Norwegians occupied positions at Krasnoye Syelo near Pushkin in February 1942. For the next two months the legion took part in the siege warfare around Leningrad. In May 1942 the legion was withdrawn for a rest, returning to the front lines in June 1942. It again became involved in major combat in February 1943, as the Soviets mounted an offensive across Lake Ladoga. The legion left the front line in the spring of 1943, having suffered over 180 casualties in a year. During that period it had been reinforced by the 1st *SS und Polizei-kompanie*, under the command of the head of the Norwegian *Allgemeine*-SS, Jonas Lie.

The legion was disbanded in March 1943. Although it had fought reasonably well, relations between the Norwegians and the Germans had not been good – a problem common to most of the

Left: Featuring the Norwegian colours (blue and white cross on a red background), the *Den Norske Legion* flag was one of the simplest used by foreign volunteer units.

UNIT INFORMATION

Commanders
Legion-Sturmbannführer Finn Hanibal Kjelstrup
(Jun 1941 – 1 Dec 1941)
Legion-Sturmbannführer Jorgen Bakke
(Dec 1941 – 15 Dec 1941)
SS-Obersturmbannführer Arthur Quist
(Dec 1941 – Mar 1943)

Unit Strength
Aug 1941	700
Dec 1941	1218
1 Dec 1942	1000
May 1943	600

Order of Battle (Brigade)
1. *Infanterie-Kompanie*
2. *Infanterie-Kompanie*
3. *Infanterie-Kompanie*
4. *Panzerjäger-Kompanie*

legions fighting on the Eastern Front. Legionnaires returned to Norway with little good to say about the Germans, which was to cause the SS some difficulty when it tried to recruit Norwegians later in the war. Most survivors of the legion who wanted to continue fighting transferred to the 23rd *SS-Panzergrenadier Regiment Norge (Norw.Frwg.1)*, one of the regiments of the newly formed 11th *SS-Freiwilligen Panzergrenadier Division Nordland*.

Opposite: A 17-year-old volunteer (foreground) in the *Legion Norwegen* helps to manhandle an artillery piece in the field. Service in the SS appealed to such idealistic youngsters, who believed wholeheartedly in the German 'crusade' against the communists.

SS-Freiwilligen Legion *Niederlande*
SS-Freiwilligen Panzergrenadier Brigade *Nederland*

The *SS-Freiwilligen Legion Niederlande* originated when the Dutch/Belgian *SS-Freiwilligen Standarte Nordwest* was split into *SS-Freiwilligen Verband Flandern* and *SS-Freiwilligen Verband Nederland* in July 1941. It was redesignated *SS-Freiwilligen Legion Niederlande* on 24 September 1941.

The legion was sent to the Eastern Front at the end of 1941. Serving with Army Group North, it went into action against a Soviet bridgehead on the west bank of the Volkhov River in January 1942. On 10 February the legion fought off a major Soviet infantry attack, the first of several over the next weeks. Although it held its positions, combat fatigue and increasing losses affected morale badly. In the summer of 1942 the legion was attached to the 2nd SS Infantry Brigade and transferred to the Leningrad front. At the end of July the legion fought in the abortive assault on Leningrad, Operation *Nordlicht*. Over the winter of 1942–43 the legion fought around Lake Ladoga. In January 1943, operating alongside the *Legion Norwegen*, the Dutch Legion fought off a major Soviet armoured offensive.

In April 1943 the legion was pulled out of the Leningrad front. After rest and recuperation, it was upgraded to brigade size, becoming the *SS-Freiwilligen Panzergrenadier Brigade Nederland*. The former Dutch legionnaires, strengthened with new recruits from the Netherlands and Romanian *Volksdeutsche*, were assigned to III *SS-Panzerkorps* in Croatia in September 1943. The Dutch played a full part in the no-quarter war against Tito's partisans, committing numerous atrocities. The brigade was numbered 4th *SS-Freiwilligen Panzergrenadier Brigade Nederland* in October 1943 before reverting to its numberless designation on 1 August 1944.

The brigade was ordered to the Eastern Front on Christmas Day 1943, and returned to the Leningrad front. The Dutch brigade was thrown into the fierce battles around Oranienburg as the Red Army launched a major offensive to relieve the besieged city. Soviet successes meant that the brigade now had to pull back to the Narva River. In the fierce fighting on the Narva, the Dutch suffered heavy losses: between 1 January and 13 April 1944 the brigade had 87 officers, 502 NCOs and 3139 men killed, wounded or missing. In the summer of 1944 the Dutch brigade retreated into the Courland pocket along with the rest of the German Army Group North, but not before the *General Seyffardt* Regiment had been destroyed by overwhelming Soviet forces. The rest of the brigade was evacuated to the Stettin area, where it became the 23rd *SS-Freiwilligen Panzergrenadier Division Nederland (niederlandische Nr. 1)* in February 1945.

Above: Members of the *SS-Freiwilligen Legion Niederlande*, seen here in the winter of 1942–43, are congratulated after having been awarded the Iron Cross. Many of the members of the legion would die in the battle for Narva.

UNIT INFORMATION

Commanders (*Standarte Nordwest*)
SS-Oberführer Otto Reich (Apr 1941 – Jul 1941)

Commanders (Legion)
SS-Sturmbannführer Herbert Garthe   (Nov 1941)
SS-Oberführer Otto Reich   (Feb 1942)
SS-Obersturmbannführer Arved Theuermann
                                        (1 Apr 1942)
SS-Standartenführer Josef Fitzthum   (10 Jul 1942)

Commanders (Brigade)
SS-Brigadeführer Jürgen Wagner
                      (20 Apr 1944 – 10 Feb 1945)

Order of Battle (Legion)
I. Bataillon; II. Bataillon; III. Bataillon
13. Kompanie (Artillerie)
14. Kompanie (Panzerjäger)

Order of Battle (Brigade)
SS-Freiwilligen-Panzergrenadier-Regiment 48
SS-Freiwilligen-Panzergrenadier-Regiment 49
SS-Artillerie-Regiment 54
SS-Nachrichten-Abteilung 54
SS-Panzerjäger-Abteilung 54
SS-Pionier-Bataillon 54
SS-Flak-Abteilung 54
SS-Feldersatz-Bataillon 54

SS-Grenadier Regiment 1 *Landstorm Nederland*
SS-Freiwilligen Grenadier Brigade *Landstorm Nederland*

SS-Grenadier Regiment 1 Landstorm Nederland was formed in March 1943 as SS-Grenadier Regiment 1 Landwacht Niederlande and renamed on 26 April 1944. Landwacht Nederland was a home defence force not intended for foreign service.

SS-Freiwilligen Grenadier Brigade Landstorm Nederland was formed when *SS-Grenadier Regiment 1 Landstorm Nederland* was upgraded to brigade size, incorporating in the process personnel from *SS-Wachbataillon 3, SS-Flak-Batterie Glingendaal*, other Dutch *Waffen*-SS units and members of the Dutch Nazi party, the NSB.

The *Landstorm* Brigade saw action against British paratroopers at Arnhem, serving as part of the battlegroup formed by the 9th *SS-Panzer Division Hohenstaufen*. It was upgraded to 34th *SS-Freiwilligen Grenadier Division Landstorm Nederland* early in February 1945.

Above: SS troops captured by British paratroopers at Arnhem during Operation Market Garden pose for the camera, September 1944.

UNIT INFORMATION

Commanders (Regiment)
SS-Oberführer Viktor Knapp　　　　(1 Mar 1943)
SS-Obersturmbannführer Albert Doerheit
　　　　　　　　　　　　　　　(1 Apr 1944)
SS-Standartenführer Martin Kohlroser
　　　　　　　　　　　　　　　(27 May 1944)

Commanders (Brigade)
SS-*Standartenführer* Martin Kohlroser
　　　　　　　　(2 Nov 1944 – 10 Feb 1945)

Unit Strength (Brigade)
Dec 1944　　　　　　　　　　　7000

Order of Battle (Regiment)
Stabskompanie
I./1. Rgt. Landstorm Nederland
II./1. Rgt. Landstorm Nederland
III./1. Rgt. Landstorm Nederland
Flak-Batterie

Order of Battle (Brigade)
SS-Freiwilligen-Regiment 83 Landstorm Nederland
SS-Freiwilligen-Regiment 84 Landstorm Nederland
Feld-Ersatz-Bataillon Landstorm Nederland

SS-Freiwilligen Legion *Flandern*
6th SS-Freiwilligen Sturmbrigade *Langemarck*

SS-Freiwilligen Verband Flandern was formed July 1941 when *SS-Freiwilligen Standarte Nordwest* was split in two. It was redesignated *SS-Freiwilligen Legion Flandern* on 24 September 1941 and assigned to Army Group North. On 10 November 1941, the Legion moved up to the front near Novgorod. Strength at that time was 1112 men, 950 of whom were Flemish.

From November 1941 the Flanders Legion was in action in the Volkhov region, fighting off Soviet attempts to raise the siege of Leningrad. From August 1942 it occupied trenches around Leningrad, before being sucked into the fighting around Lake Ladoga. In March 1943 it was pulled back from the front, returning to Debica in Poland for rebuilding.

Combat experience

On 31 May 1943 the *SS-Freiwilligen Legion Flandern* was redesignated *SS-Freiwilligen Sturmbrigade Langemarck*, becoming 6th *SS-Freiwilligen Sturmbrigade Langemarck* on 22 October 1943. The *Sturmbrigade* was assigned to operations in the Ukraine, coming under the control of 2nd *SS-Panzer Division Das Reich*. Trapped in the action at Zhitomir, the brigade fought its way out, suffering heavy casualties in the process.

After refitting in Bohemia, a *Kampfgruppe*, given the name *Kampfgruppe Rehmann*, was detached to reinforce III *SS-Germanische Panzerkorps Steiner* in Estonia. Along with many other foreign volunteer units of the SS, *Kampfgruppe Rehmann* fought through the Narva campaign and back to the Courland pocket, from where it was moved by sea to Swinemünde. On 19 October 1944, 6th *SS-Freiwilligen Sturmbrigade Langemarck* was upgraded to divisional status, becoming the 27th *SS-Freiwilligen Grenadier Division Langemarck (flämische Nr. 1)*. The new division was formed around the original 3000 men of the *Sturmbrigade*. They were augmented by up to 15,000 former Flemish *Luftwaffe* personnel as well as members of the *Kriegsmarine* without ships to crew and conscripts from the *Organisation Todt*.

UNIT INFORMATION

Commanders

SS-Oberführer Otto Reich	(Jul 1941)
SS-Sturmbannführer Michael Lippert	(Jul 1941)
SS-Obersturmbannführer Hans Albert von Lettow-Vorbeck	(2 Apr 1942)
SS-Hauptsturmführer Hallmann	(Jun 1942)
SS-Obersturmbannführer Josef Fitzthum	(20 Jun 1942)
SS-Sturmbannführer Conrad Schellong	(11 Jul 1942)
SS-Obersturmbannführer Conrad Schellong	(31 May 1943 – 19 Oct 1944)

Order of Battle (Legion)

1.Komp./SS-Freiw.Legion Flandern
2.Komp./SS-Freiw.Legion Flandern
3.Komp./SS-Freiw.Legion Flandern
4.Komp./SS-Freiw.Legion Flandern
5.Komp./SS-Freiw.Legion Flandern

Order of Battle (Sturmbrigade)

Brigade Stab
I. Bataillon
II. Bataillon
Infanteriegeschütz-Kompanie
Panzerjäger-Kompanie
Sturmgeschütz-Kompanie
Fla.Kompanie
Fla.Kompanie
Marsch-Kompanie

SS-Sturmbrigade *Wallonien*
5th SS-Freiwilligen Sturmbrigade *Wallonien*

Léon Degrelle's experience while serving with Felix Steiner's *Wiking* Division convinced the Belgian Rexist leader that his *Légion Wallonie* should become part of the SS. He convinced Himmler that the French-speaking Walloons of Belgium in fact had Germanic blood, and the *Reichsführer*-SS supported his proposal.

On 1 June 1943 *Infanterie Bataillon 373* of the German Army officially became *SS-Sturmbrigade Wallonien*. The Walloon Brigade completed its *Waffen-SS* training at Wildflecken, and was redesignated as the 5th *SS-Freiwilligen Sturmbrigade Wallonien*. On 11 November it began a move to the Ukraine, where it would come under the command of the *Wiking* Division. In January 1944, the brigade cleared a Soviet salient projecting from the Teklino. Success was short-lived, however. On 26 January, the Soviet Sixth Tank Army smashed the German front, and encircled some 56,000 German troops in the Korsun area, near the town of Cherkassy. The Germans tried to relieve the pocket, but the trapped troops had to fight their way out by themselves.

The Walloon Brigade fought through the breakout with the *Wiking* Division. Its commander, Lucien Lippert, was killed, and Degrelle (who two years before had been a private) took command. Some 30,000 of the 56,000 German troops escaped without weapons

or equipment. The Walloon Brigade lost 1100 out of 1750 men killed or captured. Degrelle became a German propaganda hero, being awarded the Knight's Cross by Hitler. Returning to training camps in Germany, the brigade was gradually brought back up to strength. During the process the brigade sent a *Kampfgruppe* to reinforce the III Germanic Corps in Estonia. Led personally by Degrelle, it fought for three weeks before being evacuated to rejoin the Walloon Brigade. In the autumn a flood of new recruits arrived, drawn from factories, POW camps and Rexist paramilitary formations. The brigade was upgraded to become the 28th *SS-Freiwilligen Grenadier Division Wallonien* in October 1944.

Left: Seen here in Brussels in 1943 after being transferred from German Army control, members of the Walloon Legion pledge allegiance to Hitler as they are sworn in as members of the *Waffen-SS Sturmbrigade Wallonien*.

Französische SS-Freiwilligen Grenadier Regiment
Französische SS-Freiwilligen Sturmbrigade
Waffen-Grenadier Brigade der SS *Charlemagne* (französische Nr. 1)

The *Französische SS-Freiwilligen Grenadier Regiment* was formed in August 1943 from French volunteers, many of whom had been members of various right-wing militias. It was enlarged and redesignated on 18 July 1944, becoming the *Französische SS-Freiwilligen Sturmbrigade*.

Also known as the *Brigade Frankreich* and the *Brigade d'Assaut des Volontaires Français*, it was sent directly to the front in Galicia to fight under the control of the *Horst Wessel* Division. On 10 August 1944, it was engaged with advancing Soviet armies in the foothills of the Carpathians. The newly formed brigade took extremely heavy casualties in a rearguard fight near Sanok. It was transferred to Schwarnegast near Danzig in East Prussia where it was merged with former members of the *Légion des Volontaires Français* in August 1944 to become the *Waffen-Grenadier Brigade der SS Charlemagne (französische Nr. 1)*.

The *Légion des Volontaires Français* (LVF), or *Infanterie Regiment 638*, as it was known to the German Army with which it served, had been formed in July 1941. It had suffered heavy losses during the Soviet winter offensive of 1941–42, during which the 2nd Battalion was almost destroyed; but a 3rd Battalion was formed from new volunteers – including some 200 colonial troops. After these losses it operated as individual battalions against the partisans. It continued fighting the partisans during 1943, but the battalions were again brought together when the LVF was attached to 286th *Sicherungs Division*.

In 1942 an attempt was made to make the LVF an official French formation, but the German Army would not release its French troops. Almost as soon as the *Charlemagne* Brigade was formed, it was reinforced with members of French collaborationist groups fleeing the Western Allies, and the remainder of 1944 was taken up with organizing a French SS division. The *Charlemagne* Brigade was upgraded to become the 33rd *Waffen-Grenadier Division der SS Charlemagne (französische Nr. 1)* on 2 February 1945.

Above: Members of the 638th German Infantry Regiment, otherwise known as the *Légion des Volontaires Français*, march to the front in Russia. As with other Army legions, the LVF was incorporated into the *Waffen*-SS in 1943.

UNIT INFORMATION

Commanders (LVF)
Major Roger Labonne   (Aug 1941)
Oberst Edgar Puaud   (Jun 1943 – 1 Sep 1944)

Commanders (Brigade)
SS-Obersturmbannführer Paul Gamory-
    Dubourdeau   (Aug 1943)
Oberst Edgar Puaud   (Late Aug 1944)

Unit Strength (*Charlemagne* Brigade)
Dec 1944   7340

Italienische-Freiwilligen Verband
SS-Bataillon *Debica* • Waffen-Grenadier Brigade der SS (italienische Nr. 1)

The rescue of Benito Mussolini in 1943 inspired Italian supporters of *Il Duce* to volunteer to join the SS. Over 1500 officers and men were sent to the training ground at Munsingen, where they formed the *Italienische Freiwilliger Verband*.

They were then sent to northern Italy as the *Italienische-Freiwilligen Legion*, where they were used on anti-partisan operations. The 1st *Sturmbrigade Italienische Freiwilligen Legion* (also known as the 1st *Italienische Freiwilligen-Sturmbrigade Milizia Armata* or *Prima Brigata d'Assalto della Legione SS Italiana*) was formed from the *Italienische SS-Freiwilligen Legion* in the summer of 1944. A second Italian SS unit was formed at the SS Heidelager training ground in Debica in Poland. The *SS-Bataillon Debica* drew its recruits from former Italian soldiers who had served with the *Lombardia* Tank Division and the *Julia* Alpine Division.

Becoming operational in March 1944, the battalion mounted anti-partisan operations south and west of Turin, before being moved south to the Anzio front, going on to fight north of Rome and on the Gothic Line at Florence. On 7 September, the *Debica* Battalion joined with the 1st *Sturmbrigade* as constituent parts of

UNIT INFORMATION
Commanders
SS-Obergruppenführer Karl Wolff   (Mar 1944)
SS-Brigadeführer Peter Hansen   (Summer 1944)
SS-Standartenführer Gustav Lombard (Oct 1944)
SS-Oberführer Constantin Heldmann
(Nov 1944)
Order of Battle (Brigade)
Waffen-Grenadier-Regiment der SS 81
Waffen-Grenadier-Regiment der SS 82
Waffen-Artillerie-Regiment der SS 29
Füsilier-Bataillon 29
Panzerjäger-Abteilung 29
SS-Pionier-Kompanie 29
SS-Nachrichten-Kompanie 29

the new *Waffen-Grenadier Brigade der SS (italienische Nr. 1)*. It was upgraded to the 29th *Waffen-Grenadier Division der SS (italienische Nr. 1)* on 10 February 1945.

SS-Sonderkommando *Dirlewanger*
SS-Regiment *Dirlewanger* • SS-Sturmbrigade *Dirlewanger*

SS-Sonderkommando Dirlewanger (also known as *SS-Sonderbataillon Dirlewanger* and *Sonderkommando der Waffen-SS Lublin*) was formed from *Wilddiebkommando Oranienburg*. This was a small anti-partisan unit made up from poachers and SS disciplinary prisoners trained by *SS-Totenkopf* members.

After the invasion of the USSR, numbers were increased by recruiting former Soviet soldiers, convicts and concentration camp volunteers. The unit was used in anti-partisan operations in Poland and Byelorussia, where it gained a murderous reputation. *SS-Regiment Dirlewanger* was formed in August 1944 when *SS-*

Sonderkommando Dirlewanger was upgraded to a regiment. It took part in fighting against the Polish Home Army in Warsaw, where its brutality and general criminal behaviour shocked even other SS units.

SS-Sturmbrigade Dirlewanger was formed in December 1944 when *SS-Regiment Dirlewanger* was enlarged. The brigade was intended for anti-partisan and security operations, but the advancing Red Army meant that it soon found itself in front-line combat. Some sections of the unit had fighting ability, but many deserted. The unit was nominally upgraded to 36th *Waffen-Grenadier Division der SS* in February 1945.

Its brutal commander, Oskar Dirlewanger, tried to escape to western Europe after the end of the war, but he was recognized by former Polish POWs in France, and was subsequently beaten to death.

Above: An SS man executes a suspected 'partisan' while a crowd of SS and *Werhmacht* soldiers look on. Dirlewanger and his men were brutal participants in the savage struggle between Soviet partisans and the German invaders.

UNIT INFORMATION

Areas of Operations

Poland	(Sep 1940 – Feb 1942)
Byelorussia	(Feb 1942 – Aug 1944)
Warsaw Uprising	(5 Aug 1944 – 15 Aug 1944)
Slovak National Uprising	(Oct 1944)
Hungary	(Dec 1944)
Germany (Silesia)	(Feb 1945)

Commanders

SS-Obersturmbannführer (later *Oberführer*) Dr
   Oskar Dirlewanger   (1940 – 20 Feb 1945)

Order of Battle (Brigade)

SS-Regiment 1 SS-Sturmbrigade Dirlewanger
SS-Regiment 2 SS-Sturmbrigade Dirlewanger
SS-Aufklärungs-Abteilung SS-Sturmbrigade
   Dirlewanger
Nachrichten Kompanie SS-Sturmbrigade
   Dirlewanger
SS-Sanitätskompanie SS-Sturmbrigade Dirlewanger
SS-Verwaltungs-Kompanie
SS-Ersatz-Kompanie

Waffen-Gebirgs Brigade der SS (Tatar Nr. 1)

The *Waffen-Gebirgs Brigade der SS (Tatar Nr. 1)* began forming in May 1944 with the merger of Crimean Tatar *Schuma* (security) battalions.

However, there was little equipment to spare, which delayed completion of the operation. Unit formation was abandoned at the end of 1944 and the men who had already been gathered were transferred to the *Osttürkischen Waffen-Verbände der SS*.

UNIT INFORMATION

Commanders
SS-Standartenführer Fortenbacher

Unit Strength
Dec 1944   3518

Osttürkischen Waffen-Verbände der SS

The *Osttürkischen Waffen-Verbände der SS* was originally formed in 1944 as the *1st Ostmussulmanische SS-Regiment*. Heinrich Himmler's fascination with Islam was encouraged by the Grand Mufti of Jerusalem, Hajj Amin al-Husseini.

The Mufti sponsored the regiment, with the hope that it might eventually grow to be a division. The core of the *Mussulmanischen SS-Division Neu-Turkistan* was provided by troops transferred from Turkic *Osttruppen*

and *Hilfswillige* units under Army command, filled out by prisoners of war and labourers working in Germany. It was trained for anti-partisan operations,

Below: The pro-Nazi Grand Mufti of Jerusalem visits a Muslim unit of the *Waffen*-SS. In 1940, he requested that Hitler 'Settle the question of Jewish elements in Palestine and other Arab countries … along the lines similar to those used to solve the Jewish Question in Germany and Italy'.

but was not reliable: the German commander executed 78 men suspected of inciting mutiny. After serving in Byelorussia from February 1944, the division was one of the SS units attached to the *SS-Sturmbrigade Dirlewanger* which was used to put down the Warsaw Rising. Transferred to Slovakia in the autumn of 1944 after the Slovak National Uprising, it was renamed the *Osttürkischen Waffen-Verbände der SS*.

In December 1944 a large number of men deserted, although some 300 later returned. The Azerbaijani regiment was transferred to the *Kaukasischer Waffen-Verbände der SS* on 30 December 1944. Troops from the disbanded *Waffen-Gebirgs Brigade der SS (Tatar Nr. 1)* were assigned as replacements early in 1945. The *Waffen-Verband* was sent to Austria for further training, which remained uncompleted at the war's end.

UNIT INFORMATION

Commanders		Unit Strength	
SS-*Obersturmbannführer* Andreas Meyer-Mader		Feb 1944	3000
	(Jan 1944)	Sep 1944	4000
SS-*Hauptsturmführer* Billig	(28 Mar 1944)	Apr 1945	8500
SS-*Hauptsturmführer* Hermann	(27 Apr 1944)		
SS-*Sturmbannführer der Reserve* Franz Liebermann		**Order of Battle**	
	(Jun 1944)	*Waffen-Gruppe Turkistan*	
SS-*Hauptsturmführer* Reiner Olzscha	(Sep 1944)	*Waffen-Gruppe Idel-Ural*	
SS-*Hauptsturmführer* Fürst	(Jan 1945)	*Waffen-Gruppe Aserbaijan*	
		Waffen-Gruppe Krim	

Kalmüken Verband

Kalmüken Verband Dr Doll was formed in October 1942 from Kalmyk volunteers. At its core was a nucleus of special troops used by the *Abwehr* – German Army intelligence – known as *Abwehrtrupp* 103. At that time it consisted of two cavalry squadrons.

As with many of the early Russian units on the German side, its creation was authorized by a front-line commander – in this case, the commanding general of 16th *Infanterie-Division (mot)* – who needed mobile troops to cover his vulnerable supply lines. The *Kalmüken Verband* was also referred to as the *Kalmüken Legion* or the *Kalmüken Kavallerie Korps*. 'Dr Doll' was the codename of its first commander, *Sonderführer* Othmar Rudolf Werba. In January 1945, it was

Right: The Kalmyks were nomadic Mongols from central Asia who had settled in the Volga delta in the seventeenth century. They suffered greatly under Stalin in the 1930s and volunteered for German service in some numbers.

intended that the Kalmyks should be assigned to the *Kaukasischer Waffen-Verband der SS*, but as its constituent units were scattered in the face of the advancing Red Army, this never occurred. The *Kalmüken Verband* was eventually concentrated at the Neuhammer training area, where it was to be reorganized as a reinforced cavalry regiment. In March,

it was transferred to Croatia were it was subordinated to the XV *SS-Kosaken Kavallerie Korps*. However, the war was pretty much lost, and so the units retreated towards Austria. Many troopers were captured by the partisans, and those that reached Austria to surrender to the British were handed over to the USSR after the war. Most were executed or sent to the *Gulag*.

Waffen-Grenadier Brigade der SS (weissruthenische Nr. 1)

Waffen-Grenadier Brigade der SS (weissruthenische Nr. 1) was formed out of the more reliable troops left over after the 30th *Waffen-Grenadier Division der SS (russische Nr. 2)* was disbanded in December 1944.

Although it was not of divisional size, it was redesignated as the 30th *Waffen-Grenadier Division der SS (weissruthenische Nr. 1)* in February 1945. The name change from 'Russian' to 'White Russian' has not been satisfactorily explained, but possibly it was to differentiate the unit from its earlier incarnation, which had almost mutinied.

UNIT INFORMATION

Commanders
SS-*Standartenführer* Hans Siegling (Dec 1944)

Order of Battle
Waffen-Grenadier-Regiment der SS 75
Artillerie-Abteilung
Panzerjäger-Abteilung
Reiter-Schwadron

Waffen-Sturm Brigade *RONA*

Bronislav Kaminski, a former engineer who had fallen foul of the Soviet system and was an ardent anti-communist, took command of the local pro-German militia in the town of Lokot, south of Bryansk, when the mayor and council were massacred by partisans.

Kaminski offered his militia for partisan operations, pointing out their local knowledge could be useful to the Germans. In June 1942 they were used in Operation *Vogelsang*, in the forest near Bryansk. The Kaminski militia was split up into company-sized units

UNIT INFORMATION

Unit Strength			
Dec 1941	400 – 500	Aug 1943	6000
Jan 1942	800	Sep 1943	12,000 – 15,000
Feb 1942	1200	Jul 1944	4000 – 5000
Mar 1942	1650		
Jul 1942	5000	**Order of Battle**	
Dec 1942	8000 – 10,000	*Stab*	*Panzer-Kompanie*
Feb 1943	9000 – 10,000	*1. Regiment*	*2. Regiment*
Mar 1943	8000	*3. Regiment*	*4. Regiment*
		5. Regiment	

Above: One of the many thousands of *Osttruppen* who fought for the German Army on the Eastern Front. RONA, commanded by Bronislav Kaminski, was one of the few former Soviet units which was eventually to join the SS.

serving as translators, guides and auxiliary combat troops for the German force. The official results of this operation, the first major one in which Kaminski's troops participated, were 1193 partisans killed, 1400 wounded, 498 captured, and 12,531 civilians 'evacuated'. The Axis troops suffered 58 killed and 130 wounded. Kaminski renamed his forces RONA – *Russkaya Osvoboditelnaya Narodnaya Armiya*, or Russian National Army of Liberation. It is sometimes referred to as POHA – which is what RONA looks like in Cyrillic script. The Germans referred to it as the Kaminski Brigade. Anti-Soviet volunteers flooded in.

During the summer of 1943 the Kaminski Brigade was targeted by the partisans, and desertions became more frequent. Nevertheless, it took part in numerous actions on the fringes of the great battle of Kursk. However, Soviet advances after Kursk meant that Kaminski and his men had to leave their home area, fleeing westwards on foot. The unit was renamed *Volksheer-Brigade Kaminski* shortly before being taken over by the *Waffen*-SS July 1944. The SS renamed it *Waffen-Sturm-Brigade RONA*, with Kaminski himself receiving the rank of *Waffen-Brigadeführer der SS*.

The brigade took part in several anti-partisan operations during 1944, but it is notorious for the wave of drunken looting and murder which it perpetrated during the crushing of the Warsaw Rising. Too much even for the Nazis, Kaminski was shot, possibly by the Gestapo, in August 1944.

Waffen-Grenadier Regiment der SS (bulgarisches Nr. 1)

Waffen Grenadier Regiment der SS (bulgarisches Nr. 1) was formed when Bulgaria left the Axis and joined the Allies in September 1944. It was made up of up to 600 Bulgarian workers and soldiers who did not agree with their government's decision.

Most of the volunteers were in Germany at the time or were attached to German military units, and all were willing to keep fighting with Germany against the communists.

The unit was re-equipped with anti-tank weaponry in April 1945 and was renamed the *SS Panzer Zerstörer Regiment (bulgarisches)*. The Germans hoped the regiment would provide the nucleus of a *Waffen-*

UNIT INFORMATION

Commanders
SS-Standartenführer Günter Alhalt (13 Nov 1944)
SS-Oberführer Heinz Bertling   (1945)
SS-Oberführer Bogosanow   (1945)
SS-Oberführer Rogosaroff   (1945)

Grenadier Division der SS (bulgarische Nr. 1), but manpower was lacking and nothing could be done before the end of the war.

1st Ungarische SS-Sturmjäger Regiment

The 1st *Ungarische SS-Sturmjäger Regiment* is believed to have been made up of approximately 5000 Hungarian volunteers who joined the SS after Germany occupied the country in 1944.

Raised on 8 January 1945 by the merging of 1st and 2nd *Ungarische Schibataillons*, the regiment was attached to IV *SS Panzerkorps* at the end of the war, serving under the command of the 5th SS Panzer Division *Wiking*. The panzer corps had been transferred from France to Hungary, but could do little to stop the advancing Soviet armies.

Losses and retreat

After suffering heavy losses in January, the *Sturmjäger Regiment* was transferred to 3rd Panzer Division of III *Korps*, where it was used as infantry. Over the next weeks the regiment was switched between commands several times. During the repeated retreats which took place in spring 1945, the different parts of the

regiment lost contact with each other, but the combat units continued fighting independently. In the last days of the war, some members of the regiment reached Austria, where, once more attached to *Wiking*, they surrendered to the Americans.

UNIT INFORMATION
Order of Battle
Stab
I. Ungarische SS-Sturmjäger-Bataillon
II. Ungarische SS-Sturmjäger-Bataillon
Dolmetscher-Zug
Nachrichten-Zug
Kradmelder-Zug
Feldgendarmerie-Zug
Stab-Sicherungs-Zug

Waffen-Grenadier Regiment der SS (rümanisches Nr. 1)

The *Waffen-Grenadier Regiment der SS (rumänisches Nr. 1)* was formed out of members of the 4th Romanian Infantry Division, which had been refitting in German territory when Romania signed a ceasefire agreement with the Russians.

The regiment also included members of the fascist Iron Guard, which had always had a close relationship with the SS. It was attached to the III Germanic Panzer Corps, and fought on the Oder front until the beginning of March. It was then transferred to the eastern approaches to Berlin, where it was smashed by the Soviet offensive which was launched against the city on 16 April. Most of those regimental personnel who escaped fled westwards, where a number managed to reach the Americans to surrender.

Construction battalions

It was hoped by the Germans that this unit would form the basis of a *Waffen-Grenadier Division der SS (rumänische Nr. 1)*, and to that end a second regiment

UNIT INFORMATION
Commanders
(Nr. 1) SS-Sturmbannführer Gustav Wegner (Nov 1944)
(Nr. 2) SS-Standartenführer Albert Ludwig (Jan 1945)
Order of Battle
I. Bataillon   *II. Bataillon*

was raised. *Waffen-Grenadier Regiment der SS (rumänisches Nr. 2)* began forming up at Dollersheim in Austria. However, by this stage in the war there was no fuel for vehicles, little food, and no weapons or ammunition for the new regiment. In April 1945 the two battalions which had been formed were used as construction battalions.

SS-Standarte *Kurt Eggers*

SS-Standarte Kurt Eggers was formed in January 1940. Originally known as the *SS Kriegsberichter Kompanie*, it was the parent unit of all SS combat correspondents. Its *Züge* – or detachments – were assigned to the four *Waffen*-SS units that fought in the Low Countries and France in 1940, and in the Balkans in 1941.

The unit was upgraded to the battalion-sized *SS-Kriegsberichter Abteilung* in August 1941, after the first major expansion of the *Waffen*-SS created more units for the *Kriegsberichter* (war correspondents) to cover. It was further enlarged to regimental size in 1943.

SS-Standarte *Kurt Eggers* was named after the former editor of the SS magazine *Das Schwarze Korps*.

Eggers was serving with the *Wiking* Division when he was killed in action near Kharkov in 1943. *SS-Standarte Kurt Eggers* was an all-volunteer formation, which placed a premium on press skills but which also had a requirement for multi-lingual members. Several foreign volunteers served with the regiment, usually attached to their national formation.

However, a number of correspondents were from nations with no national SS formations, and they were treated just like their German colleagues, being assigned to one of the regular *Waffen*-SS units. At least two US citizens served in this unit, as well as several from the UK and one from New Zealand.

UNIT INFORMATION

Commander		*Abschnitt Russland-Süd*
SS-Standartenführer Günther d'Alquen		*Abschnitt Lettland und Lettische Einheiten*
		Abschnitt Südost
Unit Strength		*Abschnitt West*
Dec 1943	141	*Sonderunternehmen Südost*
Jun 1944	1180	*Kommando Oslo*
		Kommando Kopenhagen
Order of Battle		*Kommando Frankreich*
Abteilung Verwaltung		*Kommando Brüssel*
Gruppe Wort		*Kommando Südost*
Gruppe Bild		*Kommando Adria*
Gruppe Rundfunk		*Gruppe Kampfpropaganda*
Abschnitt Russland-Nord		*Sonderunternehmen 'Südstern'*

Britisches Freikorps

The *Britisches Freikorps* was formed in January 1943 as *St. Georgs-Legion* (Legion of Saint George). It was made up of British and Commonwealth volunteers recruited from amongst the POWs captured in Norway, Belgium, France, Greece and North Africa.

The forming of such a British volunteer force was the idea of John Amery, son of Leo Amery, Secretary of

State for India in Winston Churchill's war cabinet. Amery, who had been in Paris when it was occupied by the Germans in 1940, managed to find just one volunteer. Himmler became interested in the concept and a renewed attempt to find volunteers was made. Around 300 soldiers expressed an interest, but the Germans felt that most of these were simply looking for a way to get out of their POW camps for a while.

Eventually, 58 volunteers were accepted as genuine (including three Canadians, three Australians, three South Africans and one New Zealander).

Some were former members of the British Union of Fascists and were genuinely committed to the fight against communism. Others were simply bored with life as a POW and were looking for excitement. The legion was renamed the *Britisches Freikorps* in January 1944, and it was nominally attached to III *SS-Panzerkorps* in February 1945, primarily for propaganda purposes. The unit never saw any action, but a handful of British SS men are believed to have fought with 11th *SS-Freiwilligen Panzergrenadier Division Nordland* in the battle of Berlin. Amery was arrested in Milan at the end of the war. He was found guilty of treason and hanged.

Indische Freiwilligen Legion der Waffen-SS

Infanterie-Regiment 950 (indische), or *Legion Freies Indien*, was formed on 26 August 1942 from Indian Army soldiers who had been captured while fighting for the British in North Africa.

Trained in Germany, the legion was used for garrison duty in Holland before being sent to man coastal defences in the Bordeaux area. The unit was transferred to the *Waffen-SS* in August 1944, where it received a new name, becoming the *Indische Freiwilligen Legion der Waffen-SS*. Allied advances out of Normandy threatened to cut off German troops in the south, so the legion was ordered to move from southern France to Germany, travelling by road from 15 August onwards. The unit was harassed by French resistance fighters and regular French troops *en route*. The Indians remained in German training facilities until March 1945. With Allied victory imminent, the legion tried to reach neutral Switzerland but eventually was compelled to surrender to American and French troops.

UNIT INFORMATION

Commanders (SS)
SS-*Oberführer* Heinz Bertling
(8 Aug 1944 – 8 May 1945)

Order of Battle
I. Bataillon; II. Bataillon; III. Bataillon
13. Infanteriegeschütz-Kompanie
14. Panzerjäger-Kompanie
15. Pionier-Kompanie
Ehrenwachkompanie

Right: Indian SS men undergo training in the handling of the 7.5cm (3in) LeFh Model 16 light field gun. The Indian volunteers were followers of nationalist leader Subhas Chandra Bose, who wanted to rid India of British rule.

FOREIGN *WAFFEN*-SS DIVISIONS, KNIGHT'S CROSSES AWARDED

Title (nominal divisional strength, 1945)	Knight's Crosses awarded	Title (nominal divisional strength, 1945)	Knight's Crosses awarded
5th SS-Panzer Division *Wiking* (14,800)	55	24th Waffen Gebirgs Division der SS (3000)	0
6th SS-Gebirgs Division *Nord* (15,000)	4	25th Waffen Grenadier Division der SS *Hunyadi* (15,000)	0
7th SS-Freiwilligen Gebirgs Division *Prinz Eugen* (20,000)	6	26th Waffen Grenadier Division der SS (13,000)	0
8th SS-Kavallerie Division *Florian Geyer* (13,000)	22	27th SS-Freiwilligen Grenadier Division *Langemarck* (7000)	1
11th SS-Freiwilligen Panzergrenadier Division *Nordland* (9,000)	25	28th SS-Freiwilligen Grenadier Division *Wallonien* (4000)	3
13th Waffen Gebirgs Division der SS *Handschar* (*kroatische* Nr. 1) (12,700)	4	29th Waffen Grenadier Division der SS (*russische* Nr. 1) (not known)	0
14th Waffen Grenadier Division der SS (22,000)	1	29th Waffen Grenadier Division der SS (15,000)	0
15th Waffen Grenadier Division der SS (16,800)	3	30th Waffen Grenadier Division der SS (*russische* Nr. 2) (4500)	0
18th SS-Freiwilligen Panzergrenadier Division *Horst Wessel* (11,000)	2	30th Waffen-Grenadier Division der SS (*weissruthenische* Nr. 1) (not known)	0
19th Waffen Grenadier Division der SS (9000)	12	31st SS-Freiwilligen Grenadier Division *Böhmen-Mähren* (11,000)	0
20th Waffen Grenadier Division der SS (15,500)	5	33rd Waffen Kavallerie Division der SS (not known)	0
21st Waffen Gebirgs Division der SS *Skanderbeg* (5000)	0	33rd Waffen Grenadier Division der SS *Charlemagne* (7000)	2
22nd SS-Freiwilligen Kavallerie Division *Maria Theresa* (8000)	6	34th SS-Freiwilligen Grenadier Division *Landstorm Nederland* (7000)	3
23rd Waffen Gebirgs Division der SS *Kama*	0	36th Waffen Grenadier Division der SS (6000)	1
23rd SS-Freiwilligen Panzergrenadier Division *Nederland* (6000)	19	37th SS-Freiwilligen Kavallerie Division *Lützow* (not known)	0

SS RANKS

German	British Army	US Army
Anwarter	Private	Private
Sturmann/Mann	—	Private First Class
Rottenführer	Lance-Corporal	Corporal
Unterscharführer	Corporal	Sergeant
Scharführer	—	Staff Sergeant
Oberscharführer	Sergeant	Technical Sergeant
Hauptscharführer	Staff Sergeant	Master Sergeant
Sturmscharführer	Regimental Sergeant Major	Warrant Officer
Untersturmführer	Second Lieutenant	Second Lieutenant
Obersturmführer	Lieutenant	First Lieutenant
Hauptsturmführer	Captain	Captain
Sturmbannführer	Major	Major
Obersturmbannführer	Lieutenant-Colonel	Lieutenant-Colonel
Standartenführer	Colonel	Colonel
Oberführer	Brigadier	Brigadier-General (1 star)
Brigadeführer	Major-General	Major-General (2 star)
Gruppenführer	Lieutenant-General	Lieutenant-General (3 star)
Obergruppenführer	General	General (4 star)
Oberstgruppenführer	Field Marshal	General of the Army (5 star)
Reichsführer-SS	—	—

SS UNIT ORGANIZATION TERMS & DEFINITIONS

German term

English equivalent

INFANTRY
Divisionen
SS-Divisionen
SS-Panzergrenadier-Divisionen
SS-Grenadier-Divisionen
SS-Gebirgs-Divisionen

Brigaden
SS-Brigaden
SS-Panzergrenadier-Brigaden
SS-Grenadier-Brigaden
SS-Gebirgs-Brigaden
SS-Sturm-Brigaden

Regimenter
SS-Standarten
SS-Regimenter
SS-Infanterie-Regimenter
SS-Polizei-Regimenter
SS-Panzergrenadier-Regimenter
SS-Grenadier-Regimenter
SS-Gebirgsjäger-Regimenter

Abteilungen/Bataillone
SS-Bataillone
SS-Panzergrenadier-Bataillone
SS-Gebirgsjäger-Bataillone
SS-Schi-Bataillone
SS-Jäger-Bataillone
SS-Fallschirm-Jäger-Bataillone
SS-Fla-MG-Bataillone
SS-Jagdverbände
SS-Sonderverbände
SS-Begleit-Bataillon 'RFSS'
SS-Legionen
SS-Freikorps
SS-Waffengruppen
SS-Waffenverbände
SS-Kampfgruppen

ARMOURED AND MOTORIZED TROOPS
Divisionen
SS-Panzer-Divisionen
SS-Kavallerie-Divisionen
SS-Kosaken-Kavallerie-Divisionen

Brigaden
SS-Panzer-Brigaden

Regimenter
SS-Panzer-Regimenter
SS-Schützen-Regimenter
SS-Kradschützen-Regimenter
SS-Kavallerie-Regimenter
SS-Kosaken-Reiter-Regimenter

Abteilungen/Bataillone
SS-Panzer-Abteilungen
SS-Panzerabwehr-Abteilungen
SS-Panzerjäger-Abteilungen
SS-Panzer-Aufklärungs-Abteilungen
SS-Aufklärungs-Abteilungen
SS-Radfahr-Aufklärungs-Abteilungen
SS-Radfahr-Bataillone

Divisions
SS Divisions
SS Armoured Infantry Divisions
SS Grenadier Divisions
SS Mountain Divisions

Brigades
SS Brigades
SS Armoured Infantry Brigades
SS Grenadier Brigades
SS Mountain Brigades
SS Assault Brigades

Regiments
SS Regiments
SS Regiments
SS Infantry Regiments
SS Police Regiments
SS Armoured Infantry Regiments
SS Grenadier Regiments
SS Mountain Regiments

Battalions
SS Battalions
SS Armoured Infantry Battalions
SS Mountain Battalions
SS Ski Battalions
SS 'Hunter' Battalions
SS Paratroop Battalions
SS Anti-Aircraft Machine gun Battalions
SS 'Hunter' Groups
SS Special Units
SS Escort Battalion 'RFSS'
SS Legions
SS Free Corps
SS Combat Group
SS Combat Group
SS *Ad hoc* Combat Groups

Divisions
SS Armoured Divisions
SS Cavalry Divisions
SS Cossack Cavalry Divisions

Brigades
SS Armoured Brigades

Regiments
SS Armoured Regiments
SS Mot. Rifle Infantry Regiments
SS Motorcycle Regiments
SS Cavalry Regiments
SS Cossack Rider Regiments

Battalions
SS Armoured Battalions
SS Tank Destroyer Battalions
SS Anti-Tank Battalions
SS Armoured Reconnaissance Battalions
SS Reconnaissance Battalions
SS Bicycle Reconnaissance Battalions
SS Bicycle Battalions

GLOSSARY

Einsatzgruppen: Mobile armed units, consisting of military police, SS and *Gestapo* personnel, used to round up and execute enemies in the conquered territories in the East. Their main targets were Jews, communist officials – such as commissars – gypsies, political leaders, and the intelligentsia. Each unit was made up of a number of companies known as *Einsatzkommando*.

Freiwillige: Literally, 'volunteer'. Used mainly by the *Waffen*-SS to denote units composed of foreign volunteers. For a time it was applied to non-German but Germanic volunteers (e.g., *Volksdeutsche*, Norwegians, Danes, etc.), but was later applied to denote non-Germanic units (Ukrainians, etc.) as well.

Hilfswillige: Auxiliary volunteers. After the invasion of the Soviet Union, many thousands of Soviet citizens volunteered to fight the Soviet regime. At first, the German Government refused to use them, but later relented (no doubt in the face of mounting casualties) and allowed the German Army to use them in non-combat roles. *Hilfswillige*, or *Hiwis*, served as auxiliaries to the front-line troops on various support tasks such as construction or carrying ammo.

Legion: Often used for units composed of foreigners in German service. Used by both the German Army and *Waffen*-SS. A legion had no fixed size and usually ranged in size from a battalion to a brigade.

Osttruppen: Eastern troops. Initially the Germans refused to arm Soviet citizens who volunteered to fight the Soviet regime after the German inviasion in 1941. Later in the war as German casualties continued to soar the official German stand changed. Eastern troop units were formed *en masse*. An *Ost-Bataillon* meant an infantry battalion of Eastern troops.

Reichsführer-SS: Heinrich Himmler's title as the supreme commander of the SS and *Gestapo*.

Schutzstaffel (SS): Meaning 'Protection Squad', the SS was originally the bodyguard of Adolf Hitler. Himmler transformed them into an army within the Army. Up to 40 SS divisions were created, especially as the war on the Eastern Front accelerated.

Volksdeutsche: This term was used for ethnic Germans living outside and east of Germany. This is in contrast to the *Reichsdeutsche* (literally 'Germans of the realm'), who were citizens of eastern German lands. Prior to World War II, well above 10 million ethnic Germans lived in Central and Eastern Europe. They constituted a significant minority far into Soviet Russia. The Nazi regime popularized the term *Volksdeutsche* and also exploited this group for their own purposes. They were heavily recruited to serve in every arm of the *Wehrmacht* and the *Waffen*-SS.

Wehrmacht: The umbrella term for the armed forces. This included the three major groupings of the German military: the *Heer* (Army), *Luftwaffe* (Air Force) and *Kriegsmarine* (Navy), as well as the *Waffen*-SS, which – although commanded by Himmler – was tactically a part of the *Wehrmacht*.

LIST OF ABBREVIATIONS

BK:	*Balli Kombetar* (Albanian National Union party)	NSKK:	*Nationalsocialistische Kraftfahrkorps* (Nazi party motor transport organization)
BSRN:	*Boyevogo Soyuza Russkaya Naroda* (Fighting Union of Russian Nationalists)	OKH:	*Oberkommando des Heeres* (Army High Command)
DAF:	*Deutsches Arbeits Front* (German Labour Front)	OKW:	*Oberkommando der Wehrmacht* (Armed Forces High Command)
DNL:	*Den Norske Legion* (Norwegian Legion)	POW:	prisoner(s) of war
DNSAP:	*Danmarks Nationalsocialistiske Arbejder Parti* (Danish National Socialist Workers Party)	PPF:	*Parti Populaire Français* (French collaborationist party)
GSSN:	*Germanske SS Norge* (Norwegian SS organization established by the Germans)	RAD:	*Reichsarbeitsdienst* (Reich Labour Service)
		RFSS:	*Reichsführer-SS*
HSSPF:	*Höhere SS-Polizei Führer* (Higher SS and Police Commander – the highest German police authority in a region)	RNNA:	*Russkaya Natsionalnaya Narodnaya Armiya* (Russian Nationalist Patriotic Army)
KONR:	*Komitet Osvobozhdeniya Narodov Rossii* (Committee for the Liberation of the Peoples of Russia)	RNP:	*Rassemblement National Populaire* (French collaborationist party)
LAF:	*Lietuviu Aktyvistu Frontas* (Lithuanian Activist Front)	ROA:	*Russkaya Osvoboditelnaya Armiya* (Russian Army of Liberation)
LVF:	*Légion des Volontaires Français* (French Volunteer Legion)	RONA:	*Russkaya Osvoboditelnaya Narodnaya Armiya* (Russian National Army of Liberation)
MSR:	*Mouvement Social Revolutionnaire* (French collaborationist party)	RSHA:	*Reichsicherheitshauptamt* (Reich Main Security Office)
MVSN:	*Milizia Voluntaria Sicurezza Nationale* (Italian Fascist militia – the 'Blackshirts')	SA:	*Sturmabteilung* (Nazi 'Brownshirts')
		SD:	*Sicherheitsdienst* (SS Security Service)
NCO:	non-commissioned officer	SS:	*Schutzstaffel* ('Protection Squad')
NS:	*Nasjional Samling* (Norwegian National Unity Party)	STO:	*Service du Travail Obligatoire* (French forced labour service)
NSUF:	*Nasjonal Samlings Ungdomsfylking* (Norwegian NS Youth Organization)	USSR:	Union of Soviet Socialist Republics
NSB:	*Nationaal Socialistische Beweging* (Netherlands National Socialist Movement)	VDB:	*Volksdeutsche Bewegung* (Luxembourg national socialist party)
NKVD:	*Narodnyy Kommissariat Vnutrennikh Del* (Soviet 'Peoples' Commissariat for Domestic Affairs' – the Secret Police)	VT:	*Verfügungstruppe* (armed SS units that were the forerunners of the *Waffen*-SS)
		WKB:	*Wehrbezirkskommando* (Military District Headquarters)

BIBLIOGRAPHY

Abbott, Peter. Men-at-Arms 131. *Germany's Eastern Front Allies, 1941–1945*. London: Osprey, 1983.

Ailsby, Christopher. *Hitler's Renegades: Foreign Nationals in the Service of the Reich*. Washington, DC: Brassey's Inc (USA), 2004.

Anders, Wladyslaw. *Russian Volunteers in Hitler's Army*. Bayside, NY: Axis Europa Books, 1998.

Forbes, Robert. *Pour L'Europe: The French Volunteers of the Waffen-SS*. Self-Published, 2000.

Jurado, Carlos Caballero. Men-at-Arms 147. *Foreign Volunteers of the Wehrmacht, 1941–1945*. London: Osprey, 1983.

Kleinfeld, Gerald R. and Lewis A. Tambs. *Hitler's Spanish Legion: The Blue Division in Russia*. Carbondale,

IL: Southern Illinois University Press, 1979.

Littlejohn, David. *Foreign Legions of the Third Reich, Volume 1: Norway, Denmark, France*. San Jose, CA: Bender Publishing, 1979.

Littlejohn, David. *Foreign Legions of the Third Reich, Volume 2: Belgium, Great Britain, Holland, Italy, Spain*. San Jose, CA: Bender Publishing, 1981.

Littlejohn, David. *Foreign Legions of the Third Reich, Volume 3: Albania, Czechoslovakia, Greece, Hungary, Yugoslavia*. San Jose, CA: Bender Publishing, 1985.

Littlejohn, David. *Foreign Legions of the Third Reich, Volume 4: Poland, Ukraine, Bulgaria, Romania, Free India*. San Jose, CA: Bender Publishing, 1987.

Munoz, Antonio J. *Hitler's Eastern Legions, Volume 1: Baltic Schutzmannschaft*. Bayside. NY: Axis Europa Books, 1998.

Munoz, Antonio J. *Hitler's Eastern Legions, Volume II: The Osttruppen*. Bayside. NY: Axis Europa Books, 1997.

Munoz, Antonio J. *Forgotten Legions: Obscure Combat Formations of the Waffen SS*. Boulder: Paladin Press, 1991.

Nafziger, George F. *German Order of Battle in World War II, Volume 7. Foreigners in Field Gray: Russians, Croats, and Italians*. West Chester, Ohio: Nafziger Collection, 1995.

Rikmenspoel, Marc. *Soldiers of the Waffen-SS: Many Nations, One Motto*. Winnipeg: J.J. Fedorowicz, 1999.

Thomas, Nigel. Men-at-Arms 363. *Germany's Eastern Front Allies (2): Baltic Forces*. Oxford: Osprey Publishing, 2002.

Weale, Adrian. *Renegades: Hitler's Englishmen*. London: Pimlico, 2002.

Williamson, Gordon. *Loyalty is my Honor*. Osceola MI: Motorbooks International. 1995

Websites

Axis and Foreign Legion Militaria
axis101.bizland.com

Axis History Factbook
www.axishistory.com

www.feldgrau.com

Waffen-SS Order of Battle
www.wssob.com
www.gutenberg-e.org

INDEX

INDEX